Beyond the Frontier

Beyond the Frontier
Exploring the Indian Country

By Stan Hoig

University of Oklahoma Press : Norman

Also by Stan Hoig

The Sand Creek Massacre (Norman, 1961)
The Battle of the Washita (New York, 1976; Lincoln, 1979)
The Peace Chiefs of the Cheyennes (Norman, 1980)
The Cheyenne (New York, 1989)
Jesse Chisholm, Ambassador of the Plains (Niwot, Colo., 1991)
Peoples of the Sacred Arrows: The Story of the Southern Cheyennes (New York, 1992)
Tribal Wars of the Southern Plains (Norman, 1993)
Sequoyah, the Cherokee Genius (Oklahoma City, 1995)
Night of the Cruel Moon: The Trail of Tears and Cherokee Removal (New York, 1996)

Library of Congress Cataloging-in-Publication Data

Hoig, Stan.
    Beyond the frontier: exploring the Indian country / by Stan Hoig.
        p.   cm.
    Includes bibliographical references (p.   ) and index.
    1. Oklahoma—Discovery and exploration. I Title.
    F697.H68   1998
    976.6'01—dc21   97-49152
    ISBN 0-8061-3046-6 (cloth)   CIP
    ISBN 0-8061-3052-0 (paper)

1 2 3 4 5 6 7 8 9 10

Contents

Contents

➤ _____

Illustrations

Figures

➤ _____

Preface

This book intends to consolidate in historical sequence
the major explorations and expeditions into, across,
and bordering the territory that was once the Indian
Territory and is now essentially the state of Oklahoma;
to provide an overview of the region when it was the
habitat of the Native Indian; and to reveal life as it was
in the region before the white man's influence became
pronounced. The book also calls attention to the white
men who first came forth to view this land and make
record of it. In doing so, this book hopes to bring to the
reader some of the adventure of Oklahoma's day of
revelation and introduce the main participants in this
pageant of Western history.

Although the central attention in the pages that
follow is upon the region that is presently Oklahoma,
the movements of exploring parties are followed beyond
the present borders of the state, particularly into the
Texas Panhandle. Some explorations and events of
adjacent areas are presented in order to gain a fuller
picture of those, both Indians and non-Indians, who

played significant roles in the area's history. The early residents of the Plains recognized no such artificial limits as state boundaries, nor did the explorers. Prior to the Civil War the lands of the West were still largely known even to the white man in terms of rivers, mountains, and other conspicuous landmarks. Further, many of the tribes originally residing just outside of Oklahoma's border were involved in the early history of the state where eventually they came to reside.

At one time, of course, all of America was residence to the Native Indian. However, for the purposes of this book, the general region of exploration attention—the Indian Territory and beyond—is referred to loosely as the "Indian country," even as it was during the Western frontier period. In this book the word *discover* is used in the sense of "first witnessing" and not in the sense of "being the first to witness."

Embodied in these accounts are details of Indian life and of the frontier that are often overlooked in scholarly studies, details that give a more intimate look at life in the Oklahoma area that preceded white civilization. Even the least eventful exploration is often interesting in the portrait it presents of life at that time.

The Civil War, 1861–1865, marks a definitive break in the inquiry by non-Indians into what was then known as the Indian Territory. Although only a temporary interlude in exploration, the Civil War provides an appropriate point at which to separate the early phase of Anglo-American intrusion from that following the war. These narratives include most of the known visitations to Oklahoma prior to 1861; but there were many other experiences by hunters, trappers, explorers, gold seekers, immigrants, runaway slaves seeking their freedom, adventurers, renegades, deserting soldiers, merchants, parties of eastern Indians on hunting forays, and military units for which we have no record.

A brief biography of the principals involved in Oklahoma exploration, many of whom went on to become notables of American history, is included in the Appendix. Their lives in themselves are intriguing stories of American history, particularly in regard to their involvement in wars with Mexico and between the states and in the explorations of other areas of the world. There were, of course, many other lesser-known participants accompanying these explorations who receive no mention but fully shared the experience.

It is hoped that this intermediate treatment of Oklahoma history, standing as it does between the broader historical text and the more detailed studies of specific events, will prove both entertaining and educational and keep alive a period of history that has long been overlooked and generally forgotten. These accounts of exploration and discovery by daring, resolute men reveal a colorful world that was and will never be again. Without question, Oklahoma's period of early exploration is one of its most adventurous and exciting eras. It is a story worth knowing.

Beyond the Frontier

Introduction
A Land Apart

Indian Territory, now the state of Oklahoma, was one of the last frontiers in the United States. As a treaty-promised haven for the displaced American Indian, it stood apart from the rest of the nation for much of the nineteenth century, obscure and mysterious to the outside world. Beyond today's urban centers remnants of a past era live on. Dance drums still throb into the night in Native communities, keeping alive the pulse of Indian heritage and the image of teepee crosspoles against the sky. The Western hat and boot reflect the colorful era of the open range and the free-spirited cowboy.

The land itself, its broad horizon broken here and there by time-carved buttes and rocky escarpments, still swells upward toward the Rocky Mountains with the promise that lured generations of Americans westward. Forested hills remain to be explored, and stretches of the old buffalo prairie have never been turned. Gone are the elk that once grazed these meadows, as well as the black bear, the wild horse, and the great, earth-blanketing herds of buffalo. But the deer, coyote, rabbit, wild turkey, prairie chicken, quail, dove, and crow continue as the occupants they have always been.

These life forms were all here when European explorers first came to explore the land; when bawling Texas cattle herds were driven through on their way to Kansas railheads or halted to graze and fatten on the grassy pasturelands; and when in 1889 and later the government opened the country to non-Indian occupation and eager settlers rushed pell-mell for homesteads to erect their rural and small town habitations. Even today this native wildlife survives amid an era of modern cities and highways that interlace the land.

Indian Territory comprised most of the country immediately west of present-day Arkansas between Kansas and Texas to the 100th meridian. In the eastern half of the territory were the forested mountains; to the west, the rolling, short-grassed plains. These were almost equally divided by an ocher-soiled strip of scrub oak and underbrush known as the Cross Timbers. Among the territory's principal geographical features were the rivers that set boundaries of proprietorship and danger for nomadic tribal bands and guided travelers across the townless wilderness. The Arkansas, Canadian, and Red rivers were of particular consequence in both respects; the Washita, North Canadian, Cimarron, Verdigris, Grand, and Kiamichi also served as arteries of exploration and travel.

The same rivers and creeks run their courses today, many with dams now holding back their created lakes. Once these streams were vital passageways of the frontier. Now they are mostly seen from the windows of speeding automobiles as flicking images over the railing of a roadway bridge. It is a far different perspective from that of the environmentally seasoned men who first trekked along their banks wondering what discovery or peril might lay just around the next bend or beyond the next hill.

When humans first came to this region is not recorded. Archaeological clues give evidence not only of giant mastodons and other primeval animal life but also of foraging hunter bands, prehistoric pole-and-thatch villages, and great burial mounds. It is even possible that exploring Vikings were in this area as early as the eleventh century. One of the region's most intriguing mysteries that may well bespeak such prehistoric visits is the ancient rune stone near Heavenver.

Written records, however, begin with the arrival of the first Europeans. Through these accounts we can see the concourse of explorers who made their way into and across the region before the Civil War erupted in 1861, temporarily halting such intrusions and marking an end to the initial age of exploration.

The Spanish were the first Old World visitors to these Central Plains of the United States. Shipwrecked on the Texas Gulf Coast, Álvar Núñez Cabeza de Vaca spent six years wandering among the prairie tribes of lower Texas before making his way to Mexico in 1536. Francisco Vásquez de Coronado marched from New Mexico to Kansas across what are now the Texas and Oklahoma Panhandles and back in 1542. Juan de Oñate did the same in 1601, his course being a bit more easterly.

From the records of these journeys we learn something of the peoples who resided in this region at that time. The Spanish accounts, however, leave the boundaries of tribal occupation generally unclear except to note that the people known today as the Wichitas were then firmly established along the Arkansas River of present-day Oklahoma and Kansas.

Before Coronado left Kansas, he planted a cross, at the foot of which was chiseled a message proclaiming the fact of the Spaniards' visit.[1] In accordance with the world-power notion of ownership by discovery, Coronado's visit and that of other Spaniards established the region north from New Mexico to southern Kansas as being under Spain's jurisdiction.

In the spring of 1719, French trader Claude Charles Du Tisné made a solitary journey from the Osage villages of southwest Missouri to a Wichita (to him, Pawnee) encampment in either south-central Kansas or northern Oklahoma. While there, he raised the French banner and laid claim to the country in the name of France by erecting a cross inscribed with the insignia of King Philip V.[2]

Later that same summer and fall, Frenchman Bernard de la Harpe led an exploring expedition northwestward across Arkansas and well into eastern Oklahoma. Upon reaching a large Wichita camp, on the Arkansas River it is believed, he ordered a post carved with the arms of the king of France and planted in the center of the village. The carving included notice of his company and the day and year of possession—September 10, 1719.[3]

Still another French claim to the land of eastern Oklahoma is displayed on the expedition map of Captain Zebulon Pike's exploration of 1806. The notation indicates that "at the mouth of the Canadian river the Ensigns armorial of France were buried in a leaden box at the foot of a great oak in 1742."[4] Just who did this is not certain; but it was probably Fabré de la Bruyere, a French officer who, guided by Pierre and Paul Mallet, had set out up the Canadian River for New Mexico the year before.

Within the period of modern history, the eastern portion of Indian Territory was originally populated or hunted by the Caddos of the Red River, the Osages of Missouri, and the Quapaws of Arkansas. The Caddos are the likely descendants of the mound-building society that once existed in the vicinity of present-day Spiro, Oklahoma. The Spiro Mounds provide our clearest look into ancient cultures of the region.

During the first half of the nineteenth century, the tribes that were removed by the United States from east of the Mississippi River—particularly the Cherokees, Creeks, Choctaws, Chickasaws, and Seminoles—

arrived to dominate the eastern half of the territory. They brought with them their own tribal traditions and customs and established new forms of American Indian society that utilized Euro-American experience.

The prairies of the western portion were home to the Plains tribes, which thrived on the vast bison herds that roamed up and down the Central Plains. Many of the tribes, lured to the region by the buffalo and the wild horse, lived in transportable teepee villages and competed fiercely among one another not only for territory and game but also as a matter of tribal rivalry in war.

Member bands of the large Wichita confederacy, however, held to permanent grass huts and supplemented their hunt with garden plots of maize, melons, and beans. The Wichitas were often under attack by the Osages and by Apache raiders from New Mexico and Texas who came to capture victims for the Indian slave trade that flourished both along the French-held Mississippi River and in Spanish-dominated Mexico.

In the latter part of the eighteenth century, the Comanches and Kiowas migrated down from the north to drive back the Apaches and eventually to ally themselves with the Wichitas. Later, the Cheyennes and Arapahos also became active south of the Arkansas River. Parties of Kaw Indians from Kansas, Osages from Missouri, and Pawnees from Nebraska commonly invaded the region to hunt, conduct war, or raid the abundant horse herds of the resident tribes.

Prior to the Civil War, Indian Territory remained excluded from the main thrust of the American westward movement even as the areas surrounding it advanced into the mainstream of national life. By treaty and theory, though not entirely by practice, the territory provided an inviolable haven for Native peoples. Despite the presence of military forts and the social progress of the removal tribes, the region was restricted by law from white intrusion and settlement. On the

Prior to the Civil War, the Native tribes of the Plains existed almost entirely upon the buffalo. (R. I. Dodge, *The Plains of the Great Southwest*)

north in Kansas, ox-drawn wagon trains lumbered along the Santa Fe and Oregon Trails carrying merchant goods and home seekers to Oregon, California, and other areas of the Far West. To the south, Texans pushed aggressively against the Comanche-dominated frontier.

Even as the prairie tribes held their territorial claims by virtue of inhabitance and possession, France, Spain, and the United States vied with one another for ownership by right of discovery, exploration, conquest, and international agreement. The land north of the Red River was once considered to be a part of the Louisiana country claimed by France. In 1763 France ceded this vast, ill-defined territory to Spain, which sold it back to France on April 30, 1803, with the stipulation that it not be relinquished to a third party.

When France broke this agreement with its sale of Louisiana to the United States seven months later on November 30, 1803, Spain declared the action to be invalid except for a section of land lying along the west bank of the Mississippi River. Spanish officials continued to contest the sale until 1819, when the two nations signed the Adams-Onis Treaty by which Spain recognized the U.S. claim to virtually all of the Louisiana Purchase lands except Texas and eastern New Mexico. The present-day Oklahoma Panhandle was also excluded.[5]

Of special issue in this contest between the United States and Spain were the eastern and northern borders of present Texas. Spanish concern became acute when Thomas Jefferson dispatched an exploring expedition under Meriwether Lewis and William Clark to the northwest, another under Zebulon Pike to the central Rockies, and a third under Thomas Freeman and Peter Custis up the Red River. Seeing these moves as threats to its possession of Texas and New Mexico as well as its claim to the American northwest, New Spain sent out armies to intercept the Americans. Several Spanish attempts to locate Lewis and Clark failed.[6] However, Pike was found and arrested in Colorado, and the Freeman-Custis party was turned back by New Spain military as it reached the southeastern tip of present-day Oklahoma.[7]

It was not until February 22, 1819, that the two countries resolved their differences. At that time a pact was signed in Washington, D.C., by which Spain would cede the disputed Florida lands to the United States. In return the United States relinquished its claim to Texas but extended its title northward to include the Oregon country. The agreement defined the area relating to present-day Oklahoma in part by extending the boundary westward along the Red River and turning to the north up the 100th meridian to the Arkansas River.[8]

The purchase of Louisiana spawned a notion among American leaders for solving the problem of Indian presence in the newly founded states of the Atlantic seaboard. To politicians and citizens alike, it seemed

altogether plausible to remove the tribes to an assigned area of the uncharted wilderness beyond the
Mississippi.

At first the concept of an "Indian country" involved
a broad removal zone west of the Mississippi River. As
the United States expanded, however, the region assigned to the Indians became smaller and smaller. In
1825 Congress officially decreed "Indian Territory" to be
composed of the country west of Missouri and Arkansas between the Platte and Red rivers.[9] This area was
continually redefined as western areas such as Nebraska
and Kansas were infiltrated by white settlers.

The original idea of Indian removal to the West
devised under President Thomas Jefferson was based
on voluntary consent.[10] President James Monroe proposed a plan to make landowners of individual Indians,
believing that they would eventually meld into white
society. He met strenuous opposition, however, particularly from the state of Georgia. In 1802 that state had
ceded its western landholdings that now comprise the
states of Alabama and Mississippi to the United States.
In turn the federal government promised to extinguish
all Indian title to land within Georgia. This was to be
done as soon as it could be achieved peacefully and at
a reasonable cost.[11]

The purchase of Louisiana, Georgia argued, made
such government action possible. State officials were
not concerned that to carry out this agreement, the
United States would be required to break solemn
treaties that it had made with the Indian tribes that
were the original occupants. Unwilling to do this,
Monroe was forced to abandon his hopes of Indian
integration. He now offered a systematic plan for voluntary resettlement of all eastern tribes to west of the
Mississippi River.[12]

Some Indians, wishing to escape the march of white
civilization, were amenable to moving west. Most
Native peoples, however, were strongly opposed to

giving up their homelands and did so only under military coercion. In 1817 Monroe addressed a group of the Cherokees who had since moved to Arkansas, telling them:

> You are now in a country where you can be happy; no white man shall ever again disturb you; the Arkansas [River] will protect your southern boundary when you get there. You will be protected on either side; the white man shall never again encroach upon you, and you will have a great outlet to the West.
> As long as water flows, or grass grows upon the earth, or the sun rises to show your pathway, or you kindle your camp fires, so long shall you be protected by this Government, and never again removed from your present habitations.[13]

President John Quincy Adams continued support of the voluntary removal concept. But not so Andrew Jackson, who became president in 1829. Jackson, a southerner, had had a lifelong experience with the Indians in Tennessee and during his years as a soldier. His rise to national fame had been helped considerably by his defeat of the Creek Red Stick uprising in Alabama during the War of 1812. His victory came in part from the fighting support he received from other Creeks and a large Cherokee contingent at the 1814 Battle of Horseshoe Bend.

Whatever debt Jackson owed the Indians, he held a frontiersman's attitude toward them. He readily accepted the argument that they and their homelands were inescapably doomed by the march of the American frontier—that it would be best for all, including the Indians, if they were sent off to the west. Siding with Georgia and other southern states in their quest to rid themselves of Indians, Jackson quickly introduced a bill to Congress for Indian removal.[14]

Andrew Jackson as a soldier. (Library of Congress)

"As a means of effecting this end," Jackson said in his address to Congress, "I suggest, for your consideration, the propriety of setting apart an ample district west of the Mississippi, and without the limits of any State or Territory now formed, to be guaranteed to the Indian tribes as long as they shall occupy it, each tribe have a distinct control over the portion designated for its use."[15]

Debate on the Indian removal bill was intense and far from one-sided. One opposing congressman insisted: "As for the idea that this retreat west of the Mississippi is to be a safe and undisturbed abode, the facts show that this is a mere mockery. We see one unfortunate remnant driven from a reservation which six years before had been spared to them out of a vast territory, and on the condition that their reservation should not be intruded on."[16] "By persuasion and force," Jackson himself admitted regarding the Native bodies, "they have been made to retire from river to river, and from mountain to mountain, until some of the tribes have become extinct and others have left but remnants."[17]

Despite such arguments, the Indian bill narrowly passed. New treaties were quickly initiated with those tribes still situated east of the Mississippi River. Indians from the northeast would be assigned to lands above the thirty-seventh parallel, which today marks the Kansas-Oklahoma border. Tribes from the southeast were to be relocated below that line.[18]

It was easy for even well-intentioned U.S. officials to conclude that by removal to the west, the white man was really doing the Indian a favor. To reinforce this belief, it was common practice for officials, including presidents, to promise faithfully that the tribespeople's new home in the west would forever be "a territory set apart and dedicated to their use and government forever."[19] Inherent in such promises was the concept of a separate, inviolable homeland over which the tribes would hold total jurisdiction. This notion would soon be overwhelmed by the incessant passion of whites for land.

The United States was particularly interested in confirming the Red River as a southern boundary to the Louisiana Purchase. However, it made little effort to explore the interior of the territory and establish proprietorship over the resident Plains tribes until 1834, when the Leavenworth expedition marched from Fort Gibson to the Wichita Mountains. U.S. interest in the region prior to the Civil War centered largely on the issue of potential transportation routes westward.

Attempts were made to work out peace agreements with the Plains tribes mainly to safeguard citizen travelers and trade.

Perhaps the territory's most unique quality was its contradictory position of dual ownership. Although the United States had by treaty expressly promised that various areas belonged to individual tribes, it was clear that both government officials and U.S. citizens considered the territory to be occupied by those tribes only at the will and consent of the United States. The promise of tribal separation retarded but did not stop outside intrusion. Both the United States and the Republic of Texas felt free to invade the Indian homeland when their interests were threatened.

The concept of exclusion for Indian Territory had, in fact, been doomed from the very start. Both the United States and the various tribes independently considered themselves to be lords of the land. Furthermore, the march of white settlement onto Native-held areas was virtually unstoppable; it merely swept past Indian Territory for a time, inevitably to return. The final barriers were broken by the Civil War, which spawned military invasion and punitive postwar treaties that essentially ended tribal autonomy over the land.

The era of the Indian Territory frontier produced few lasting physical mementos. Some still remain: a buffalo wallow indentation, the restored ruins of a military fort, a once-stately tribal edifice, a country schoolhouse, a crumbling log-cabin homestead or caved-in dugout—even the railroad depots are now antiques of a bygone age.

The imprints of the past, however, are not as invisible to the eye as they may initially seem. Resting in our historical archives are the journals, diaries, and records of those who made that history. Here rest the testaments of men who first explored the raw country that once was Indian Territory.

We are fortunate, indeed, that many of those who first came left behind diaries, memoirs, letters, books, and other accounts of their experiences and the world they knew. In fact, Americans of the nineteenth century were far better recorders of the everyday life around them than we are in today's overfictionalized America. Even the barely literate Jacob Fowler penned a spacious view of his experiences in the primordial West. Of particular consequence were West Point graduates, officers such as Randolph B. Marcy who were often the educated elite of the frontier. But others, such as merchant Josiah Gregg, artist George Catlin, British scientist Thomas Nuttall, government official George Sibley, and Indian trader Thomas James, added enormously to the lore of the early West.

There were those who left behind no written accounts but imparted their discoveries to others by word of mouth. Men such as the Chouteaus of Missouri, Indian trader Jesse Chisholm, and military scout Black Beaver— one of many Delaware Indians who explored western America widely—saw and knew the country of Indian Territory as well as any and helped to guide military expeditions, peace commissioners, surveying parties, and others into uncharted and often perilous areas.

The early explorers came for a variety of reasons. Some came to garner great mineral wealth, some to investigate scientifically the natural habitat, some to develop peaceful relations and trading operations with the resident tribes, some to open transportation routes, and others merely to traverse the area on their way to distant lands. Lurking all too surely in the historical distance was the white man's desire to reap of the land and eventually to possess it. Although no move was made prior to the Civil War to open Indian Territory to non-Indian occupation, there can be no doubt that each intrusion contributed inexorably to the end of tribal sovereignty. Each was preface to the inevitable political conquest of the territory and to its social and economic incorporation into the United States.

Nevertheless, whatever fate awaited the region in the years ahead, this was the day of hardy men who, by foot or by horse, pushed with resolve and courage into the wilds of the American West. Theirs was a fascinating period of American history distinguished by the impelling force of adventure in exploring a land filled with mystery and danger and wonders of discovery.

The Spanish and the Prehorse Plains

If the Indians on the mid-Plains of North America had had calendars and recorded history, they might well have marked July 2, 1541, as a significant date. It was on that day that a party of Indian hunters, with some of their women, were killing and butchering buffalo along the Arkansas River between present-day Kingsley and Larned, Kansas. They looked up to see a strange and disturbing sight coming toward them along the river from the southwest.

What they saw was a group of alien beings, some walking and some riding on the backs of equally strange animals. Two or three wore long black frocks that reached to the ground. Most of the others, however, were clad in hats and coats that glistened blindingly in the sun. They carried objects that had the appearance of being weapons, and they, too, glistened. The hunters were badly frightened and began to run away in terror. Then they heard a voice from the group call out to them in their own language. The owner of the voice proceeded to harangue them until their fears were calmed. Finally they came forth to meet and talk with the strange men in the shining hats and coats.[1]

The intruding aliens were the Spanish command of General Francisco Vásquez de Coronado, who was searching for a city of gold called Quivira. It was the arrival of this Spanish *entrada* (entrance) onto the Central Plains of North America, some eighty years before the Pilgrims landed at Plymouth Rock, that began the recorded history of the region. Even though Coronado and his men crossed Oklahoma only at the Panhandle, the accounts of their journey were the first to introduce to the world the Indian tribes then living in the Texas Panhandle and southern Kansas; these tribes were simultaneously native to Oklahoma.

Born about 1510 in Spain, Coronado was made governor of Nuevo Galicia, Mexico, in 1538. Hearing tales of the dazzling wealth of the Seven Cities of Cíbola, he led a great expedition north into southeast Arizona. He discovered the Grand Canyon but failed to find the great riches he sought. Establishing a base for his army near present-day Albuquerque, New Mexico, Coronado lorded for a time over the Native Pueblo tribes, draining them so of food and other resources that they finally rose up in rebellion.[2]

Coronado now looked hopefully to the northeast for the wealth he yearned desperately to find. On April 23, 1541, he marched from Tiguex, New Mexico, with an army of 1,500 men accompanied by a herd of 500 cattle, 500 sheep, and 1,000 horses. The expedition was inspired

→

Spanish and French Visitations *(opposite page)*

1. Coronado—1541
2. Oñate—1601
3. Baca—1634
4. de Vargas—1638
5. La Harpe—1719
6. Du Tisné—1719
7. Mallets/Fabry—1740–1742
8. Sandoval—1749
9. Parrilla—1759
10. Gaignard—1773
11. De Mézières—1778
12. Vial—1786
13. Malgares—1806

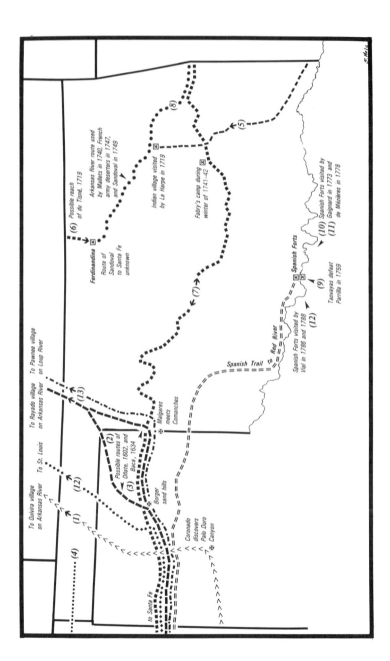

To Quivira village
on Arkansas River

To St. Louis

To Rayado village
on Arkansas River

To Pawnee village
on Loup River

(4)

(1)

(12)

(13)

(3)

(2)

Possible routes of
Oñate, 1602, and
Baca, 1634

to Santa Fe

Coronado
discovers
Palo Duro
Canyon

Borger
sand hills

Malgares
meets
Comanches

Spanish Trail

Red River

To Spanish Forts visited by
Vial in 1786 and 1788

(12)

Spanish Forts

(9)

Taovayas defeat
Parrilla in 1759

(10) Spanish Forts visited by
(11) Gaignard in 1773 and
de Mézières in 1778

(7)

Fabry's camp during
winter of 1741–42

Indian village visited
by La Harpe in 1719

Ferdinandina

Route of
Sandoval
to Santa Fe
unknown

(6) Possible reach
of du Tisné, 1719

Arkansas River route used
by Mallets in 1740, French
army deserters in 1747,
and Sandoval in 1749

(8)

(5)

by an Indian guide known to them as the Turk, a Plains Indian who had been victimized by the slave-taking habits common among the competing tribes.

For over a month the Turk beguiled the Spaniards with tales of a city of gold named Quivira. He led them aimlessly about the vast, treeless prairies of the Texas Panhandle before the conquistadors realized their error. During this month of wandering, Coronado and his men encountered several tribes of Indians.

Near the New Mexico–Texas border, the Spaniards met two Indian villages, both bands of a people known to them as the Querechos. It is generally accepted that they were branches of the Apache Nation. These people, who were somewhat taller than the Pueblo Indians of New Mexico, were deeply enmeshed in a buffalo-hunting culture, depending on the animal for virtually all of their needs.

The entire substance of the animal was put to use. Its skin was used to stretch about poles for homes as well as for robes, ropes, shoes, and various articles of clothing. The sinews were made into thread. The bladders served as containers for water and for the blood of the buffalo, which the Indians drank. The meat was eaten slightly cooked or raw, often with chunks of uncooked tallow. Some of the meat was dried and ground into a mash, then boiled in a pot to produce a pemmican that could be taken along on extended journeys.

The brains of the buffalo were used to dress and soften the hides, and hooves were used for glue on arrows. Horns of the animals were fashioned into ropes and girths, and the fur from the animals' forequarters was turned into belts and ornaments. The Querechos traded their buffalo hides among the Pueblos for corn, cloth, and pottery.[3]

Dogs were used extensively by the tribe for hauling goods, sometimes being fitted with cinched packsaddles and at other times hitched to long travois poles. These

For gold and God—the Spanish came to the Central Plains to find gold and to Christianize the Natives of the New World. (Isidro Felix de Espinosa, *El Peregrino Septentrional Alante*, WA1849, Research Publications, Inc.)

large, wolflike dogs often moved in trains, growling fiercely at any interference and setting up a terrific howl whenever their thirty- to forty-pound load would slip. Often the dogs were taken along on hunting missions, either to carry provisions or to haul back the kill.[4]

Still following the misguidance of the Turk, Coronado and his army stumbled upon the immense abyss of Palo Duro Canyon. Here, encamped on the floor of the chasm, was the village of another Indian band known to Coronado as the Teyas. Some scholars believe that this band was related to the Tejas of eastern Texas, from whom Texas got its name. These Indians also followed the buffalo, though they were enemies to the Querechos. The Teyas were a large people who painted their faces and bodies liberally. They knew about the Native tribes to the north that Coronado would soon encounter.[5]

Having now placed the Turk in chains and taken up the truer lead of an Indian guide named Sopete, Coronado ordered his army to return to New Mexico. At the same time, he led a select group of thirty horsemen, six unmounted soldiers, Fray Juan de Padilla, and servants—a total of forty persons—northward out of Palo Duro. Following his compass almost due north, Coronado crossed the Oklahoma Panhandle and reached the Arkansas River near present-day Ford, Kansas.

After marching eastward down the river for three days, he encountered the Indian hunters. He then followed the river three more days past its great bend to arrive at the Indians' village near Lyons, Kansas. There, at the Turk's Quivira, the Spanish governor met a tribe of Indians who were much different from those previously encountered. The Spaniards called them the Quiviras, but scholars generally agree that these were the ancestors of the Wichita Indians.

These Indians did not move with the buffalo but lived in permanent villages of round, grass-thatched huts with long, low entrance ways. Inside there were no dividing walls, but each contained a loft where the family resided and kept its belongings. The Quiviras were both hunters and planters, raising maize, beans, and melons. They baked bread beneath their lodge fires.

Quivira, however, was a great disappointment to the Spaniards, who had hoped to find a city of enormous wealth. Marching on northward into central Kansas still in search of gold, they met another band of Indians called the Tabas, thought by some to be the later-known Taovayas of Oklahoma and Texas.[6] After a month of futile searching for riches, Coronado held a conference with his men.

They agreed that it would be best to turn back for Tiguex. In revenge for the lies the Turk had told them, he was put to death by Coronado's officers. The act was committed at night by means of a garrote about the Turk's neck. He was buried secretly, so that the Indians would not know. Then in mid-August 1541, with six young Quiviras as guides, the Spaniards began their return to Nueva Galicia, none the richer except for having been the first Europeans to enter the Central Plains of North America. Following this adventure, Coronado became involved in a fruitless war with the Indians of Mexico. He was dismissed as governor in 1544 and spent the remainder of his life in obscurity in Mexico City, dying in 1554.

At the same time that Coronado was marching to Quivira and back, another Spanish soldier of fortune, Hernando de Soto, was conquering his way from Florida to northeastern Arkansas. De Soto encountered mound-building tribes in Louisiana and eastern Arkansas. On the upper Ouachita River, he was attacked by Natives who lived in grass-thatched huts and whose weaponry included lances made from long poles with tips hardened by fire. Although de Soto died in Louisiana on May 21, 1542, his men continued on to explore eastern Texas, where they encountered the Tejas Indians.[7]

The Spanish reentered southern Kansas that same year when Fray Juan de Padilla, reputedly a "fighting priest," led a small missionary group back to the Quivira villages. After working there to Christianize the Indians for a time, Padilla decided to extend his efforts to the northeast. He set out to attend a group of Indians known as the Guas, who were likely the Kansa, or Kaw, Indians. But after only a few days on the trail, Padilla's party was attacked by hostile Indians and murdered. This is believed to have taken place near Herrington, Kansas, where a marker has been erected to note the event.[8]

It was 1592 before the region was visited again, this time by thirty men under two Spanish officers, Antonio Gutiérrez de Humaña and Francisco Leyva de Bonilla, who departed New Mexico to escape arrest for taking cattle and servants away from the citizens of New Mexico. The party headed for Quivira in search of the "gold mines of Tindan,"[9] guided by an Indian called Joseph, the only member of the Padilla party to return after a year's time to tell the story of the ill-fated *entrada*.

Traveling for a month through great herds of buffalo and Indian villages in the Texas Panhandle, the group turned northward. The thirty men journeyed fifteen more days, undoubtedly passing through present-day Oklahoma, to a large Indian village. There the houses were built on a frame of stakes with straw roofs.[10] This is believed to have been Quivira.

When, like Coronado, the travelers found no gold, they continued on to the north. Three days past the village, the two Spanish officers quarreled. Gutiérrez stabbed Leyva to death with a knife after the other had threatened him with a stick. Burying Leyva there, Gutiérrez continued on, reaching a large river that was over half a mile wide and so deep and sluggish that he dared not try to cross it. On returning to the Indian village, the Spaniards were attacked by Indians, who set the grass on fire around the expeditioners and burned all but Joseph and one or two others to death.[11]

Another Spanish thrust onto the Central Plains occurred in 1601 when Juan de Oñate, governor and capitán-general of New Mexico, set out once more to locate Quivira. He was still hopeful of finding great mineral wealth, but he also wished to teach the Holy Gospel to "the barbarous nations, now in the power of Satan."[12]

Oñate took with him Gutiérrez's guide, Joseph; seventy well-equipped men; over seven hundred horses and mules; six carts drawn by mules; two drawn by oxen; a retinue of servants; four pieces of artillery; and baggage. Two Franciscan friars accompanied the expedition, as did Oñate's son and two nephews.

Leaving San Gabriel, New Mexico, on June 23, 1601, Oñate and his party moved leisurely eastward across the Texas Panhandle following the Canadian River. Encumbered by livestock, the expedition seldom made more than 10 miles a day. Accounts of the journey state that after traveling 111 leagues (estimated to be around 333 miles), Oñate encountered sand dunes where he turned from east to north and traveled a few days between two small streams that flowed to the east.

Oñate scholars have commonly identified these sand dunes as Antelope Hills. These hills, however, are not sand dunes any more than are other buttes the expedition had already passed along the Canadian. It seems plausible to reason that Oñate left the Canadian at the sand hills just west of what is now Canadian, Texas. This would have taken the expedition on a northeasterly course between Wolf and Kiowa Creeks of the Texas Panhandle and northwestern Oklahoma.[13]

Now moving across level ground teeming with buffalo, the Spanish army began to meet Indians who made signs of peace by extending a hand toward the sun and then placing it on their chest, exclaiming, "Escanjaque!" It was by this word that the Spaniards identified the tribe, which undoubtedly populated northwestern Oklahoma at that time.[14]

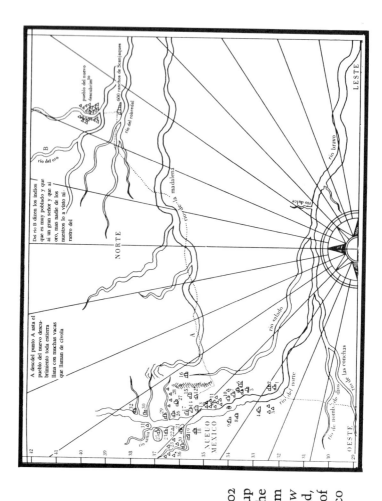

Juan de Oñate's map of 1602 indicates the route he took up the Canadian River to the Rayado villages. (Adapted from *The Rediscovery of New Mexico*, George P. Hammond, ed., and used by permission of the University of New Mexico Press)

The Escanjaques, whose social characteristics were much the same as those of the Apaches of New Mexico but who spoke a different language, resided in a village of some five to six thousand inhabitants. Their circular huts were made of branches and poles covered with buffalo hides and stood ten feet high, ninety feet in circumference. The Escanjaques indicated that there were more of their villages in the vicinity, making them a sizable tribal unit.

These tall, well-proportioned people lived by the hunt and practiced no agriculture. They ate their buffalo meat without bread, but with roots and fruit. Seen as they were in the summertime, the Escanjaque men went about largely unclothed. The women wore only small pieces of soft skin over their pubic areas. Their faces, bare breasts, and arms were painted profusely with stripes. The men, who were still horseless, carried bows and arrows and hardwood clubs headed with large pieces of flint. A strap attached to the handles of their clubs prevented their being lost in battle. A large buffalo-hide shield gave the warrior protection for his entire body.

They were at war, the Escanjaques said, with a tribe to the north. Because these people painted stripes horizontally across their cheeks from ear to ear, the Spaniards called them Rayados. The Rayados are believed to have been Wichitas. When the Escanjaques learned that the Spaniards wished to have revenge for the killing of Gutiérrez, they claimed the Rayados were the guilty ones and eagerly offered to go along and help. It was an offer that Oñate was reluctant to reject, though he did not wish to accept either.

Followed by the Escanjaques, Oñate continued on north, coming onto a Rayado village after traveling some twenty to thirty miles. Because of the Escanjaque presence just behind the Spaniards, they were met with hostility by the Rayados. Rayado warriors appeared on the hilltop before Oñate's line of march. They were armed with bows and arrows, shields, and war clubs. Their warriors challenged the intruders to battle by shouting, twanging their bow strings, and tossing handfuls of dirt into the air, the universal sign of war on the Plains.

The Spaniards managed to persuade the Rayados that their intentions were friendly, and the Indians' attitude changed to one of peace. They came forward to take strings of beads from their own necks and place them around those of the Spaniards. Others brought huge round loaves of bread, and Oñate's men made them presents of knives, tobacco, and other items.[15]

On the following morning, the Escanjaques arrived, fiercely painted for war. They began shouting insults and challenges at the Rayados. Wishing to find out if it had been the Rayados who killed Gutiérrez, Oñate took prisoner eight Rayados who arrived bringing gifts of corn and placed them in chains. When questioned about Gutiérrez's death, the prisoners insisted that the Spaniard had been killed eighteen days' march from there. They also told Oñate that he should not believe the Escanjaques, who practiced cannibalism and were their mortal enemies.[16]

Taking his prisoners, Oñate advanced into the village only to find that the inhabitants had deserted it and fled. The Escanjaques now rushed up and began setting fire to the grass houses, but Oñate ordered his men to stop them. He permitted the Escanjaques only to take some of the corn stored in the village after a recent harvest.

The Rayado village consisted of twelve hundred grass-thatched houses situated on the banks of a good-sized river. This is thought to have been the Arkansas River either in present-day northern Oklahoma or southern Kansas.[17] The huts were much as those Coronado had encountered—round, built with forked wooden poles that were joined by sticks and covered on the outside with straw. They were two lances high and large enough inside to hold eight to ten persons, being seventy to eighty feet in circumference. Bunklike beds were made of poles and cross-laid with sticks.

Some six feet above ground level were balcony platforms that the occupants reached from the outside by portable ladders. The Spanish thought that the Indians probably slept there in hot weather, particularly since the lower parts of the houses were often infested with fleas. Gardens of beans and melons along with corn fields surrounded the village. Most of the houses contained a flat stone and a smaller one for grinding corn, a supply of which was stored in separate silo structures.[18]

Like the Escanjaques, the Rayados wore virtually no clothing during the summer. What they did wear was of animal skin, the Spaniards finding no evidence of cotton material such as was used in the New Mexican pueblos. The men were well built, the stripes across their faces giving them an especially fierce look. They carried bows with very short, flint-headed arrows—too short, the Spaniards judged, to be effective at long range. Some of the Indians wore sea shells from some distant ocean on their foreheads.[19]

Oñate released six of the eight prisoners, telling them to inform their people that it was safe for them to return to their village. The Rayados did not return, and that night the other two hostages escaped. Having also released Joseph, Oñate was without a guide. Seizing several Escanjaques who were looting the Rayado village, Oñate queried them regarding the land beyond the river. The Indians told of even larger settlements farther up the river. When Oñate showed them several gold pieces and a silver pin, they showed no familiarity with either form of metal.

Nonetheless, the Spaniard took up his march, heading north and east for a short distance. The explorers found more and more villages. Naked warriors were seen dashing furtively about, and Oñate's officers began to fear an ambush. They presented Oñate with a petition asking that they withdraw, saying it was too much risk for such a small force.

Oñate conceded and turned about, the day being September 29. But as his advance guard approached the deserted Rayado village, it was met by some twenty-five hundred to three thousand Escanjaques amassed in battle array. The Indians began firing at them, but the Spaniards formed in ranks and marched on, making signs of peace as they advanced. The Escanjaques continued to attack, forming in a semicircle and sending a barrage of arrows at the conquistadors. The Spaniards began firing their harquebuses and artillery, knocking down and killing a few of the Indians. The others retreated into some rocks. A three-hour battle ensued, and several Escanjaque women and boys were captured before Oñate finally ordered a withdrawal. The Escanjaques contented themselves by burning some more Rayado huts as the Spaniards, who suffered only slight wounds, marched off to the south.[20]

After his trip to Oklahoma and Kansas, Oñate led an expedition west to the Colorado River, following it to lower California. He resigned as governor in 1609. Because he had found no gold, he was convicted on charges of misconduct in 1614 but was eventually pardoned before his death in 1624.

Oñate's exploration across Oklahoma into neighboring Kansas is the only well-recorded look we have of the region during the seventeenth century. Another intrusion was made in 1634 when Captain Alonzo Baca, accompanied by Indian allies, trekked some three hundred leagues eastward from Santa Fe. Like Oñate, Baca arrived at a large river that his guides would not cross. When the Indians warned that the Spaniards would be killed by the Quiviras, Baca decided that his force was too small to take the risk and turned back. Thus far no revealing accounts of Baca's trip have come to light, so his route and details of the Indians he met remain mysteries.

In 1606 a Quivira chief arrived at Santa Fe with six hundred warriors to request help against the Ayjaos, who may have been the Escanjaques. The chief promised friendship and land in return for Spanish help against these enemies. What came of this tribe is not known, almost the entire century to follow being silent on Spanish contact with the Plains tribes.[21]

In the fall of 1696 the Spanish governor of New Mexico, Diego de Vargas, set out across the Taos Mountains to capture a group of Pueblo Indians who had refused to accept Spanish domination. The chase took de Vargas into what is now the Oklahoma Panhandle, where the rebellious Natives were captured. The excursion took only seventeen days, two of which were spent in camp during an early Plains blizzard. The distance traveled was eighty-four leagues, or just over two hundred miles.[22]

Virtually nothing concerning the Plains tribes came to light from the de Vargas excursion, and the century came to a close with little more known about the Oklahoma region and its inhabitants than had been revealed by Coronado and Oñate. However, when exploration resumed during the eighteenth century, it became apparent that numerous changes had taken place among the Natives of the region.

Arrival of the French

The story is told that the Osages sent word to the Pawnee Picts of a Frenchman who was coming among them for the purpose of stealing their young boys and selling them into slavery, as the French were known to do. When Claude Charles Du Tisné appeared, the Pawnee Picts advanced toward him with their tomahawks ready to do him in. But Du Tisné, a small-of-stature Parisian who had once been rejected for service in the French army, stood his ground without fear. As a Pawnee Pict raised his tomahawk to crush Du Tisné's skull, the Frenchman suddenly discarded the wig he wore to reveal his shaved, completely bald head.

Throwing the hairpiece onto the ground in front of the Indians, Du Tisné exclaimed: "There! You will have my scalp, then take it up if you dare to do it!" The warriors were taken aback in astonishment, providing Du Tisné the opportunity to convince them that he came on friendly terms and was not there to take their children for slaves. Later he further amazed the tribesmen by pouring brandy in a pot and setting it on fire.

He claimed that he had the power to set the water in their lakes on fire and burn their canoes.[1]

The Spanish of New Mexico had lifted the curtain of the mid-Plains and provided written history with the first brief glimpse of the boundless prairies and their inhabitants. Nothing more would be revealed until the year 1719, when two French military officers, Bernard de La Harpe and Claude Charles Du Tisné, entered the Arkansas River country of Kansas and Oklahoma — from different directions but coincidentally in the same year and month and without knowledge of the other's activities.

During the first half of the eighteenth century, the rivalry between the Spanish of New Mexico and Texas and the French of Louisiana and Illinois brought the area that is now Oklahoma into special importance. René Robert Cavelier, sieur de La Salle, had explored the great Mississippi River in 1682 and laid claim to Louisiana for the king of France.

Many of the streams spanning westward from the Mississippi offered routes for travel and trade between the French settlements at St. Louis and New Orleans and the Spanish settlements at San Antonio and Santa Fe. Furthermore, there was a wealth of furs, robes, horses, mules, and Indian slaves to be obtained in this Spanish-claimed wilderness. The French were anxious to exploit this potential market and to reach the mineral-rich lands of New Mexico.

However, the warring Indian tribes of the Plains presented a barrier to French trade expansion. The factionalism and hostility among the many Indian nations caused each to resent and distrust the French. The Osages did not want them to trade with the Pawnee Picts; the Pawnee Picts did not want them trading with the Comanches; and the Comanches did not want them trading with the Apaches. Especially, these tribes did not want guns and ammunition to reach their enemies. To overcome this, the French made strong efforts to develop alliances with various tribes, and their traders aggressively moved out to contact the Indians.

In 1714 some French traders had joined with a group of Jumano (possibly Wichita) Indians in attacking a Cuartelejos settlement in New Mexico, killing thirty people and carrying off twenty-eight captives, who were probably sold into slavery. The Spanish attempted to counter the French intrusion with a 1720 military expedition under Pedro de Villasur, who penetrated as far north as the Platte River. However, the Spanish command was virtually wiped out by a combined force of French-allied Otoes and Pawnees of that area.[2]

The French effort to secure pacts with the Indians of the Plains brought Bernard de La Harpe, former commandant at Natchitoches, Louisiana, to Arkansas and Oklahoma in 1719. La Harpe, who had been granted a concession for a post on the Red River by the French government, erected a log-house fort called the Masonite Post near present-day Fulton, Arkansas. After making first contacts with several of the Caddoan tribes of the region, La Harpe set out to meet other Indian bands, display the goods he could offer for trade, and make alliances with them. This effort would take him into present-day Oklahoma.[3]

Departing his Arkansas post on August 11, 1719, with some twenty-two horses loaded with provisions and trade goods and accompanied by two French companions, three soldiers, three Indian guides, and two Negro servants, La Harpe moved up the Red River and crossed into present-day Oklahoma on August 13. The eleven-man party sought to avoid the hostile Lipan Apache Indians of Texas, who had the advantage of many good horses, while their enemies had few. On the night of August 14, La Harpe camped near the site of present-day Idabel.

From there he made a steady march toward the north, noting the lay of the land and its potential mineral content. He hunted as he went, bagging a large bear as well as deer. On August 21, the men met with a band of thirty Caddoan hunters who were returning to their village after killing forty-six buffalo. The Caddos were fearful of meeting Osages, who had already become an intimidating influence in Oklahoma as far south as the Red River.

On August 26, La Harpe's small band came face to face with a band of Osages who had their tomahawks ready for attack. Putting on a bold front, La Harpe and three of his party, all well armed, advanced to meet the war party. The Osages, surprised as much by this act as by seeing white men in the area, tendered the peace pipe instead of the tomahawk. This meeting may have taken place just east of present-day McAlester. Still moving to the north along the course of Gaines Creek, the French party met another band of Caddos, who accompanied them as they crossed the Canadian River near the site of today's Eufaula and moved on to a large Indian encampment east of present-day Bixby, arriving there on September 3, 1719.

This temporary confederation of some nine different Wichita bands included the Ousita (Wichita proper), Touacaro (Tawakoni), Toayas (Taovayas), Ascani (Yscani), plus other bands soon to lose their identities. La Harpe estimated their number at six thousand. The French party was greeted by a Tawakoni chief whose party was mounted on beautiful horses with Spanish-style saddles and bridles. After being feasted generously on corn-meal bread and smoked meat, La Harpe was placed on a handsome horse and escorted into the village. There he was carried bodily on the shoulders of two Indians into a lodge and deposited at its center on a buffalo hide.

After the principal men of the various bands extended their hands as a sign of friendship, they took seats in a circle about the Frenchman. The trader presented them with gifts of bullets, powder, hatchets, knives, and other goods. The Tawakoni chief, a young man in his midtwenties, responded with a gift of a bonnet of eagle feathers and two calumet plumes. One, he said, stood for peace and one for war.

All of the following day was consumed by a peace-making ritual. It was a long day, indeed, for La Harpe, with the ceremonies beginning at eight o'clock in the morning and still continuing when he finally retired two hours past midnight. With the arrival of an unidentified roving band, the number of Indians who feasted, sang, and danced grew to an estimated seven thousand. Some of the older chiefs performed dexterous plume rites and harangued the assembly on the value of an alliance with the French, who could provide them with arms and trade goods. Others told the visitors of their fighting power and listed the many scalps they had taken in battle.

The next morning La Harpe was carried on a buffalo hide to a foliage-covered bower. After painting his face with a blue pigment, the Indians presented him with buffalo robes, rock salt, tobacco, and even an eight-year-old Lipan Indian slave boy. The boy was minus his two little fingers. They had been eaten by his captors to indicate that he someday might well serve as food for the cannibalistic tribe. Chief Togas told La Harpe that if he had arrived one day sooner, he could have participated in the public feast of seventeen captives that they had recently devoured!

Although La Harpe went no farther inland than this village on the Arkansas, he did learn of some of the Indian nations to the north and west. He was told that the Arkansas River formed two branches, one leading to the country of the Padoucas, as the Comanches were known to other tribes. The Comanches, whose villages extended far to the north, were enemies of the eastern tribes as well as of the northern Pawnees. The prairies to the west were covered with horses and buffalo, the Indians said; and they told La Harpe of a place where a lot of salt could be found. This was likely either the Salt Plains near what is now Cherokee, Oklahoma, or the saline north of Woodward. However, it was risky to go there, the Indians said, because of the Lipan Indians who often passed by from Texas to make war on the Comanches.

The tribes of eastern Oklahoma, the Frenchmen found, made an annual habit of leaving their villages in October to spend the winter hunting, for buffalo mainly. They returned only in March to plant their crops of maize, beans, pumpkins, and tobacco. The cabins of these Indians were built of straw and reeds that were covered with dirt to form a dome shape. Over the entrance to each hut were leather patches on which had been painted the symbols of each band. Usually the paintings were of the sun, moon, stars, or various animals. Dining plates were made of reeds so tightly woven that water would not penetrate. Wild game and the abundant fish in the rivers provided the principal food source. A meal consisted of greens, smoked meat, and a maize–beef marrow mixture.

La Harpe found the Indians to be people of good judgment and, he decided, more clever than others he had met. The men were, however, prone to indolence and spent much of their time eating, smoking, playing, and—evidently from his description of them as "libertines"—engaged in sexual indulgence. The Indian women, whom La Harpe found quite attractive, did their utmost to please the visitors. La Harpe felt the Indians were largely hedonistic in their attention to worshiping pleasures of the body. However, they did recognize and worship a "great spirit" to whom they paid homage with gifts.

The Indians were drawn in particular to the two black men with La Harpe's party, perhaps in part because of tribal religious beliefs. The tribes' concept of life after death involved a trip aboard a great canoe. The canoe was guided by a black man who had horns.

Those who had lived their lives well and had been good warriors would be put ashore in a prairie country filled with game. But those who had not lived a good life or served their people well would be left in an arid land where they would live in misery forever.

Before departing the Indian villages, La Harpe had one of his men carve on a post the coat of arms of the king of France and plant the post at the center of the village. He explained to the Indians that it was a symbol of their new alliance with the French.

Even as La Harpe was departing on September 13, taking with him beans and maize provided by the Indians, Du Tisné was on his way to visit the Pawnee Picts. Scholars are uncertain as to the location of the Pawnee Pict village.[4] Some think it was in northeastern Oklahoma, but this appears to be much too close to the enemy Osages for a Wichita village. Others think it was either in north-central Oklahoma or just across into southern Kansas near the Arkansas River.

Du Tisné had left the Illinois country during the spring of 1719 carrying trade goods with which he hoped to establish commercial relations with western tribes. He was received kindly at an Osage village in Vernon County, Missouri. The Osages were well supplied with horses, which they stole from the Pawnee Picts, and were willing to sell them. The Osages were also interested in establishing trade relations. But when Du Tisné indicated that he wished to go on to the villages of the Tattooed Pawnees to the southwest, the Osages objected strongly. They finally permitted him passage only when he agreed to leave his trade goods behind.

Taking three guns for himself and his guide, Du Tisné traveled forty leagues to two Pawnee Pict villages. In his records, he states that the salt plains were two days' journey to the west and six hours' journey to the southwest. This indicates that the villages were in or very close to northern Oklahoma.[5]

The Pawnee Picts received the Frenchman with displeasure, the Osages having sent word ahead that he was after slaves. But Du Tisné was able to convince them that he wished to conduct trade. On September 27, he succeeded in making a pact with the Indians. Although there were about three hundred horses in the two villages he visited, they were so highly prized that the Pawnee Picts would not give them up. However, Du Tisné managed to trade three guns, powder, a pickax, and a knife for two horses and a mule with a Spanish brand. The trader wished to continue on to visit the Comanches on the western prairie, but the Pawnee Picts also opposed his visiting their mortal enemies. He returned to Missouri, apparently having heard nothing from the Indians of La Harpe's recent visit a short distance to the south.

La Harpe returned to Oklahoma in 1721, but some degree of mystery surrounds this visit, for no diary or log of the journey has come to light. Only two brief and unidentified accounts by men who were with La Harpe as he boated up the Arkansas River give clue to the exploration. The time of year and circumstances of the trip are far from clear, but one account has it that the excursion was made in search of an emerald rock rumored to be somewhere along the Arkansas. With twenty-two men, La Harpe ascended the river for more than 250 leagues, then moved 50 leagues more by land. La Harpe's party most likely went as far as the Three Forks of the Arkansas River near present-day Muskogee or Fort Gibson—only a few miles from where he had met with the Indians in 1719.

La Harpe reportedly met several bands of Quapaws on his journey. But no records exist to provide further details regarding the adventures of this expedition. We are told only that La Harpe and his crew saw a beautiful country whose vast flower-covered prairies teemed with buffalo, stags, does, and other wild life. There was, of course, no emerald rock.[6]

While visiting a forward settlement on the Arkansas, La Harpe was informed that during the preceding year five Frenchmen had headed up the river to trade for horses with the Indian nations on its headwaters. They had been murdered by Osages.[7]

In 1721 a Spanish caravan of three hundred persons — men, women, soldiers, and at least one priest — set out from Santa Fe on a journey across the uncharted prairies for the Missouri River. They took with them droves of horses, cattle, and other livestock. Their purpose was to win the friendship of the Osages in an effort to set them against their French allies. However, when the Spaniards encountered a village of the Missouri tribe, they mistook it to be Osage and disclosed their scheme. As a result, the Missouris attacked the Spaniards and drove them back to New Mexico. In doing so, they captured the "ornaments of the chapel" belonging to the Spanish priest and carried them in triumphant display to the French of Illinois.[8]

The French were soon to extend themselves even farther west beyond the Missouri River into Kansas. By doing so, they contacted Indian tribes that also ranged across present-day Oklahoma. In 1724, after having established Fort Orleans in Carroll County, Missouri, Frenchman Étienne Veniard de Bourgmond organized an expedition to contact the Comanches, whose warfare with the Missouri River tribes was a principal barrier to French trading efforts to reach Santa Fe. Accompanied by eighty-eight Missouri Indians and sixty-eight Osages, Bourgmond's party reached a Kansa village on the Missouri River. The Kansa smoked the pipes of peace with Bourgmond, regaled him and his men with large quantities of grapes, and agreed to accompany the group to treat with the Comanches.[9]

On July 24 Bourgmond rode off to the west with a small army of nineteen Frenchmen, some three hundred Kansa and Missouri warriors, and over eight hundred Indian women and children. The Frenchmen were amazed at the loads carried on the march by the women and impressed with the train of over three hundred dogs that pulled the travois loaded with baggage. After six days on the trail, Bourgmond became so ill that he was carried back to Fort Orleans on a litter. His men went on, however, and met with the Comanches, who were highly pleased at the return of two Comanche captives whom Bourgmond had ransomed from the Kansa. The Comanches and the Kansa now made friendship visits to each other's villages.

Recovered from his illness, Bourgmond set out again in October with a party of forty men and several pack horses loaded with gifts—guns, sabers, axes, knives, combs, awls, kettles, bells, beads, cloth, rings, boxes of vermilion, etc. Advancing westward over sixty-five leagues (about 170 miles), they found the grass burned before them. The caravan signaled its approach by setting fire to unburned patches of grass. On October 18 a large answering smoke cloud was seen ahead, and presently an entourage of Comanche warriors came galloping toward the French party. Bourgmond ordered his men to take up arms as a precaution and saluted the Comanches with the French flag.

The Indians answered by raising their robes over their heads three times as an indication of peace. After smoking the peace pipe with Bourgmond, the Comanches mounted the visitors on horses and led them to their encampment. On the following day a grand chief and two hundred others came to the French camp, where Bourgmond had laid out his gifts on display. After another smoke the gifts were distributed. The Comanches were given a French flag and exhorted to live in peace with their neighbors.

The chiefs agreed to do this and offered the services of their warriors if they were needed by the French. One Comanche chief said that his people traded with the Spanish, who were twelve days away. They exchanged buffalo hides and other animal pelts for horses, which the Spanish had in great numbers. Seven mounts were presented to Bourgmond. The Comanche chief complained that the Spanish had traded hatchets made of soft iron and knives whose points would break off easily. He said his tribe was well supplied with horses, which they would trade to the French.

Despite the promises made in this meeting, the Comanches remained at war with the Indians to the east as well as with the Apaches to the south and persisted as a hindrance to the French traders. In 1739, however, Pierre and Paul Mallet and six others departed the French settlements of Illinois on an exploring-trading expedition up the Platte River (which they named). Turning southwest across western Kansas, they found stones with Spanish inscriptions, possibly in Ford County. Following the Arkansas River into Colorado, they encountered a Comanche village near present-day Lamar.

The Mallets continued on from there to Santa Fe, where they spent the winter in cordial reception by the Spanish authorities. On making a return in the spring of 1740, the party divided in the Texas Panhandle. Three of the group to Illinois returned by way of Kansas. The Mallets and two companions followed the course of the Canadian and Arkansas rivers to Arkansas Post (established in 1686 at the tri-juncture of the Arkansas, White, and Mississippi rivers by Henri de Tonti) and on to New Orleans.[10]

During the ensuing year, 1741, Governor Jeanne Baptiste de Moyne Bienville of Louisiana dispatched Fabry de la Bruyère, guided by the Mallets, to ascend the Canadian River for the purpose of opening a route to Santa Fe. The river soon became too shallow for their pirogues. Attempts to procure horses from the Indians failed, and finally Fabry returned east for the animals. Despite orders to wait for his return, the Mallets pushed on to Santa Fe on foot. Fabry returned to his camp, which is believed to have been near the

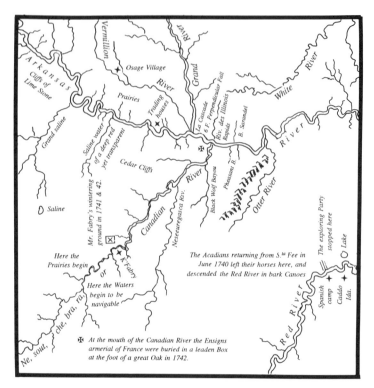

Zebulon Pike's map of 1806, as reflected in this rendering, indicates the then-known sites of present-day eastern Oklahoma as well as activity of the Mallets and Fabry, including the burial of a leaden box at the mouth of the Canadian River. (Adapted from Pike's Chart in Donald Jackson, *The Journals of Zebulon Montgomery Pike*)

boundary separating present-day McIntosh and Hughes Counties of Oklahoma, and spent the winter there. He later traveled from the Canadian to the Red River, where he visited among what were perhaps the same Indians La Harpe had met on the Arkansas. Pierre Mallet returned in 1751 with three other Frenchmen, traveling up the Red River before swinging southwest across Texas to New Mexico.[11]

Six years later three Spanish deserters from Arkansas Post set out up the Arkansas headed for Santa Fe.

Somewhere, either in Oklahoma or Kansas, they came to a Wichita village. From there they were conducted to a Comanche encampment and eventually taken on to Santa Fe.[12]

Felipe de Sandoval visited this same Wichita village in 1749. The Spaniard left Arkansas Post with a small party of Frenchmen and canoed up the river with Taos as his destination. After fifty days they reached two adjoining villages of grass huts that were defended by stockades and ditches. A French flag flew over the settlement, and evidence indicated that the French carried on a brisk business with the Indians. Although they grew corn, beans, and melons, these Indians were "fierce cannibals," Sandoval said. He claimed that he had seen them eat two of their captives. The Wichitas had only a few horses, these stolen from the Comanches to the west.

From the village Sandoval and two of his companions were guided to a Comanche camp. Already present were a French priest and several French traders who were bartering guns and goods for horses, hides, and Indian slaves. The Spanish had now become concerned about the French intrusion, and Sandoval was arrested and interrogated at length by authorities at Santa Fe. The Wichita village was reached by the Spanish again in 1759 when a military expedition was sent in pursuit of marauding Comanches.[13]

The location of the villages visited by Du Tisné in 1719, by the three deserters in 1747, and by Sandoval in 1749 will never be known with certainty. However, there is good reason to speculate that one or all may have been the Pawnee Pict–French settlement on the Arkansas River known as Ferdinandina. Existence of the trading center, located just south of the Kansas-Oklahoma line on the west bank of the Arkansas, has been verified by archaeological evidence. Scholars think that Ferdinandina lasted only from the late 1740s to past midcentury.

Hundreds of relics of French-Indian trade have been found at the site of Ferdinandina in Kay County: parts of flintlock guns, flints, lead bullets, gun trim, adzes, knives, porcelain beads, scissors, copper bells, copper and brass ornaments, glass, potsherds, flint scrapers, skinning knives, arrowheads, Indian pipe bowls, hatchets, and many other items that indicate an active trading operation.[14]

Little is known about Ferdinandina directly, but it is a matter of record that many of the traders on the Arkansas River were renegade deserters from the French army or from ships docking at New Orleans. Men who had committed robberies, rapes, or murders were now engaged in kidnapping and slave trading on a grand scale. Not unlikely, some of these men found their way up the Arkansas to Ferdinandina to help build the block house, log cabins, stockade, and surrounding moatlike ditch that archaeologists indicate once existed there.

But whether this was an official or a renegade French operation, it was destined to come to an end sometime in the late 1750s. Again, warring among the Plains Indians was the cause. The Osages, now well armed from British trade, had begun exerting themselves even more powerfully on the Plains. In 1751 they wiped out a Pawnee Pict village already decimated by measles and smallpox. The Pawnee Picts sought and obtained the help of the Comanches in making a vengeance raid on the Great Osage villages in Missouri. In a bloody battle some twenty-two Osages were killed, while the attackers lost twenty-seven of their own men.

The Osages retaliated for the attack with such force that the Pawnee Picts and other Wichita bands were forced to abandon Ferdinandina. They retreated south, eventually settling in two villages on the Red River. They fortified these villages much as they had Ferdinandina, evidently with the help of the French who moved with them. The villages became a consolidation

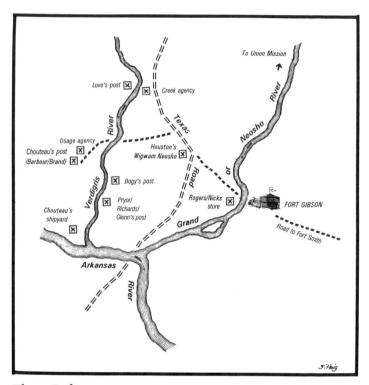

Three Forks

of the main Wichitas proper and the more militant Pawnee Picts, who were now known as the Taovayas. Here they conducted trading relations with the French of Louisiana and, later, the Spanish of Texas.

The first permanent white entry into the region of present-day Oklahoma was made by Jean Pierre Chouteau. A pioneer fur trader of Missouri who had a long acquaintance with the Osages, Chouteau first came to the Grand River in 1796 and established a trading post. Because there were no tribes native to the area, however, the venture was unsuccessful, and Chouteau returned to Missouri.[15]

In 1802 Spain replaced France in control of the Missouri country, and the great fur-trading monopoly formerly owned by the Chouteaus was transferred to Spaniard Manuel Lisa. To counter this transfer, Jean Pierre Chouteau persuaded some three thousand Osages under Chief Clermont to migrate to the Grand and Verdigris rivers of present-day northeastern Oklahoma. In partnership with Indian half-blood Joseph Revoir, Chouteau established himself at La Salina, now known as Salina, Oklahoma.

After Revoir was killed by Cherokee Indians in 1821, Chouteau and his son, Colonel Auguste Pierre Chouteau, purchased the trading house of Brand and Barbour where the Verdigris and Grand rivers joined the Arkansas to form what became known as Three Forks. The area soon became a thriving center of frontier commerce and the launching base for explorations westward.

——————————————————

Citadel on the Red River

During the mid-eighteenth century, the two Red River villages of the Wichitas, known as Spanish Forts, became the focus of Spanish and French attention. Both military and trading sojourns to them provide excellent revelations of Native life and events that dominated the region. The accounts of these visits tell us much not only about the Wichitas but also about the Comanche Nation that ruled over what is now western Oklahoma and much of Texas during that period.

The villages, located across from each other along the Red River near present-day Fleetwood, Oklahoma, and Spanish Fort, Texas, soon developed into a thriving trade center. Here the Wichitas proper and their Taovaya branch lived in an uncomfortable alliance with the powerful and demanding Comanches, to whom they traded French weapons and goods in exchange for stolen Spanish horses, mules, and captive children, mainly Apaches. These last were bartered in turn to French traders for more weapons and goods.

The consolidated bands of the Wichita confederacy were estimated to have a warrior force of from one to three thousand.[1] But it was the Comanche Nation of several tribal divisions that controlled the vast region south of the Arkansas River well into southern Texas and portions of New Mexico. Of them a Spanish official wrote with a mixture of despair and awe: "They are a people so numerous and so haughty that when asked their number, they made no difficulty of comparing it to that of the stars. They are so skillful in horsemanship that they have no equal; so daring that they never ask for or grant truces."[2]

In efforts to control the Norteños, as the Spanish called the collective tribes to the north, Spain established the remote post of San Saba on the tributary of that name west of present-day Temple, Texas, in 1757. The Comanches and Wichitas, resenting the post's affiliation with their great enemy the Apaches, lost little time in raiding the settlement. They brutally murdered a number of people, including two priests at their altars, one of which they beheaded.

This attack plus rumors that the Norteños were planning a combined assault on both San Saba and San Antonio led Diego Ortiz Parrilla, the Spanish governor of Texas, to organize a military expedition against the northern tribes. He marched from San Saba in August 1759 with 130 garrison presidials, 241 militia, and 120 Tlascalteco and Mission Indian allies. Two Franciscan friars accompanied the caravan, which was supported by two cannons and herds of over sixteen hundred horses, mules, and cattle.[3]

Because the Comanches were believed to be located too far north of the Red River to strike, the prime targets of the expedition were the bands on and south of the river. On October 2 the Spanish army surprised a village of Tonkawas just north of the Brazos and in the ensuing fight killed several warriors and took 149 prisoners. Forcing the captives to serve as guides,

Parrilla headed on toward the Taovaya villages on the Red River.

As Parrilla's army approached, sixty or more Indian warriors swooped down on fast-flying ponies to attack the vanguard of the Spanish army. When the mounted presidials gave chase, the Indians retreated into a small forest, and the Spanish cavalry plunged headlong after them, emerging suddenly onto a level plain alongside a wide-bedded river. They were just in time to see the Indians disappear into a well-fortified village on the banks of the river.

The village was surrounded by a deep ditch and a stout stockade wall. The winding path of approach was well defended by a body of warriors, while all along the pole palisade were others armed with muskets. Above the stockade could be seen the tops of the tall, rounded grass huts of the Taovayas. Over them waved a French flag. Across the river near another grass-hut village gleamed the conical teepees of a Comanche encampment. The presidials suddenly realized they had found more Indians than they really wanted.

Parrilla moved forward and went into camp while he and his officers debated their strategy. Even as they deliberated, they were attacked by repeated sallies of mounted warriors. Other Indians on foot kept the attackers well supplied with a reserve of loaded guns. One chief, who carried a shield of white buckskin and wore a helmet of the same with a plume of red horsehair, fought with great valor before being knocked from his stallion by Spanish musketry. When the Spaniards brought up their two brass cannons and fired ineffectively at the Indian fort, those inside laughed and jeered at each shot.

At night the Indians in the fort held a war dance by a huge bonfire to display their contempt for their attackers. The raw recruits of the Spanish army became badly demoralized, and the Indian allies of the Spaniards began deserting. Finally at the insistence of his officers, Parrilla ordered a retreat. It became so precipitous, however, that the army's baggage and two brass cannons were left behind.[4]

The military defeat long embarrassed the Spanish and denied them control of the region. Parrilla blamed his defeat by the Taovayas on the French traders, who, he felt, had had a strong hand in fortifying the village and developing a defensive plan. He also recognized that the Indian warriors had exhibited excellent battle discipline. During the year following the battle, a Spanish missionary was sent to the Wichita village to work out a truce with the Indians.

Another witness to the Wichitas in their Red River village was a Spanish lieutenant, Antonio Trevino, who was captured by the tribe in 1763. Although the Taovayas were noted for their cruel treatment of prisoners, Trevino had put up an especially courageous stand against them before being captured badly wounded. Because the Taovayas greatly respected bravery, they took the Spaniard in, nursed him back to health, and accepted him in their midst as a friend. After two years of captivity, he was escorted safely back to San Antonio.

In his testimony regarding his ordeal, Trevino described the fortifications of the Taovaya villages. The deep ditch in front of the palisade would stymie any attempt to charge the location on horseback. Inside, four great underground houses provided safety to occupants during a siege. Furthermore, much to Parrilla's chagrin, Trevino said that the French traders had shown the Taovayas how to fire the two captured cannons, which were now mounted at the entrance to the fort.[5]

The Seven Years War in Europe between the French and the British ended with the defeat of the French in 1763. As a result, virtually all of the territories west of the Mississippi River, including the area of Oklahoma, became Spanish possessions. In 1769 Frenchman Athanase de Mézières was appointed lieutenant gover-

The Norteños—tribes from north Texas and the Red River—
were occasional friendly visitors to the Spanish citadel of
San Antonio. (Homer S. Thrall, *A Pictorial History of Texas*)

nor of Natchitoches in Louisiana and, as such, became
the principal Spanish agent of an area that included
north Texas and Oklahoma. He immediately set out to
improve relations with the Norteños. In 1770 de
Mézières held a peace council near present-day Texarkana, Texas, with chiefs of the Taovaya, Tawakoni,
Yscani, and Kichai (Keechi) tribes and signed friendship
treaties with them.[6]

In 1773, while de Mézières was in Europe, a trader
named J. Gaignard was sent up the Red River from
Louisiana to make a treaty with the Comanches. By
this move Spanish authorities hoped to blunt the thrust
of the Missouri-based Osages, who were intruding
farther and farther west and south. Only recently it had
been reported that the Osages had killed a French
trader named de Quindel and four other men on the
Washita River.[7]

Gaignard arrived at the Taovaya villages to find the Wichitas angry that their horse and slave trade had been cut off by the Spaniards. They refused to allow Gaignard to continue on to the Comanches and treated him roughly. They took away his goods and even his sleeping blankets during winter weather. The trader, in fact, had little good to say for the tribe. Enemies who were captured, he wrote, were horribly tortured, broiled, and feasted upon; both the men and women were cruel-natured.

Gaignard had a much better view of the Comanches, who came to the village, four thousand strong, to trade with him. He found them to be fine men and great fighters and less barbaric in that they killed their grown captives without torture and kept the young ones for slaves. Although an unsettled and warring nation, the Comanches abhorred the Taovaya practice of cannibalism. While Gaignard was at the village, two parties of unlicensed French traders arrived from the Arkansas River country to trade for horses, mules, and slaves.

De Mézières himself led a peacemaking expedition to the Wichita villages in 1778 in an effort to counter the increasing influence of British traders. The English were now extending their operations into the Oklahoma region as far south as the Red River. Only recently, de Mézières learned, two Englishmen had entered the Taovayas' country and attempted to establish trading relations with the tribe. However, the Taovayas had taken their goods and forced them to leave.[8]

De Mézières confirmed much of Gaignard's description of the Taovayas and Comanches and added more. He was more generous in his estimation of the Taovayas, seeing them as "cheerful, affable, and docile in their manner, compassionate toward the sick, orphans, and widows, respectful to their elders, generous toward strangers, kind to guests." But he also noted that they were "more revengeful for injury than grateful for benefits, as is proved by the atrocities which their prisoners experience, which are so great as to relate them would cause horror."[9]

The Spaniard described the two Red River thatched-hut villages as consisting of 37 houses on the north bank and 123 on the south. De Mézières named them San Theodoro and San Bernardo. Each house, he said, contained ten to twelve beds. He estimated the number of potential warriors in the villages at more than eight hundred.

There were also a large number of women and children. Their dress, as seen in the spring, consisted of shirts, leggings, and moccasins—all made of leather, as were their battle shields, horse equipment, and a thick leather cap worn as a battle helmet. Each house was well stocked with watermelons and tobacco. Like the Indians met by La Harpe, the Taovayas used tightly woven mats in their food service. Although the river offered an abundance of fish, the Indians did not eat them. The water course did serve as a perpetual snare for the buffalo, deer, and bear that came there to drink. A convenient quarry provided round rocks for corn grinding, white stones for lances, and flint for arrowheads.

The women of the tribe were allotted some say in tribal government—this, in addition to their regular duties of tanning, sewing, dressing skins, fencing fields, planting and harvesting crops, gathering firewood, preparing food, erecting houses, rearing children, and giving constant attention to the pleasures of the men of the house. The men were solely hunters and warriors. They gained their wealth through horse stealing and won tribal position through battle. The Taovayas indulged in no defined religion, though they did believe in afterlife rewards for their deeds. They revered fire and held strong superstitions.[10]

Although conveniently and comfortably established, the Taovayas still lived in constant fear of the marauding Osages, with whom they were perpetually at war. They maintained a tentative peace with the Comanches, who visited them under the guise of friendship to steal their horses and corn. The Taovayas pretended not to notice this pilfering, well aware that they could hardly afford to make enemies of such a large and powerful nation.[11]

Like Gaignard, de Mézières thought highly of the hostile Comanches. He admired their modesty in dress, hospitality to guests, humanity toward captives, and bravery in battle—with the women sometimes participating.[12] Skilled in arms and keen of intellect, the Comanches were happy natured and had a moral code that severely punished adultery. However, de Mézières noted, their propensity for stealing tended to obscure their good qualities. Their nomadic habits of following the buffalo north in the winter and south in the summer caused them to lose many of their horses. They made up the loss by raiding Spanish ranches in Texas and Mexico.

The Comanches were dexterous in the use of the bow and arrow, lance, sword, dagger, and firearms. They were also highly skilled as horsemen and at horse raising. They waged unending war with the Apaches, whom they had driven farther and farther south. The Spanish saw the Comanches as masters of the Plains northward to the Missouri River.[13] De Mézières thought the best way to nullify the Comanches as a barrier to Spanish expansion northward would be to take them as companions on military campaigns. Such comradeship among the prairie Indians, he observed, brought about ties of friendship. The Indians termed this alliance *Techán,* "allies" or "friends."

De Mézières recounted how a Wichita chief proved his friendship for the white people during a July 1777 hunting trip to the Arkansas River. On the way the chief rescued four destitute and bewildered white hunters who had been robbed of their weapons, ammunition, and clothing by a band of Osages. The Wichitas then followed the Osage party, killed five of them, and recovered the spoils of their robbery. While in the north, the chief had learned of a place on the Arkansas River called El Cadron—an early Arkansas trading post—where a group of Englishmen maintained a store with a large quantity of goods.

Because Spanish authorities were greatly concerned about British and Osage encroachment, they laid plans for a combined Spanish-Indian strike against the Osages in Missouri. However, because of Spain's involvement in the American colonial wars, the campaign never developed.[14]

De Mézières died from a fall while visiting another Indian village the following year. Another Frenchman now became the principal witness to the Indians of the Oklahoma-Texas-Kansas region through his efforts to discover new lines of transportation across the southern Plains. In 1785 Pedro Vial was sent with former captive Francisco Xavier Chaves to contact the Taovayas and the Comanches on behalf of the Spanish government at San Antonio.[15]

He did so successfully, and the following year Vial was commissioned to explore a new route from San Antonio, Texas, to Santa Fe, New Mexico. Following the Colorado and Brazos Rivers northwest, Vial reached the Red River. There he visited villages of both the Wichitas and Comanches before continuing on across the Texas Panhandle to Santa Fe the following spring. He returned to the Wichitas again in 1788 while traveling from Santa Fe to Natchitoches.

The Frenchman made a much more perilous trip in 1792 when he was commissioned by the governor of New Mexico to explore and open a trading route from there to the Missouri River. Vial and two companions set out from Santa Fe on May 21, 1792, taking much the same route as that followed by Oñate in 1601. Little had changed during the interceding two centuries as the three Frenchman marched steadily across the Texas Panhandle along the Canadian River before turning northeast to strike the Arkansas River on June 27.[16]

Here they discovered the carcasses of recently killed buffalo and set out to find the hunters. When they did so, the Frenchmen soon had cause to regret it. The Indians, a band of the Kansa (Kaw) tribe, immediately gathered about them, taking their horses, guns, and other possessions. Then the warriors used their knives to cut every last stitch of clothing from the three, leaving them totally naked on the empty prairie.

Some of the Indians wanted to kill the men. But even as they were arguing over whether to do this with guns or knives, one "highly esteemed" Indian rode up and lifted Vial up behind him on his horse. Nevertheless, the others persisted, and one tried to lance Vial from behind. He was saved again when another Indian came up and ordered the attackers to stand back. The Indian, who had once been a slave-servant in St. Louis, knew Vial. He quickly took the Frenchman to his lodge and fed him. "It is the custom and law," the man said, "that after having eaten no one is killed."[17]

Vial's companions went through similar harrowing experiences, but they, too, survived. One was saved from a knife attack by an Indian who suffered a badly slashed arm in warding off a death blow aimed at the Frenchman. The three men were forced to accompany the Indians to their village on the Kansas River. Here they remained still unclothed until September 11, when a French trader came upstream in a pirogue and provided them with garments. A few days later they were picked up by three other traders on their way downstream. Finally on October 6, the three explorers reached St. Louis.

Vial, his two companions, four other white men, and two Indian guides left St. Louis during the summer of 1793 and journeyed westward to a Pawnee village on the Republican River of Kansas. The Pawnees, they found, were at war with the Osages, Wichitas, and Comanches but on friendly terms with the Spanish. Vial remained with the village until October, when, with ten horses and seven Pawnee guides, he traveled south to the Arkansas River, striking it just west of what is now Dodge City, Kansas. From there the group moved across the Oklahoma Panhandle to the Canadian River and followed that stream on to Santa Fe, arriving there on November 15. Credit goes to Vial and his companions for opening the important and much-to-be-used trade route between Missouri and New Mexico.[18]

The Vial effort marked the finale of the Spanish exploration of the Central Plains. The turn of the century and the purchase of the Louisiana Territory by the United States were in the offing. A new set of participants, known as Americans, would soon replace the French and the Spanish as the principal actors on the stage of the great American prairies.

During the early 1800s, U.S. Indian agent John Sibley administered relations with the tribes of Louisiana, Arkansas, and Oklahoma from his agency at Natchitoches, Louisiana. He was strongly interested in maintaining contact with the Indians who resided so far up the Red River, still the main route from the American frontier to those tribes as well as the dividing line between American and Spanish authority.

Sibley's opportunity came in the spring of 1808 when Wichita chief Awakahea issued an invitation to him to send someone to a big trade rendezvous that the chief planned to host that coming summer. Sibley was eager to comply not only because the Wichitas were the key to entry onto the Comanchería but also because there were rumors of silver ore having been found in that far-off, unknown land.

Sibley proceeded to make arrangements with a Mississippi Irishman named Anthony Glass to go to the Wichita-Taovaya villages.[19] The agent helped to outfit Glass with horses and trade goods. With interpreter Joseph Lucas and nine others, two of whom had been to Wichita country before, Glass set out from Natchitoches on July 5, 1808. Of forty-eight horses, sixteen were loaded with trade goods. A Mexican merchant in Natchitoches sent word to Spanish authorities that the Americans were on their way to mine silver and warned that a stampede of people might result. Sibley reassured the Spanish that there would be no invasion of their territory.

Glass and his party arrived at the Taovaya villages on August 11. He would remain there through the winter, and his journal provides still another extensive look at Wichita/Taovaya and Comanche culture during the exploration period of the Oklahoma frontier.

The men were received with great hospitality by the Wichita chief, who hoisted his own American flag above his village in response to the one flown at Glass's camp. A band of Wichita women was sent to clear away the grass and weeds around the Americans' campsite, and an abundance of green corn, beans, and melons was brought to the visitors' tents. In council the next day, Glass responded with presents of tobacco for the chief and his warriors, saying that he had other goods to be exchanged for horses with the Wichitas and their brothers, the Comanches.

Awakahea, the great chief of the Wichitas, presided over the village on the Oklahoma side of the river. From him Glass learned that the chief, who was then about fifty, had been born on the Arkansas River, where his nation lived at the time. Because of the Osages, Awakahea said, the Wichitas had moved south, first to the Brazos and then to their present site. A part of their nation, the Tawakonis, still resided on the Brazos.

Invited by the chief of the village on the south side of the Red River to come and trade, Glass found sixty-five thatched huts that were much like those on the north. They had the same cultivated fields of corn, beans, pumpkins, and melons. This south-bank village was divided into two parts, with Kachatake the chief of one and Kittsita the headman of the other. The Wichitas' highly respected warrior leader Chichiskinik had only recently visited the governor of Texas province, Antonio Cordero, at San Antonio. Cordero had advised him against maintaining a friendship with the Americans.

Even on the Red River, the Wichitas were subject to horse-stealing raids by the Osages. On one occasion the Osages came in such numbers as to brazenly plant a pair of flags between the villages while driving off five hundred horses; the Wichitas did not dare to venture out in challenge. Glass joined one chase after a small Osage party, but it moved ahead too quickly to be caught. On another raid an Osage was killed when his war party attempted to drive off some Wichita horses.

Unlike the Comanches, the Wichitas were not given to jealousy. Wives were purchased with horses, generally one or two, from a brother or uncle of the woman. Strangers often had to pay more in blankets, scarves, vermilion, or beads. The Wichita men could take as many wives as they wished and discard them whenever they desired. The women had the same privilege of backing out of a marriage. Chiefs and head warriors had the choice of any women they wanted, and it was not unusual for a man of fifty or sixty to have a wife not more than fifteen. Nor was it uncommon for a man to lend or hire out his wife to others, particularly to strangers in camp.

The Comanches, Glass found, were not so generous in marital affairs. One man who caught his wife in bed with another of his tribe immediately shot the culprit dead and then killed the wife. Comanches so often killed their women, Glass reported, that the tribe had more men than women, while among the Wichitas there was a majority of women over men.

The Comanches were very fond of gambling. Virtually every night a small group of Comanche men could be found squatting and playing "hide the bullet," with large numbers of horses and mules being won or lost; this simple game required the opponent to guess which hand the bullet was in. The Comanches were very dexterous at the maneuver, but somehow the Wichitas were generally the winners. The Comanches and Wichitas also enjoyed foot and horse races. The Comanches were great riders, Glass noted, but when beaten they gave up their stakes willingly.

The Wichita men worked in the fields along with the women, planting crops, harvesting, and making fences by driving stakes into the ground three or four feet apart and weaving brush into them. The tribe's principal crop was corn, much of which was traded to the Comanches for horses and mules. Scaffold-dried corn was buried secretly in buffalo skin bags for winter keep. Pumpkins were preserved in long strips that were then woven into a sort of mat. The Wichitas ate buffalo mainly, never the deer that grazed about the village almost like domesticated animals.

On one occasion when Comanche parties arrived at the village for trading, Glass dispatched some of his men with trade goods to go out and barter for horses. The party returned, however, when their guide refused to take them to the Comanche camp. Meanwhile, Glass had heard stories of a strange "medicine rock" that the Wichita Indians had found several days' journey to the south on the Brazos River of Texas-Mexico. Determined to learn more about the metal rock that the Indians believed was potent in curing diseases, Glass finally persuaded the finder to take him to it. They were escorted by an encampment of nearly one thousand people and some three thousand horses and mules.

After visiting the medicine rock, which eventually proved to be a large meteorite, Glass continued on with the Indians to the Colorado River, trading and chasing wild horses unsuccessfully. It was mid-February 1809 before he again reached the Wichita villages on the Red River. The Osages had conducted a horse-stealing raid only a few days before. Glass remained at the villages until March 21, when he and his party began the long trip back to Natchitoches. There the chips of metal he had taken created quite a stir, though no one was quite certain what sort of metal they were.

Members of Glass's group vied with one another in their attempts to obtain the meteorite. In August 1809 one group made a trip into the Comanche country, found the metal rock, and hid it. A second group came behind the first, searched the countryside, and found the meteorite. Carting it to the Red River by wagon, this group floated the piece of metal downstream in a large pirogue to Natchitoches, reaching there on June 4, 1810. The pilferers were doomed to the disappointment of learning that the meteorite had little monetary value, though it did prove to be the largest meteorite discovered to that date. Today the "Red River Meteorite" is owned by the Peabody Museum of Natural History at Yale University.

The Wichitas, meanwhile, had joined the Comanches in another consolidated attack against the Osages. When the Spanish sent out a force in November 1809 to search for the Americans they had heard were in Texas, they found the Wichita stronghold deserted and in ruins. Later accounts show that the tribe moved west to a sheltered point on the North Fork of the Red River to reestablish itself.

▶ 4

The Wilkinson Party

In 1806, at the Red River at the southeastern corner of present-day Oklahoma, units of the U.S. and Spanish governments came close to engaging in battle and thereby igniting a war between the two countries. On the one side were the Jefferson-sent explorations of the new Louisiana Territory, designed to establish boundaries of this great land purchase from France and to discover its content. On the other were the forces of New Spain, which suspected the United States of designs on Texas and other Spanish dominions.[1]

The Jefferson explorations were threefold: that of Lewis and Clark up the Missouri River to the Pacific Ocean, the Freeman-Custis survey up the Red River, and the Pike expedition up the Platte River to the Rocky Mountains. Each of these latter two would involve the area that is now Oklahoma and bring both American and Spanish witnesses to add to its revelation.

Because no one knew precisely what territory France once had just claim to in North America, the exact boundaries of the Louisiana Purchase were vague. Spain still felt it held a proprietary right to much of the region. The conspiracy of Aaron Burr to invade Mexico, the connivance by General of the Army James Wilkinson (who was also in the pay of Spanish authorities as a spy and was doing much to foster suspicion between the two countries), and the natural competition between the Old World throne of Spain and the upstart American democracy all created talk of war.

Lewis and Clark had set out up the Missouri River in 1804, meeting and treating with the Indian tribes along the river. They spent the winter at the Mandan villages in North Dakota before moving west in the spring of 1805 on several barges and small boats. However, it was May 3, 1806, before the Red River expedition under surveyor Thomas Freeman and naturalist Peter Custis would get organized and depart from Fort Adams near Natchez, Mississippi. Its military escort of a lieutenant, two noncommissioned officers, seventeen privates, and a black slave was under the command of Captain Richard Sparks.[2]

The expedition leaders hoped to move undeterred to the Wichita/Taovaya villages, where they would leave their river craft and proceed on horseback. The group reached Natchitoches on May 19. There the expeditioners learned that the Spanish at Nacogdoches, Texas, were making plans to intercept them. Accordingly, the expedition took on another twenty soldiers from the garrison at Natchitoches, Louisiana—this even though their orders instructed them to turn about if confronted by a larger military force.

On June 2 the party set out again. On June 7 it was overtaken by an Indian guide dispatched by Indian agent Sibley at Natchitoches. The guide carried a letter from Sibley that again warned the expeditioners that a large force of Spanish dragoons was on the march in their direction. Undaunted, the group continued on. But it soon encountered a serious obstacle of a different nature. Just above the site of present-day Shreveport, Louisiana, an enormous and impenetrable blockage of fallen trees and other debris known as the Red River Raft totally prevented boat passage. However, a series of swamps, ponds, and bayous ran parallel to the river, and the expedition finally discovered a narrow but unobstructed passageway through. After fourteen days of incessant fatigue, danger, and uncertainty, the party reentered the main channel of the Red River.

Twenty miles above the raft, the Americans reached the village of the Coashatay Indians. They were met there by a messenger who informed them that some three hundred Spanish dragoons with about four to five hundred horses were encamped at the Caddo village some thirty miles to the west. On July 1 a Caddo chief with forty men arrived at the Coashatay village. He related how the Spaniards had demanded to know if he loved the Americans and wished to take their side. The chief had answered that if the Spanish wished to fight with the Americans, he hoped they would go to Natchitoches to do it.

He said that the party might be harassed by the Osages, who had always been the inveterate enemies of his nation. Should the party kill any of them, he would dance for a month; and if they killed any Americans, he would turn out with his warriors, although few; make his cause; and get revenge.[3]

On July 11 the explorers reembarked on their journey, now finding the Red River extremely winding and its water so low that the boats were often grounded. On July 26 three Caddo Indians intercepted them to report that the Spanish dragoons had been reinforced and now numbered 1,000 strong. The Spaniards had cut down the American flag flying at the Caddo village and stated their intention to destroy the American expedition. They were now encamped ahead on a bluff waiting for the Americans to arrive. The Caddos begged the party to turn back, but the leaders refused.

An Osage chief of the Three Forks region. (*Catlin's Notes of Eight Years' Travel*)

At sunset on the evening of July 28, the men on the boats heard the sounds of gunfire ahead. Realizing that this would be the Spaniards, the party went into camp for the night. On the following morning, the explorers continued their advance. Freeman, Sparks, and an Indian guide walked ahead of the boats with guns in hand. When tracks were discovered, the party halted, and arms were put to readiness. Now with all aboard the boats again, they continued on. Eventually an advance guard of the Spanish camp spied them coming and fled to give alarm to the camp, which was situated on a prominent rise along the river's south bank known as Spanish Bluff.

The explorers had halted and kindled fires for their noon meal when a large detachment of mounted Spanish dragoons suddenly made its appearance in a charge down the riverbed. Dust obscured their full number. The Americans immediately took up positions in a thick cane brake on the bank of the river. A noncommissioned officer and six men were sent to circle behind the advancing Spaniards.

The two sentinels posted to guard the boats called out a challenge to the horsemen, ordering them to halt. The dragoons did so, deploying in formation some 150 yards away. Their commander, veteran officer Don Francisco Viana, advanced to parley with Sparks and Freeman. Viana indicated his determination to stop the Americans at all cost. Outnumbered twenty to one and remembering their orders not to oppose a superior force, the Americans gave in without a fight. They turned about and headed back to Louisiana.

This meeting with the Spaniards, which occurred very near the far southeastern tip of Oklahoma, stymied U.S. exploration of the upper Red River and left the region a lingering mystery for years to come. Americans on the southern frontier were outraged at the Spanish interference, and war appeared imminent. One newspaper commented, "Something energetic will take place at no great distance of time."[4]

U.S. officials did not then know that another Spanish effort had been launched to intercept and stop American explorations. Even as the Spanish Bluff drama was being played out, an army was being assembled in Santa Fe, New Mexico, under Lieutenant Don Facundo

Malgares. A Spanish soldier of much distinction as well as an educated man of wealth, Malgares would later become the governor of Spanish New Mexico.[5] In addition to stopping the Americans, Malgares hoped to establish better relations with the Comanches, Wichitas, Pawnees, Kansa, and other tribes of the area west of the Missouri River as a buffer against the Americans.

The Spanish army consisted of 100 mounted dragoon regulars and 500 mounted militia who had been pressed into service from New Mexico residents. Each man led two horses and one mule, making well over two thousand animals in the expedition. The dragoons wore short blue coats with red capes and cuffs, blue velvet waistcoats and trousers, jackboots with glistening spurs, and broad-brimmed, high-crowned hats banded with brightly colored ribbons adopted in gallantry for their ladies. Many of them sported long mustaches and side whiskers that covered most of their faces. As they rode, their lances gleamed aslant above them. One Indian observer later described them as looking like "a flock of bluebirds on the prairie."[6]

The dragoons carried their fusils slung in leather cases at the right side of their high-pommeled saddles, while behind the saddles were tied a small bag and two pistols. Every man carried a rounded shield of three-doubled sole leather, bent to deflect arrows. Gilded in gold on each were the arms of Spain and the name of Don Carlos IV, king of Spain. Their saddles were ornately trimmed in silver and gold, while their stirrups were of wood carved to the shape of the head of a lion or some other animal.

In June 1806 Malgares led his army east from Santa Fe to the headwaters of the Canadian River, which he apparently mistook for the Red River. After the army had followed that river eastward for several days across the hot, desertlike Texas Panhandle, provisions began to run short. The disgruntled militiamen who had been pressed involuntarily into service demanded to know where Malgares was taking them. The Spanish nobleman replied haughtily, "Wherever my horse leads me."[7]

A few mornings later a militia spokesman came to the officer with a petition signed by 200 others. It demanded that they return home. Malgares called a halt and ordered a gallows erected on the prairie. The drummers beat out the call to arms. When the troops had fallen in, Malgares separated out the petitioners from the others. He then had the man who had presented the petition bound and given fifty lashes. Malgares warned that any further insurrection would result in death on the gallows to those who defied him. This quieted the rebellion.

Somewhere along the Canadian River, quite possibly on the soil of present-day Oklahoma, the Spaniards made contact with the Comanches. A council was arranged in the broad expanse of an open meadow. The result was a pageant of two contrasting cultures, one European and the other American Plains Indian, meeting in a dusty but dazzling display of mounted pomp and ceremony.

The blue-uniformed Spanish dragoons performed their military maneuvers smartly before the tribesmen to the rolling commands of a drummer corps. The Comanches were not to be outdone. They came as lords of the vast domain over which they reigned to flaunt their numbers, their wealth of horses (many of them wearing Spanish brands), and the riding and battle skills of their warriors. They galloped forward en masse, a mighty throng of some fifteen hundred warriors on their war-painted ponies, whooping their war yells. Some wore brightly colored robes and some, mere breechclouts with their bronze skins daubed and streaked with fanciful design. All were armed with bows, arrows, lances, and war shields. They performed the feats of horsemanship that marked the Comanches as the most skillful riders on the Plains. Behind them came the women with dog travois, quickly erecting on the edge of the meadow a small city of leather lodges with their crosspole tops. Lastly came the young boys of the tribe, driving with them the immense Comanche horse herds.

Malgares met with the Comanche chiefs, smoked the calumet, and presented them with medals and commissions from the king of Spain, a Spanish flag, and four mules for each chief. The Spanish officer reiterated the hope of his government for friendship with the Comanches. He also asked that the warriors refrain from raids such as the recent one on the Spanish village of Agua Caliente. Some two thousand head of horses had been driven off.[8]

After treating with the Comanches, Malgares moved northward to the Arkansas River. There he met and talked with a band of Pawnees. The Indians came back later that night and ran off many of the Spaniards' horses. Already food supplies had run out, and the soldiers of the expedition were eating their weaker animals. Halting his march, Malgares sent an officer and 300 of the dragoons to visit a Pawnee village on the Republican River in present-day northern Kansas. The officer presented the Pawnee chiefs with medals, mules, and a Spanish flag. He promised that a larger army would be coming later to establish a fort and trading post in Pawnee country.[9]

Meanwhile, an American expedition to explore the southwestern regions of the Louisiana Purchase had been organized in St. Louis under Captain Zebulon M. Pike. His mission was more than mere exploration, however. Pike was also serving as a spy for General Wilkinson. The captain was to explore the upper Arkansas and Red rivers to the Rocky Mountains and establish relations with the Comanches, Osages, and Pawnees who dominated the region.

Pike was to advance to the Rocky Mountains, divide his party, and explore back down the Red and Arkansas

Zebulon M. Pike. (*Appleton's Cyclopaedia of American Biography*)

rivers. He set out on July 15, 1806, with a party of twenty-five men—including the "Dam'd set of rascels" who had been with him on an earlier exploring expedition to the upper Mississippi River in 1805.[10] He also took with him the Little Osage chief Tuttasuggy, or the Wind, and fifty Osage and Pawnee men, women, and children. These Indians had been rescued from the Pottawatomie Indians, who had taken them in a raid the previous year, and were now being returned to their tribes in southwestern Missouri.

The captives, being impatient to return home, were permitted to go ahead under the escort of Lieutenant James Biddle Wilkinson, son of General Wilkinson. Wilkinson reached the Osage village after a six-day march across open prairie. The former captives were met by some 180 horsemen, each painted and decorated in gala fashion. As the returnees entered the village, they were greeted by a salvo from four swivel cannons, which the Osages said had been taken from an old Spanish fort (not impossibly, the Spanish Forts of the Wichitas). The Indians exhibited great emotion when reunited with loved ones.

Pike arrived later to be feasted on green corn, buffalo meat, and watermelon. Tribal priest-magicians, who swallowed knives, ran sticks through their noses and tongues, and performed other stunts, entertained the visitors. While at the Osage village, Pike conducted a census of the tribes, counting 214 lodges and 1,695 persons, who were about equally divided between male and female.

The Osage dwellings varied in length from 36 to 100 feet. Built on a center pole with smaller roof poles extending out to the wall stakes, the lodges were covered with mats made of rushes. Usually doors opened on both sides of the structures, and a hole in the roof vented the smoke from lodge fires.[11] No regularity was apparent in the placement of the houses,

——————————————————————————➤

Explorations Prior to the Formation of Indian Territory
(opposite page)

1. Chouteaus—c. 1800
2. Wilkinson (Pike)—1806
3. Custis-Freeman—1806
4. Glass—1808
5. Sibley—1811
6. Bingier—1816
7. Long—1817
8. Bradford/Nuttall—1819
9. Miller—1820
10. Nuttall—1820
11. Long/Bell—1820
12. Bell—1820
13. James McKnight—1821
14. Glenn/Fowler—1821
15. James McKnight—1823
16. Pryor/Chisholm—1826

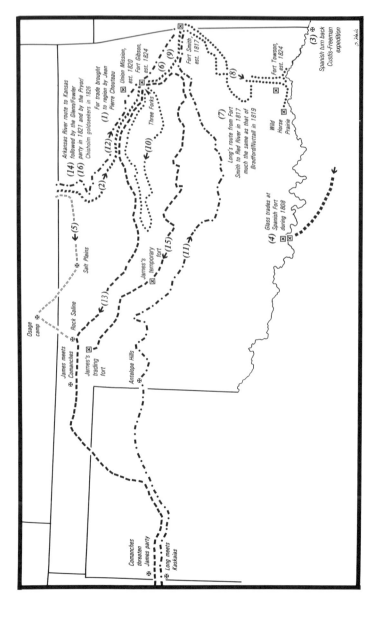

D. Heis

(3) Spanish turn back Custis-Freeman expedition

Fort Towson, est. 1824

(8)

Wild Horse Prairie

Fort Smith est. 1817

(9)

(6)

Union Mission, est. 1820

Fort Gibson, est. 1824

(12)

Three Forks

(10)

(7) Long's route from Fort Smith to Red River in 1817 much the same as that of Bradford/Nuttall in 1819

Fur trade brought (1) to region by Jean Pierre Chouteau

(14) Arkansas River route to Kansas (16) followed by the Glenn/Fowler party in 1821 and by the Pryor/ Chisholm goldseekers in 1826

(2)

(4) Glass trades at Spanish Fort during 1808

(5)

Salt Plains

Osage camp

Rock Saline

James meets Comanches

James's trading fort

James's temporary fort

(13)

(15)

(11)

Antelope Hills

Comanches threaten James party

Long meets Kaskaias

while stock pens were located within the village to permit the safety of stock at night.

Being appreciative for the return of the captives, the tribe supplied Pike with guides and pack animals for the trip to the Pawnee villages on the Republican River. The Osages were at war with the Kansa Indians, so their guides carefully avoided the Kansa range in northeastern Kansas, leading Pike and his men well to the south across the headwaters of the Grand and Verdigris rivers.

As the Americans marched, they were witness to a virtual Eden of animal life: deer, elk, buffalo, antelope, panthers, among others. Turning north, Pike crossed the Smoky Hill and on September 25 reached the Pawnee village that Malgares had visited only a short time before. Pike and his men were greeted by a charge of three hundred mounted, war-whooping Pawnees. The warriors were naked except for breechclouts and dabs of white, yellow, blue, and black clay over their bodies. The Spanish flag left by the Spaniards waved above the town.

The Americans were welcomed by Chief Characterish, or White Wolf. Wearing his Spanish medal, he greeted Pike by stretching out his hand and saying, "*Bon jour.*"[12] The chief told Pike that the Spanish had said that, even though the Americans were a "little people"—small in number—they were enterprising and would soon come to take the Indians' land and drive away the game. "And how very true," Characterish observed, "has the Spanish chief spoken!"[13]

Pike presented the chief with a double-barreled gun and a gorget neckpiece. He persuaded the Pawnee to take down the Spanish banner, and he raised the U.S. flag in its place. But he could not offset the impression of comparative power that the Spanish force had made over his small group of men.

Pike found the Pawnees to be better at horse raising than the Osages. Owners of large numbers of the animals, the tribe kept breeding mares to one side. Despite this wealth of horses, the Pawnees habitually went to war on foot in the prehorse style, usually in masses of two to three hundred. At this point in their history, they possessed firearms secured in trade with the French and English, while their enemies fought mostly with bows and arrows, lances, and slings. This band of Pawnees, by Pike's count, numbered 1,618 persons, who resided in forty-four lodges.

The houses of the village were round and covered with grass and dirt. The floors of the huts were some two to four feet below ground level, and their support consisted of poles planted into the soil. In the winter months, partly because the grass at the village site could not support the horse herds, the tribe quit its permanent site, buried its corn to keep until spring, and went on the hunt. The tribe, too, lived principally from the buffalo it killed. In trade with the Spanish, the Pawnees profited only in horses and blankets.[14]

Characterish objected strongly to the exploring party's continuing on any farther toward Mexico. He threatened to use force to prevent it, as he had promised the Spaniards he would. He also refused to provide horses, which Pike needed badly.

"You are a brave young warrior," he told Pike that night before his departure. "I respect you; I love brave men. Do not oblige me to hurt you. You have only twenty-five men while I can command a thousand. You must not pass."[15]

But Pike refused to turn back. He insisted that on the following morning he would continue on his way to the Mexican mountains. True to his word, the morning sun found him and his men all mounted, their firearms primed and ready. All the men had their swords drawn, except for Pike. When he drew his, it would be a signal to begin fighting.

The Pawnees surrounded them, over five hundred warriors with their bows strung and their spears, tomahawks, and guns ready. The old warrior chief walked up to the side of Pike's horse and made an emotional appeal for him not to continue on. But Pike pointed toward a small blue speck in the eastern sky. He declared that when the sun reached that point, he and his men would start on their way. "I will start," he said, "I and my brave comrades here, and nothing but death can stop us. It is my duty, as I have told you. If you think it yours to obey the Spaniard and stop me, be it so, but the attempt will cost the lives of some brave men, that you may be sure of."[16]

It was a pivotal moment that well may have ended in a bloody battle that only the exploring party could have lost. But Pike's determination had won the admiration of the old chief. Waving his warriors back, he said to the officer, "Were I now to stop you by destroying you, I should forever after feel myself a coward."[17] After this the Pawnee chief loved to tell the story of the brave Americans, as he did to the visiting George C. Sibley five years later.

Picking up the trail of the Spanish entrada, Pike followed it to the Great Bend of the Arkansas River. During the march, the explorers encountered herds of elk and buffalo. On one occasion they were witness to a buffalo hunt staged by the Pawnees, who were following behind them for a time. They watched with awe as the Indian hunters drove their arrows "up to the plume" in the furry forequarters of their prey.[18]

At the Great Bend, Pike directed Lieutenant Wilkinson to lead an eight-man exploring unit of the expedition back down the river through present-day northeast Oklahoma to Arkansas Post, while Pike continued on to the west. This had been prearranged by General Wilkinson, who wanted the Arkansas route explored as a potential passageway to New Mexico in the event of war with Spain.

The general also harbored concern for his son and his military career. Two months before he had been assigned the task of establishing a fort at the mouth of the Platte. After a fight on the Missouri River with Indians, resulting in the death of one soldier, the younger Wilkinson had been unable to command the will of his men. The party of would-be fort builders straggled back to St. Louis, their assignment unfulfilled.[19]

In addition to Wilkinson, the men who made up the Arkansas River detachment included five seasoned frontiersmen—including Sergeant Ballinger, who was assigned by General Wilkinson to look out for his son—and two Osage scouts. In assigning the men, Pike had foreseen potential problems: securing of meat, attacks by Indians, and the difficulties of river travel in general. The journey would prove to be far more difficult than anyone realized, however, and young Wilkinson's metal would be tested to the extreme.

In preparation for the trip down the Arkansas, the men felled a large cottonwood tree and hewed out a canoe from it. They made another boat from the hides of four buffalo and two elk that they had killed. Lieutenant Wilkinson was sorely vexed over being sent back and over receiving such limited resources from Pike. In a letter to General Wilkinson, his son complained: "I have a small skin canoe, of 10 feet in length, with a wooden one of the same length capable to carry one man and his baggage—not more I believe—I have 5 men, whose strength is insufficient to draw up my skin canoe to dry— and which must necessarily spoil. I have no grease to pay the seams of my canoe, and was obliged to use my candle, mixed with ashes, for that purpose. My men have no winter clothing, and two of them no blankets."[20]

Wilkinson was also concerned about the potentially dangerous tribes that he might meet along the river. Thus far the weather had been good, though rainy; but on the night before Wilkinson was to depart, a snowstorm blew in and the temperature fell below freezing.

Farewells were said, and the Arkansas River contingent made ready to shove off. Wilkinson, three soldiers, and an Osage guide were in the skin canoe, another soldier and an Osage were in the wooden canoe with the baggage, and still another soldier was marching on shore. Men of both parties gave a final wave as Pike turned upriver toward the mountains and Wilkinson's men took to the river.

Wilkinson's boats soon became grounded in the ice-clogged stream. The men were forced to haul the boats over sand and ice for five miles. With the river completely frozen on November 30, Wilkinson decided to abandon the canoes. Discarding all spare clothing and provisions except for a dozen tin cups of hard corn for each, the party continued its march on foot along the barren banks of the stream. The marchers were amazed at the abundance of wild game, particularly buffalo. "I do solemnly assert that, if I saw one, I saw more than nine thousand buffalo during the day's march," Wilkinson commented in his diary on November 8.[21]

Reaching the mouth of the Little Arkansas River, the group rested, replenished its supply of meat, and hewed out two more cottonwood logs for canoes. Moving on down the ice-crusted river in frigid weather, the expeditioners had just passed the mouth of the Ninnescah when the heavy canoes became mired on a midstream sandbar. Barefooted and barelegged, the men waded into the icy stream with ropes over their shoulders and hauled the canoes for several miles over sand bars until finally the river was deep enough again to float the vessels. Nevertheless, it was often necessary for the men to get out with their axes and chop a pathway through the ice.

It was then that a severe misfortune occurred. The canoe that carried the meat, the only food supply, and most of the powder and lead overturned. All of the spilled materials were lost. Wet and frozen, feet and hands numb, the men realized full well their predicament. Most of their clothes were in tatters, they had scant food and virtually no ammunition with which to procure more, and already two of them had frostbitten feet. They were in uncharted country where few white men had ever trod, still over a month's hard travel from their destination.

Their situation was desperate when on November 30 their luck suddenly improved. They met with a small group of Osage hunters from the band of Chief Tutta-suggy. The Indians insisted on providing them meat. The chief himself was very ill at his camp some twenty miles away. He had sent word that he would very much like to see Wilkinson.

Leaving his men on the river, Wilkinson followed an escort to the Osage encampment. Tuttasuggy, who had a badly swollen stomach, wished to make a complaint against Pierre Chouteau. He said that Chouteau, the Missouri trader who had persuaded a portion of the Osages to move to the Verdigris River of northeastern Oklahoma, had treated him badly. Chouteau had taken Tuttasuggy's brother, rather than Tuttasuggy himself, to see the Great White Father in Washington. Chouteau, Tuttasuggy claimed, had predicted that the Spaniards would soon take that country away from the Americans.

When Wilkinson returned to his men, he found the river again ice-drifted from a new cold wave. On the morning of December 3, having passed the site of what is now Ponca City, Oklahoma, on the day before, the voyagers found the river completely frozen over; as Wilkinson noted in his report, "The men solicited me to hut"—meaning that they wished to take shelter in the vacant Indian huts at what may have been the former site of Ferdinandina.[22]

Wilkinson refused to halt, however, and the small, badly suffering band continued on past the mouth of Red Rock Creek. The canoes still became grounded every so often, requiring the men to go into the water, ax away the ice, and drag the heavy craft for long distances. December 10 found them at the mouth of the Cimarron River, where, Wilkinson noted, the Osages usually procured their salt by scraping it off the prairie with turkey wings. On December 23, with a sleet- and snowstorm in progress, the Americans arrived at the wintering camp of Cashesegra, or Big Track, an Osage chief who resided near the mouth of the Verdigris. Big Track indicated his desire for the Americans to establish a trade factory in his country.

Wilkinson recorded that the Osage village, known as "Place-of-the-Oaks," of Chief Clermont, or Town Builder, was located some sixty miles up the Verdigris from its conflux with the Arkansas. The travelers spent Christmas Day in the Osage camp before plunging on past the mouth of the Illinois River. A short distance downriver, Wilkinson reported, were seven-foot falls. This would appear to be an overestimate of the rapids that became known as Webber's Falls.

In the area of present-day Fort Smith, Arkansas, Wilkinson and his men met James McFarlane, a trapper who had been working the Poteau River. Passing several Quapaw villages, the weary band finally reached Arkansas Post on January 9, 1807. While there, three of Wilkinson's men deserted, taking a canoe with them. The officer himself was so ill that he was confined to his blankets for the remainder of the trip to New Orleans. His health was so impaired by this journey that Wilkinson would suffer an early death in 1813. His most notable accomplishment, perhaps, was being the first American to report a voyage along the Arkansas River through Oklahoma.

In immediate terms, his account provided geographical and topographical information previously unknown. It also revealed the status of the Arkansas River for navigation. Officials now knew that navigation beyond Three Forks was questionable, though his estimation of the falls below made boat passage seem virtually impossible. In establishing friendly relations with the

Osages on the Verdigris, Wilkinson had eliminated them as a threat to U.S. military marches through the area.

On separating at the Big Bend, Pike had turned upriver to the Rocky Mountains. In late February he was captured north of Santa Fe by Spanish soldiers and held until July 1807. The turmoil with Spain over boundaries would continue to boil, but in the end war was averted. The southern boundary of Oklahoma, the still unexplored Red River, would become accepted as a line of demarcation between the United States and Spanish Mexico.

Sibley and the Salt Mountain

According to the Osages, they regularly visited a salt prairie as well as a salt mountain. Around the start of the nineteenth century, Missouri fur trader Jean Pierre Chouteau had persuaded a large portion of that tribe under Chief Big Track to move from southwest Missouri to Three Forks, where the Verdigris and Grand (or Neosho) rivers joined with the Arkansas.[1] The Osages annually visited a hunting camp to the west near a great salt prairie. Some forty miles on, they said, was a high bluff or mountain composed of a solid mass of fossil salt, at the base of which issued a large salt spring. The Indians would scrape away the thin cover of earth and then break the salt into fragments to be carried home on their horses.[2]

The story of the salt mountain was heard by Amos Stoddard from an old French trapper living at Vincennes, Indiana. He said he had once pursued the peltry trade on the Arkansas. During the winter of 1871–1872, he had ascended some eight hundred miles up that river, entering a branch of it that he said was

Red sandstone cliffs along the Cimarron mark the supposed site of Jefferson's salt mountain. Today a modern salt plant operates just to the north across the river. (Author photo)

as red as vermilion and as salty as the ocean.[3] Stoddard repeated the story in his descriptive essay to President Thomas Jefferson on the region of the Louisiana Purchase. As such, Stoddard's story gave rise to the myth of "Jefferson's salt mountain." Or was it an exaggeration? No one but the Indians seemed to really know.

In 1811 George C. Sibley, the Osage factor at Fort Osage, Missouri, became intrigued by the idea of Jefferson's salt mountain. He wished to be the first white man to visit and officially report on this mystery of the far, unexplored West. But the mountain was supposed to be deep in dangerous Comanche country. Even the Osages said that it was not safe to go there without a force of at least one hundred men.[4]

Two years after Pike and Wilkinson visited the Osage villages in Missouri, the United States established Fort Osage (also known as Fort Clark, or as Fire Prairie by the Osages) on the Missouri River forty miles east of present-day Kansas City. As factor, George Sibley was responsible for both the Kansa and Osage tribes. He initiated a treaty with the Osages whereby they ceded all claims to land east of a line from Fort Osage southward to the Arkansas River and all of the land north of the Missouri River.[5] The Osages who were located on the Verdigris River of present-day Oklahoma were not in attendance at the Fort Clark treaty council conducted by Osage agent Pierre Chouteau. Led by Chief Clermont, they were taken to St. Louis, where on August 31, 1809, after Missouri governor Merriwether Lewis had personally read and explained the treaty papers to them, they also signed the treaty.[6]

There is little doubt that trappers were working the fertile streams of Oklahoma by this time. Two trappers, John Shaw and William Miller, are believed to have trekked westward from Missouri to the Rocky Mountains along the Kansas-Oklahoma border in the spring of 1809. Others are known to have traveled from Missouri to Santa Fe by unrecorded routes. It was 1811 before another chronicled visit was made, this time by George Sibley.[7] He was the son of Dr. John Sibley of Louisiana fame and the grandson of Reverend Samuel Hopkins, a prominent Congregational minister. Undoubtedly influenced by his father's activities, Sibley gave up his work in a counting house to enter government service on the Missouri frontier. After helping to establish Fort Osage, he was assigned to the post as factor and Indian agent. Like his father, he was intrigued with exploration of the new lands that President Jefferson had recently purchased and, like other Americans of his day, the potential of U.S. expansion beyond.[8]

Sibley became so intrigued with the salt mountain that he arranged a tour into Indian country to investigate. He departed Fort Osage in May 1811 escorted by elderly Osage war chief Sans Oreille, ten other Osages, two guides, and an Irish servant. Sibley first visited a Kansa village on the Marias Des Cygnes River of

Major George C. Sibley. (Archives and Manuscripts Division, Oklahoma Historical Society)

Kansas. The Kansa and Osages, whose languages were much the same, were at this time on friendly terms.

The Kansa had once been the scourge of French traders, often beating and robbing them and, on one occasion, burning several to death. Their small but fierce warrior force, numbering about 250 men who were noted for their daring, was feared by most other Indians in the area. The Kansa demanded high prices for the beaver, otter, bear, raccoon, fox, elk, and other animal pelts they proffered. Sibley found the Kansa village abundant in horses, mules, dogs, and children.

From here Sibley's party of fifteen, now augmented with five Kansa warriors, rode northward to the Platte River of Nebraska to where the Republican River Pawnees under Characterish had relocated since Pike's visit. Also, he discovered, they had been joined by the Pawnee Loups and Skidi bands for protection from the Kansa. Sibley's was the first American visit to the Pawnees since Pike, whom the old chief remembered with affection.

Sibley, having become ill, was well treated by the Pawnee chief. After reaffirming American-Pawnee friendship, Sibley headed south to a prearranged rendezvous with the Little Osages on the Arkansas River. En route he met a Kansa hunting party that had just killed upward of one hundred fat buffalo. "Feasting and merriment were the order of the day and of the night, too," Sibley noted.[9] On the day following he found the camp of the Osages, who had just made a kill of around two hundred buffalo.

Sibley had been wanting to witness the spectacle of an Indian entourage—men, women, and children with horses, dogs, and movable effects—traversing the prairie and enjoying a summer's hunt. He had his chance as he fell in with the Osage band as it moved southward toward the Grand Saline, as the Salt Plains near present-day Cherokee, Oklahoma, were then known. Sibley also hoped to be the first white man ever to visit this popular Plains Indian site. But he had been warned that it was well in Comanche range. It would be hazardous, he was told, to go there without a sizable escort.

After crossing the Arkansas somewhere just west of present-day Wichita, Sibley accompanied the Little Osage village thirty miles southwest to a stream that was probably the Ninnescah. Wishing to visit other Osages to the south as well as the Grand Saline, Sibley and his small party left the Little Osage band here. With some difficulty, he arranged to rejoin this group at an appointed site, whereupon the band would provide him escort to the salt mountain.

Traveling on for some thirty miles to the southeast, Sibley reached the Osage hunting camp of Chief White Hair close to the present Kansas-Oklahoma border. Sibley presented White Hair with an American flag. After spending the night there, the frontier tourists continued on some twenty miles to the camp of Chief Clermont west of present Blackwell, Oklahoma. From there the party rode almost due west forty miles to the Grand Saline, the last eight miles being over a range of barren sand hills. On the way the travelers paused to enjoy the tasty sand plums from bushes scattered among the dunes. The Fort Osage agent was much impressed with the Grand Saline.

> I found myself on a level hard sandy plain, the southern side or extremity of the Grand Saline and I had leisure quietly to contemplate the wonderful scene before me, far surpassing anything that I had ever pictured to my mind from the descriptions I had obtained from the Indians. It is a perfectly smooth and nearly level plain of red sand, so hard on the surface that our horses made no impressions with their hooves, except on the thin crust of salt with which it was entirely covered.[10]

Small herds of buffalo sprinkled the salt plains. Sibley could not resist the temptation to give chase at one herd of thirty or more. He underestimated the distance, however, and it took much longer to overtake the buffalo than he had thought. He fired his pistols without effect, while a young Osage gracefully downed two of the animals.

Unknown horsemen had been spotted in the hills to the southwest. Thinking they could well be Padoucas

(Comanches), old warrior Sans Oreille advised Sibley it was time to leave. From the salt prairie, the party traveled some thirty-six miles in a northwesterly direction to rejoin the Little Osages on a stream that was probably Medicine Lodge Creek of southern Kansas. Here the Osages planned to spend several weeks, living on fat buffalo meat, tongues, marrow bones, hominy, dried pumpkins, and plums. "All was mirth and merriment," Sibley wrote. "I never witnessed so much apparent happiness so generally pervading an Indian nation."[11]

As prearranged, a war party had made itself ready to escort Sibley to the salt mountain. Although he was determined to see it for himself, Sibley had some doubts about the reports he had heard. He reasoned that they may have been exaggerated by white men in telling of the wonders of the far unexplored West. He would soon find that his suspicions were not unfounded.

On June 28 Sibley, Sans Oreille, and an interpreter set out on horseback with their escort of Osage warriors. The warriors were all on foot, as was their usual warring style. For two days the three horsemen and their escort of trotting Osages traveled southwest through harsh, ravine-slashed country that seemed "thrown together in utmost apparent confusion."[12] At times they wound along high, rocky ridges; at other times they passed through lush meadows cut by meandering, tree-lined streams. But most awe-inspiring to Sibley were the towering, rock-capped plateaus, which made him feel he was amid the ruins of an ancient city around which the earth had sunk away.

As they approached the Cimarron River, the grassland gave way to sandy hills of silver-green sagebrush. In the bottomland of a small, high-banked rivulet feeding into the Cimarron from the north, the travelers came onto a sight that excited them even more than the picturesque country they had just seen. They found themselves looking down on a herd of some thirty thousand buffalo that were grazing and watering along the stream.[13]

It was not an opportunity that the Osages would simply pass by. Surrounding the herd, they began pelting it with rifle fire. The mass of buffalo stampeded down the valley, the thunder of their hooves rumbling against the red sandstone cliffs. Two of the Osage warriors were injured in the affair, which netted twenty-seven animals.

What Sibley looked down upon from a hilltop overlooking the Cimarron River was not a salt mountain but another saline. Although not so large as the other—Sibley estimated it to be some five hundred acres—it greatly impressed the Osage agent nonetheless. The saline lay like a broad expanse of flat red land spotted with white cone-shaped hills that had built up around four salt springs. Eventually it would become known as the Rock Saline because of the thick layers of rock salt that could be found there. Known today as the Big Salt Plain, it is located a few miles west of Freedom, Oklahoma, where the Cimarron River borders Woodward and Woods Counties. Commercial salt processing has been in operation there off and on since 1919.

The Indian guides told Sibley that normally the area was a solid mass of salt several inches thick but that rains had recently washed the land clear. Sibley used his tomahawk to chip off some chunks of salt from the cones to take home as evidence. He was convinced that normally the entire saline was covered with a solid rock of salt from four to twenty inches thick. In the future, however, Sibley no longer talked of a salt mountain.[14]

Again Comanches were reported to be prowling nearby. Although the Osage warriors hoped to take a few of their enemy's scalps, Sibley insisted on heading back. After a frustrating journey in which he lost his favorite riding horse in a bog, the agent returned to Fort Osage on July 11. He had been in the field for two months.

Sibley's trip to the salines of northwestern Oklahoma excited some interest among other explorers of the West. He even visualized a commercial potential in carting the salt by wagon to the Arkansas River and floating it downriver to market. In the end, his discovery would have little effect on the course of history. Nevertheless, his was the first Anglo-American intrusion into a heretofore unknown region of the West. It pulled back the curtain of mystery about the area and provides history a record of life there we would not otherwise have.

Sibley would return to the soil of present-day Oklahoma again in the fall of 1825. As one of three commissioners appointed to survey the historically significant Santa Fe Trail, he traveled with surveyor Joseph C. Brown and a surveying party from Fort Osage across Kansas and the western tip of the Oklahoma Panhandle to New Mexico. In an entry on October 7, Sibley's diary recorded a visit to a famous camping place on the trail: "Here we found, Situated amidst huge rocky cliffs *The Upper Semerone Spring*, affording abundance of excellent Water, and the long narrow Valley that its water supplied us with plenty of Wood for fuel & pretty good pasturage for our Horses."[15] It would be over a year before Sibley returned to Fort Osage, his journal and diaries once again providing graphic descriptions of the western world he saw.

───────────────────

Exploring up the Arkansas

In America's day of river travel, the Arkansas River—especially with the Red River blocked by its great channel-clogging raft of driftwood above present-day Shreveport—offered one of the most natural and prominent routes of entry into the wilds beyond Arkansas country. Without doubt many individuals and small parties of which we know little or nothing made their way up the Arkansas River route. Evidence indicates that one of the more intriguing of these was a secret Spanish expedition in 1816 headed by the infamous Gulf of Mexico pirate Jean Lafitte, who was accompanied by Major Arsene Lacarriere Latour and Louis Bringier, the son of a wealthy Creole family of Louisiana.[1]

The purpose of the Spanish expedition was to provide information and maps that would assist Spain in exercising dominance over that portion of the Louisiana lands it still claimed. Lafitte, who had helped Andrew Jackson defeat the British at New Orleans in 1814, had not as yet won his fame as a Galveston Island brigand. Latour, formerly a chief engineer in the U.S. Army and a cartographer, was to provide the maps. But it is Bringier's narratives that reveal a visit by the party as far upstream as the Osage village on the Verdigris branch of the Arkansas. Although Bringier does not specifically say he and the party reached the Osage village, his detailed description of it clearly indicates personal observation. He wrote:

> The Osage village on the Verdigris river, contains about two hundred and fifty lodges or cabins, of about forty feet by eighteen or twenty, placed with little regularity: some are built with barks, and others with upright poles; they are all nicely covered with plated flags [flats]. The village stands in a handsome and fertile prairie, where weeds grow twelve or fourteen feet high.
>
> Near this village are three beautiful mounts [mounds], which may be eighty or one hundred feet high; the surface of one is perfectly level, and is more than 150 yards in distance. The rest of the country, for a great distance round, is almost level. The mounts afford three fine springs which yield good pure water, although the country is a calcareous one.
>
> Fifteen miles from this village, is the saline which yields the water that give one-sixth of salt. One Herhart [Earheart] had put up about thirty kettles on that spring.[2]

The Osages, Bringier reported, were a very hospitable people. When a trader's canoe stopped at the Three Forks landing, the Osage chief immediately sent people to transport his goods the forty-six miles to their village, stationed a guard over his boat, and assigned a warrior as the trader's personal bodyguard. While in the Osage village, visitors were daily brought large wooden bowls filled with such delicacies as smoked pumpkin, boiled sweet corn, buffalo meat, turkey, venison, and bear's meat.

Bringier also told of a western saline called Lake Jefferson (apparently the Great Salt Plains) and of sand hills beyond that moved about with the wind (possibly the Waynoka sand dunes).[3] Likely, he did not visit these sites but heard about them from the Osages. Bringier provided extensive, though severely biased descriptions—the Spanish Indians were all good, he said, the Indians of the United States all bad—of both the Osages and their Arkansas River enemies, the Cherokees.

Blow-for-blow warfare had persisted between the two tribes since the Cherokees had settled along the Arkansas River above Little Rock in 1812. Following a particularly vicious attack by the Cherokees on the Osages' Verdigris River village in 1817, the U.S. Army decided to establish a military post as a buffer between the two nations. Major William Bradford, a veteran of the War of 1812, and Major Stephen Long of the Topographical Corps were dispatched up the Arkansas to locate a site for the fort.

The party arrived at Arkansas Post at the conflux of the Arkansas and the Mississippi rivers on October 15, 1817. With a number of men suffering a variety of illnesses, Bradford remained behind, while Long went on ahead up the river. Ascending the Arkansas in a skiff to the mouth of the Verdigris, Long made astronomical and botanical observations. He then returned to where the river crossed the dividing line between Cherokee and Osage land. There on a beautiful bluff along the river—the site had become known to French voyagers who often camped and rendezvoused there as Belle Point—Long chose the site for a military post. He named it Camp Smith after General Thomas A. Smith of the Ninth Military District.[4] Long continued his explorations with a reconnaissance from the new site up the Poteau River to its headwaters. From there he cut across the divide to the Kiamichi and explored down that stream to the Red River.

Two years later, on April 24, 1819, riding as a passenger in the pirogue of two French trappers, botanist Thomas Nuttall arrived at what had become known as Fort

English botanist Thomas Nuttall. (*Imperial Magazine*, December 1825)

Smith. He had hopes of eventually reaching the Rocky Mountains. Born January 5, 1786, at Long Preston in North Riding, Yorkshire, Nuttall had served seven years as an apprentice printer before emigrating to the United States in 1808 at the age of twenty-two.[5] It was his love of botany, developed in part by field studies of plant life and geology of his home environment and in part by readings on North American flora, that had brought Nuttall to America.

Through the encouragement of botanist Dr. Benjamin S. Barton, Nuttall became a student at the University of Pennsylvania. His first western scientific adventure came in 1810 when he made a tour to the Great Lakes region, arriving at the fur-trading center of Michilimackinac on August 12. There he met a group of

Astorian trappers and accompanied them by canoe on a trip to Prairie du Chien, Wisconsin, and on to St. Louis, Missouri. Nuttall remained in St. Louis through the winter, and in the spring of 1811 he joined an elite trader party headed up the Missouri River under the famed Manuel Lisa. The botanist spent the summer and fall along the river, eventually reaching far-off Fort Mandan in present-day North Dakota. He remained at Fort Mandan until the year's end collecting plants, seeds, roots, and other scientific specimens.[6]

Nuttall had arrived at Arkansas Post on the Mississippi River in January 1819. Four fellow members of the American Philosophical Society donated the sum of $200 to finance his year and a half trip to reap "a rich harvest of Botanical treasure in the Arkansas" country.[7] He found the place distasteful despite the interesting Indian burial mounds in the area. After a month's stay, with peach trees heralding the coming of spring, he began a tediously slow journey upriver as a passenger on a large skiff. He and his traveling companions had to fight not only the stiff current but also swarms of mosquitoes.

The skiff had hardly made it halfway to Little Rock when Nuttall eagerly grasped the opportunity to transfer to a much larger boat owned by trader William Drope. On March 9 the boat passed by some rocky cliffs opposite the infant settlement of Little Rock. On March 27 the voyagers reached the trading post of Cadron, then being surveyed as a town site. From there it was on past Point Remove and the portion of Arkansas occupied by the Cherokees.

From Nuttall's view along the river, the Cherokees appeared to be prosperous, with "houses handsomely and conveniently furnished, and their tables spread with our dainties and luxuries."[8] The botanist paused to visit among the Cherokees, meeting and reporting to his journal on interesting personalities such as Cherokee trader Walter Webber and Chief John Jolly.

At Webber's, Nuttall hired the services of two French boatmen and a pirogue, departing there on April 20. Traveling under warm springtime skies, Nuttall basked in the beauty of nature along the river: "the melody of innumerable birds, and the gentle humming of the wild bees, feeding on the early blooming willows."[9]

At Fort Smith he was received cordially by Major William Bradford. Although Nuttall wished to continue on up the Arkansas, he decided to spend some time at Fort Smith collecting specimens of flora and fauna. Occasionally accompanied by Dr. Thomas Russell, the post surgeon, Nuttall wandered at will over the countryside examining plants and flowers through his pocket microscope. With only minimal funds and already suffering from bouts with malaria, Nuttall was unconcerned for his health and oblivious of the many dangers that threatened on all sides. His interest and his devoted intent were the observation and study of plant and animal life of the region.

Nuttall's 1819 scientific sojourn to Indian Territory produced significant botanical knowledge and specimens. But the record of his journey up the Arkansas River, published as *A Journal of Travels into the Arkansas Territory* in 1821, was perhaps even more significant in the record it offered history. Today his observations of the frontier provide a literary window through which we are given a close look at primordial Oklahoma, its early landmarks, and the rough beginnings of organized white society.

Conditioned to the dangers of the frontier, Nuttall was unconcerned about the threats of Indians or wild animals. He had a pistol, but he used it for digging up plants. Convinced that the Arkansas River drainage was a botanical Eden, he harbored plans for a trip to Arkansas Territory. In October 1818, supported by modest contributions from patrons in the Academy of Natural Sciences, he set out on his southwestern journey alone, botanizing as he went,

After a few weeks at Fort Smith, Nuttall was given the opportunity to join a party under Bradford headed down the Kiamichi River to its juncture with the Red. The officer had orders to remove the white immigrants who had settled on land that was then claimed by the Osages. The group traveled by horseback over the Winding Stair Mountains through trackless LeFlore, Pushmataha, and Choctaw Counties. The countryside, sometimes woods, sometimes grassy meadows, abounded in wild life.

Nuttall proved to be an astute observer and excellent diarist as well as a determined scientist, making precise records of plants, geological formations, and animal life. He also provided interesting sketches of curiosities of the frontier. While traveling in the vicinity of present Talihina, he wrote: "On the summit of the dividing ridge, we observed a pile of stone in the bison path that we travelled, which, I was informed, had been thrown up as a monument by the Osages when they were going to war, each warrior casting a stone upon the pile."[10]

Here Nuttall saw his first American buffalo. The soldiers with the party spotted a small herd on a prairie pasture and gave chase. Nuttall was impressed with their size and speed. "The bulls, now lean and agile, galloped along the plain with prodigious swiftness, like so many huge lions. The pendant beard, large head hid in bushy locks, with the rest of the body nearly divested of hair, give a peculiar and characteristic grace to this animal when in motion."[11]

On May 24 Nuttall's party reached the conflux of the Kiamichi and Red rivers and on up the latter some fifteen miles to Wild Horse Prairie. It was so named, he said, for the herds of wild horses that had inhabited the site until only recently.

Nuttall was hosted at the Red River home of a man named William Styles. There Nuttall was so absorbed with collecting plants that he missed the homeward departure of Bradford's party. That night Bradford's men fired four shots in an effort to locate Nuttall, but the answering shots were not heard. While waiting for someone with whom he could return to Fort Smith, the botanist occupied himself with strolls up and down the banks of the Red River investigating plants, minerals, and animal life.

Nuttall's opportunity to return north came unexpectedly on a Sunday afternoon when three white men appeared. They were leaving immediately on their way north to recover horses stolen from them by the Cherokees. With little time to find provisions for the trip, the botanist departed his hosts with feelings of much gratitude for their "sincere and unfeigned hospitality, which I so seasonably experienced from these poor and honest people, when left in the midst of the wilderness."[12]

The journey back up the Kiamichi River was torturous, in part because of the torment of large flies but also because of the rugged terrain: "We passed and repassed several terrific ridges, over which our horses could scarcely keep their feet, and which were, besides, so overgrown with bushes and trees half-burnt, with ragged limbs, that every thing about us, not of leather, was lashed and torn to pieces."[13]

Nuttall arrived back at the Arkansas fort on June 21. By July 6 he was headed out on still another scientific exploration. Traveling upriver on the trading boat of Joseph Bougie (or Bogy), the Englishman made note of landmarks of that day: the mouth of Skin Bayou; the towering rock cliffs then known as Swallow or Hirundel Rocks and later as Wilson Rock; Cavaniol and Sugar Loaf Mountains; Sallisaw Creek; the Canadian River; the Illinois River, rippling and clear in contrast to the muddy Arkansas; and four miles above it, the "cascade of two or three feet perpendicular fall" that would a decade later become known as Webber's Falls.[14] Here the boat became grounded; but after several tries and with a favorable wind, passage was achieved. Beyond the Grand River, which the Osages knew as the Six Bulls, the voyagers reached the Verdigris.

Three trading posts were operating now in the vicinity of the Three Forks meeting of the Verdigris and Grand rivers with the Arkansas. They included Joseph Bougie's, located a mile and a half above the mouth of the Verdigris; that of Nathaniel Pryor, Samuel Richards, and Hugh Glenn, a mile up the Verdigris; and one operated by Captain Henry Barbour and George W. Brand, situated on the east side of the Verdigris. Some thirty miles up the Grand was Chouteau's trading house.[15]

Nuttall continued his exploring and studies at Three Forks. He joined two men in a canoe trip up the Grand River to a salt works where only recently owner Johnson Campbell had been murdered by his partner and two other men. Nuttall was even more horrified to learn that the murderous partner was a man he had tried to hire at the Cadron.[16] Although the salt springs operation was now abandoned, Nuttall stayed for a short time at the nearby home of a hunter-trader named Slover while he overcame a bout with influenza. Nuttall did not visit the Osages, but he learned much about them from others.

> The first village of the Osages lies about 60 miles from the mouth of the Verdigris, and is said to contain 7 or 800 men and their families. About 60 miles further, on the Osage river, is situated the village of the chief called White Hair. The whole of the Osages are now, by governor Clarke, enumerated at about 8000 souls. At this time nearly the whole town, men and women, were engaged in their summer hunt, collecting tallow and meat. The principal chief is called by the French Clarmont, though his proper name is the Iron bird, a species of the Eagle.[17]

During the past two summers, an interpreter said, the Osages had hosted a general council of various

Plains tribes at the salt plains—Shawnees, Delawares, Creeks, Quapaws, Kansa, Sac and Fox, Arapahos, Comanches, and others. Their object was to form an allegiance in opposition to the Cherokees. It was said that the Osages had given the Sac and Fox over three hundred horses and won their support in the event they were needed for a fight.

Nuttall no sooner returned to Bougie's place than he was off again, this time guided by an old trapper named Lee. He led the botanist on what was to be the first chronicled visit to central Oklahoma. The two men departed alone on horseback on August 11, riding westward past the site of present-day Okmulgee and crossing the Osage buffalo-hunting trace leading southward to the Red River. As they traveled along the north bank of the Deep Fork, Lee trapped and hunted, while Nuttall examined the scientific mysteries of this new world.

The men were forced to drink the water of stagnant pools, and Nuttall suffered badly from the blistering August heat. As a result, he experienced a flareup of malaria that brought a high fever, diarrhea, and vomiting. Adding to this misery were the swarms of green blowflies that attacked the horses, invaded the clothes of the two men, and filled their meat supply with maggots.

Lee recommended that they turn back, but Nuttall, who could barely sit his horse, refused. Unable to eat for over three days, he endured the "miseries of sickness, delirium, and despondence" as well as a "kind of lethargy, almost the prelude of death."[18] The determined Englishman continued with the trapper on up the Deep Fork past present-day Bristow and on to the west until they reached the Cimarron River near present-day Guthrie. They were now well into the Cross Timbers, of which Nuttall wrote, "We saw nothing far and wide but an endless scrubby forest of dwarfish oaks, chiefly the post, black, and red species."[19]

Lee had told of some interesting "tracts of moving sand hills" a few days to the west (probably the Little Sahara near Waynoka).[20] But when the trapper's horse became mired and was lost, Nuttall finally consented to turn back. Lee hewed out a cottonwood tree canoe to carry himself and his pelts down the Cimarron. The botanist followed along on shore.

The two men were dependent on the briny water of the Cimarron for drink. As Nuttall and Lee descended the river to its conflux with the Arkansas, the tails of beaver (the rest of the animal being inedible) were their only food. Nuttall noted that the game seemed to have been driven out of this part of the country.

Nine or ten miles down the Arkansas, the two men encountered a small group of Osages. The two or three families consisted mostly of women and an old blind chief who had a paper showing that he had once been to St. Louis. One of the women, "resembling one of the imaginary witches of Macbeth,"[21] insisted that Nuttall give his horse to her daughter. He resisted the hag's demand. The old chief invited the men to his lodge to eat, feeding them a meal of boiled corn sweetened with pumpkin marmalade. But when the two men prepared to leave, the Indians made every attempt to take both their canoe and the horse.

Unable to keep up with Lee in the canoe, Nuttall decided to cut across land to Three Forks. He arrived at Bougie's store with his feet and legs so swollen from traveling through thickets that it was necessary to cut off his buckskin pantaloons. Nuttall remained with Bougie for a week, suffering a high fever and delirium. He was still feeble and afflicted by violent spasms of feet and hands when he joined an engagé in a five-day canoe trip downriver to Fort Smith. The settlement was astir with a peace council being held between the Osages and the Cherokees.

Nuttall was not alone in his illness. Over one hundred Cherokees died from an epidemic of bilious fever that swept the region. He remained at Fort Smith, sick in body and spirit, until mid-October and then moved slowly downriver, reaching Arkansas Post in December, New Orleans in February 1820, and Philadelphia the following April.[22]

Still another narrative of the Three Forks area of this period is provided by James Miller, first governor of Arkansas Territory. From 1819 until Indian Territory was created in 1824, Arkansas Territory extended some forty miles into present-day Oklahoma. During the summer of 1820, Miller made a two-month trip up the Arkansas River accompanied by two aides. His purpose was to end the bloody dispute between the Cherokees and Osages, and he persuaded four Cherokee leaders to accompany him to the Osage village on the Verdigris. In a letter to a friend, Miller described the Arkansas as a "fine navigable river" that afforded rich land on both sides and an abundance of wild game.[23] As had Bringier four years earlier, Miller found the Osages to be hospitable:

> The Osage village is built as compactly as Boston, in the center of a vast Prairie. We rode forty miles into it, before we came to the town. All the warriors, chiefs, and young men met us two miles from the town on horseback, mounted on good horses, and as fine as they had feathers or anything else to make them. They professed much friendship. I got them to suspend their hostilities. The Osage town consisted of 145 dwellings with from ten to fifteen in each house. The average height of the men is more than six feet. They are entirely in a state of nature—. Very few white people have ever been among them. They know nothing of the use of money, nor do they use any ardent spirits.[24]

Miller's visit to Three Forks came at the end of its age of innocence to the outside world. The area would soon become another foothold of white people on the Indian frontier.

The Long Expedition

Major Stephen Long, who had made his brief exploration of southeastern Oklahoma in 1817, returned in 1820, this time marching eastward along the Canadian River after exploring the eastern slopes of the Rocky Mountains. Another division of his 1820 expedition under Captain John R. Bell, which had split away from Long's segment in Colorado, retraced Wilkinson's route along the Arkansas River. Long's Canadian River trek gives us our first recorded look at this important route across the Central Plains. Bell's account of the Arkansas River leg of the journey makes note of revealing changes in the arrangement of Indian tribes since Pike's expedition of 1806.[1]

The Long scientific expedition of 1820 was one part of the U.S. government's effort to exert some degree of influence over the vast area of the Louisiana Purchase. The northern phase of this operation, known as the Yellowstone Expedition, was to move up the Missouri River under the command of General Henry Atkinson. However, this movement came to failure in the autumn

Stephen H. Long was an early explorer of the Arkansas, Red, and Canadian rivers of Oklahoma. (U.S. Army Military History Institute)

of 1818 and spring of 1819 because of difficulties in navigating the river.[2] It would be 1825 before Atkinson finally succeeded in undertaking this leg of the task. Nevertheless, in late September 1819 U.S. troops did manage to reach the Council Bluffs point on the Missouri River and establish what at first was called Engineer Cantonment or Camp Missouri, near present-day Omaha, Nebraska.

The Long party assembled there in May 1820 to pre-pare for its adventure into the western wilderness.[3] The company of twenty men included Captain Bell, expedition journalist; Lieutenant W. H. Swift, assistant topographer; Dr. Thomas Say, zoologist; Dr. Edwin James, botanist; Samuel Seymour, landscape painter; H. Dougherty, hunter; Stephen Julien, interpreter for French and Indian languages; a Spanish interpreter; a baggage master; two engagés; and seven soldiers from Camp Missouri.[4]

The expedition was equipped with twenty horses—one for each member—along with eight pack mules. The expeditioners carried with them three tents; food provisions of pork, biscuits, cornmeal, coffee, sugar, and salt; and, for the Indian tribes they would meet, five gallons of whiskey and presents: vermilion, beads, knives, combs, hawk bells, scissors, looking glasses, tobacco, hatchets, tin canisters, and a variety of other materials. Each member had a tomahawk, shot pouch and powder horn, and rifle, and most had pistols. The packhorses carried a variety of scientific equipment.

The Indians at Camp Missouri shook their heads as the group departed on June 6. The country that the expedition planned to travel through was destitute of water and grass, the Natives said, and there was no way such a small group could withstand the attacks that were sure to come from the hostile Indians who infested the land. The truth of this warning was borne out when a Sac and Fox attack on a trading boat just up the Missouri River killed one man and wounded several others. Dr. Say and a small group had also been threatened and robbed by a 140-man Pawnee war party while returning from a visit to a Kansa Indian encampment. The men felt very lucky to escape with their scalps. When the expedition visited a trio of Pawnee villages on the Loup River, a Pawnee chief remarked, "Your heart must be strong to go upon so hazardous a journey."[5]

Joined by two Frenchmen of considerable experience in hunting and trapping in the mountains, Joseph Bijeau and Abraam Ledoux, Long and his small band of explorers moved westward up the Platte River during June 1820. They reached the Rockies without incident, turning south near the peak that today bears Long's name. July 12 found the party encamped near the site of Colorado Springs, and Dr. James and two soldiers climbed Pike's Peak, the first men known to do so. Continuing on south, the group reached the Arkansas River near Pueblo and, after a sojourn upriver to the Royal Gorge, turned east.

Shortly thereafter they met an Indian—a Kaskaia who was eloping with another man's wife—from whom they purchased a horse preparatory to splitting into two groups for their return trip. That move was made on July 24 near the mouth of the Apishapa River. Long and ten of the men waved their good-byes as they moved south with six horses and ten mules to strike the headwaters of the Canadian River in northeastern New Mexico. They followed the stream to the south along the mountains until August 4, when it turned sharply eastward to cross the flat prairieland of the Texas Panhandle.

The eleven men were unsure as to exactly what stream they were following but were hopeful that it was the Red River. A week's march along the rugged, ravine-cut north bank of the river brought them to the river's northeasterly bend to the north of present-day Amarillo.[6] It was there on August 10 that they encountered a migratory village of Kaskaia Indians, now believed to have been the Plains Apaches, that was approaching the river from the south—a long, uneven string of warriors, women, and children, all on horseback and driving their horse herds with them. Some of the horses pulled travois, some carried packs of meat, and some were loaded with young children whose legs were lashed to their saddles.

As they crossed the stream, some of the Indian women paused to fill their buffalo-bladder water bags. These bags were carried on a stick that was inserted through the two orifices with the bladder dangling. In camp they were mounted on tripods in front of each lodge. When the exploring party attempted to drink from the still-odious pouch, to the amusement of the Indians they spilled more on themselves than into their mouths.

The Kaskaias, who numbered about 250 people in some thirty-two lodges, still hunted with bow and arrow. Although the Americans found a few articles of Spanish origin among the tribespeople, they displayed little evidence of trade for outside goods. The home of this tribe was at the head of the Platte and Arkansas rivers. Interestingly, the image of the Gulf Coast alligator was a fetish among the tribe. The symbol was prominent as an ornament throughout the band and was used on occasion as a cure for disease or prevention of misfortune.[7] The band said it was returning home from a hunting excursion to the headwaters of the Brazos and Colorado rivers of Texas. When queried on the matter, the Kaskaias chief, Red Mouse (or so the interpreter thought), informed Long that this river was indeed the Red.

When the American explorers prepared to depart the Indian camp, they discovered that some of their horses, camp kettles, and other accoutrements were missing. Major Long ordered his interpreter to make a complaint to the chief, but the chief's answers were vague and unaccompanied by any positive action. Already the leather lodges of the Kaskaias had been struck and loaded onto the travois, and the Indian horse herd had been rounded up and moved off a distance with the women and children.

Long knew he had to act quickly and ordered his men to take up arms. Immediately a large number of Kaskaia warriors, all of them with bows strung and an abundance of arrows in hand, surrounded the eleven white men. For a breathless moment it appeared that the Indians were prepared to fight, and the warnings of the Missouri River Indians seemed very meaningful. But eventually the chief ordered the missing property found and brought forward, much to the relief of the Americans, and the parting was a friendly one.

This would be the only band of Indians encountered by this segment of the Long expedition as it marched across the Texas Panhandle and the breadth of Oklahoma. Although the Kaskaias had reassured them that this was, indeed, the Red River and that they would soon encounter the Pawnee Pict villages, the white men saw no other tribespeople. But as the explorers neared the 100th meridian on August 15, they discovered Indian breastworks—constructed in a circular fashion and large enough to hold eighty to one hundred members of a war party.

Long and his men also saw large numbers of prairie wolves and vultures, often feeding on the carcasses of buffalo. The fresh tracks of both horses and men told the expeditioners that an Indian hunting party had been there recently. Their own hunters brought in buffalo meat. This was dried and smoked during the night, then enough jerked to provide for several days. Wild horses were becoming more numerous now, and by midday buffalo by the thousands came from all directions to find water in the stagnant pools of the drought-stricken river.

On August 16 a violent afternoon rainstorm struck, bringing with it hail an inch in diameter. The horses refused to move, and some of the mules stampeded. The men huddled in their blankets for protection, remembering stories they had heard of men and animals being killed by hailstones. The torrid sun returned, the water from the rain disappeared into the ground, and the men were soon digging holes in the riverbed once more to quench their thirst.

The Long party entered present-day Oklahoma at the 100th meridian on August 17. The expedition journal fails to make any notice of Antelope Hills, unless it was the reference on August 18 to "exposed portions of sand rock, and was often seen from a distance of several miles."[8] The explorers halted at midday to kill several buffalo in the vicinity, and feasted on wild grapes abundant in the area. The roaring of the immense herds of buffalo sounded through the night, mixing with the hooting and screeching of owls and the howling of coyotes.

As the men made their way along the Canadian between present-day Ellis and Roger Mills Counties, suspicion mounted that this was not the Red River as they had understood from the Kaskaias. They had no choice but to push on. At times the men explored beyond the river's banks. On August 19 they visited what may have been Red Rock Canyon near present-day Hinton. James wrote:

> We could distinguish the winding course of a small stream uniting numerous tributaries from the ridge we occupied, and pursuing its way towards the southeast along a narrow well-wooded valley. The dense and verdant foliage of the poplars and elms contrasted faintly with the bright red of the sandstone cliffs, which rose on both sides, far surpassing the elevation of the tallest trees, and disclosing here and there masses of sulphate of lime of a snowy whiteness.[9]

The men found their way back to the Canadian by following buffalo paths that "in this country are as frequent and almost as conspicuous as the roads in the most populous parts of the United States."[10] Swarms of blowflies had made it impossible for the men to eat their fresh meat. They resorted to eating directly from their kettle of hunter's soup. Their supplies of salt and parched cornmeal were all but gone. Gnats and ticks were a further annoyance. The sun blazed down, driving temperatures at midday to the upper nineties, and an ugly mood had grown among some of the men who had used up their tobacco supply. There were other inconveniences. "All our clothing had become so dirty as to be offensive both to sight and smell. Uniting in our own persons the professions of traveller, hostler, butcher, and cook, sleeping on the ground by night, and being almost incessantly on the march by day; it is not to be supposed we could give as much attention to personal neatness as might be wished."[11]

On August 22 a dense column of smoke was spotted rising from the summit of a hill south of the Canadian. This, plus a multicolored herd of some four to five hundred horses seen shading themselves in a grove of trees, raised expectations of meeting with Indians. Guns were put to order, but the horses proved to be a wild herd.

Reaching the vicinity of present-day Oklahoma County on August 27, the travelers witnessed numerous buffalo, wild horses, elk, and deer grazing in contentment. Black bears prowled the river's sand hills for grapes, berries, plums, and other forage. The worst encounter here was with an infestation of wood ticks that attached themselves in swarms to men, horses, and dogs alike, creating swollen, inflamed sores and great suffering.

The abundance of game continued as the explorers moved on eastward down the Canadian. The men were also finding occasional bee trees from which they procured honey. Long duly recorded in his notebook the lay of the land, the vegetation, the flocks of birds they were now seeing, and the various species of animal life. On September 6, three and a half miles above the mouth of the North Canadian, the party came across a unique sight: "A remarkable rock, standing isolated in the middle of the river . . . It is about twenty-five feet high, and fifty or sixty in diameter, and its sides so perpendicular as to render the summit inaccessible. It appears to have been broken from a high promontory of gray sandstone overhanging the river on the north side."[12]

This unique formation would be rediscovered later and dubbed Standing Rock. The expedition passed the mouth of the North Canadian on September 8 and on September 10 reached the much larger Arkansas River. It confirmed Long's worst fears. He knew for certain now that for nearly three months he had been following the wrong river. "Our disappointment and chagrin at discovering the mistake we had so long laboured under, was little alleviated by the consciousness that the season was so far advanced, our horses and our means so far exhausted, as to place it beyond our power to return and attempt the discovery of the sources of the Red river."[13]

Floating baggage and swimming the horses across the Arkansas, the already weary and disheartened party became enmeshed in a virtually impenetrable cane brake. For all of one day and part of the next, the men fought their way through the giant canes. On the morning of September 6, they met the first humans they had seen since leaving the Kaskaias in the Texas Panhandle.

These were a small hunting party of Cherokees, their horses loaded with guns, kettles, and other equipment. Although they did not speak English, the Indians told the exhausted travelers by sign language that they should reach Belle Point and Fort Smith the following morning. En route they met the first English-speaking men they had seen other than themselves in three months. It was a group under trader Hugh Glenn. He made Long's men much-appreciated presents of coffee, biscuits, and other food, plus a bottle of whiskey.

The exploring group arrived at Fort Smith on September 13. There the men discovered that the other half of their party under the command of Captain Bell had arrived ahead of them via the Arkansas River route. Major Bradford treated Long and his men to a sumptuous breakfast, though he cautioned them against eating too much bread, sweet potatoes, and other foods that they had not eaten for some time. The travelers failed to heed his advice and later regretted their lack of caution.

Of the two excursions, the one down the Arkansas had been much the more eventful. Only two days after separating from the Long group, the Bell-led party of twelve men—Captain Bell, Lieutenant Swift, painter Seymour, Dr. Say, the three guide-interpreters, and five soldiers—met a large encampment of Plains Indians near present-day Lamar, Colorado. It was an interesting encounter with several important tribes that had now moved southward to exert significant influence throughout the mid-Plains. In the encampment were Kaskaias, Kiowas, Cheyennes, and Arapahos. These tribes now dominated an area once controlled by the Apaches, Wichitas, and Comanches.

The Kaskaias evidently became associated with the Kiowas during their tenure on the headwaters of the Arkansas and Platte rivers of Colorado. The Long meeting may have come at a time when they were emerging onto the mid-Plains with the Kiowas, both tribes eventually moving into the Texas Panhandle– western Oklahoma region in association with the Comanches. The Cheyennes and Arapahos, both Algonquian-speaking peoples, had moved across the Missouri from Minnesota and the Great Lakes area during the latter half of the eighteenth century to become associated with each other in the Black Hills. This meeting with the Americans on the Arkansas is one of the first evidences of a historical split within the two tribes that would produce permanent northern and southern divisions.[14]

When the four chiefs met and smoked with Captain Bell and his party, they were informed that the white men represented the "numerous and powerful" nation whose great chief presided over all that country. The chiefs were given a few combs, knives, vermilion, and so on as presents, and the Indians responded with three or four horses, though they considered the visitors to be "tight-fisted."[15]

Most of these Indians still wore buckskin clothes, though there were some red and blue blankets and serapes visible. The explorers were told that some "Tabbaboos"—white traders—had come up the Red River during the past winter and traded cloth, beads, knives, guns, powder, lead, and vermilion for horses, mules, hides, and robes. Arapaho chief Bear Tooth appeared to hold dominant power among the tribes, though the Americans were impressed with the Cheyenne leader, a man "born to command" and endowed with unconquerable ferocity of appearance. The Cheyennes had just recently fought a big battle with the Pawnees, one of their principal enemies.[16]

As the band moved off, the young warriors displayed their war effects by riding up and down alongside the departing caravan, brandishing their bows, arrows, lances, war shields, war clubs, knives, and tomahawks. Their horse herds at this point were very large; the gun was seldom seen. The American expedition would, in fact, get a good look at the war culture of the Plains Indian during its journey down the Arkansas.

On September 30 the Bell group met a small Arapaho war party—nine men and one woman. In the group was a lone Kiowa, who tried to take a horse from the explorers. When he was repulsed and sent off fuming, the Arapahos displayed no sympathy for him. Two days later the expeditioners encountered a Cheyenne war party on its way back from a raid against the Pawnees. The party had counted coup on a Pawnee woman whom the leader had killed. In recognition of this feat, he had charcoaled his entire body a deep black. Most of the warriors carried lances decorated with strips of red and white cloth, beads, and the tail plumes of the eagle. From the lance of the leader dangled the scalp of the Pawnee woman.[17]

But even starker evidence of intertribal warring came on August 12 when near present-day Hutchison, Kansas, a Comanche war party of thirty men and five women appeared from over a hill to the north. They had been on a foray against the Osages and in the process had had three men killed and six wounded. In addition, they had lost fifty-six horses and most of their robes and clothing. One of the Comanches, in his sorrow over the loss of a brother in the fight, had slashed himself with over one hundred parallel cuts, three to four inches long, across his arms and thighs.[18]

At the mouth of the Little Arkansas, the exploring party discovered an abandoned hunting camp. The bark-covered huts were surrounded by a scattering of watermelons, pumpkins, and corn. Similarly, down-stream at what may have once been the site of Fer-dinandina, the party discovered sixty to seventy more lodges, along with several small fields of corn. Numer-ous well-worn trails leading in various directions from there indicated that this site was still popular as a planting and hunting camp location.[19]

August 28 found the party camped at the site of present Tulsa. The men threw themselves "supperless, upon the ground to repose after a fatiguing march of about twenty-nine miles, during which the greatest degree of heat was 92."[20] On the morning of August 31 near present-day Coweta, Bell awoke to a disconcerting discovery: three of the soldiers and three of the horses were missing. Also gone were saddlebags containing clothing, Indian presents, and—alas for history—the journals and notes of Dr. Say and Lieutenant Swift. These contained observations on the manners and habits of the Indians and their history, notes on the animal life witnessed on the journey, vocabularies of

Indian languages, and a topographical journal of the expedition. The notebooks would never be recovered.[21]

The presence of well-beaten trails now indicated to the men that they were nearing an inhabited area, though they erroneously thought they were approaching Fort Smith. Then on September 1 a war whoop sounded behind them. They wheeled about to see a mounted Indian on a hill. When a man was sent forward with a flag to parley, he discovered that the Indian was the son of Osage chief Clermont. The travelers were brought fresh meat by the Osages, as had been done for Wilkinson in 1806, and then were escorted to the Osage hunting camp, where they met Clermont himself. Clermont, they were told, had four wives and thirty-seven children.[22]

The chief informed them that three men were presently at the village a few miles up the Verdigris. Lieutenant Swift and the guide Julien hurried to the village in the hope of catching the deserters, only to find them already gone. After a brief visit with the Osages, who were armed with guns and were excellent hunters, the exploring party moved on to Glenn's trading house. There they enjoyed the pleasures of civilization before going downriver to Fort Smith, arriving there on September 13; as one report put it, their appearance was "a source of amazement to men and dog alike."[23]

Having not explored the Red River as assigned, Long considered his expedition to be a failure, and some historians have agreed.[24] However, Long and his men added considerably to the knowledge of the region, particularly the area that is now Oklahoma.

➤ 8

The James-McKnight
Expedition of 1821

Thomas James was no novice to the dangers of the frontier, having migrated with his family from Maryland to Kentucky, then to Illinois, and finally to Missouri in 1807.[1] A somewhat ill-natured Welshman, James was a muscular six-footer, a "coon hunter" type of man. In the spring of 1809 at the age of twenty-seven, he enlisted with a band of Missouri Fur Company traders under Manuel Lisa and Pierre Chouteau to return the Mandan chief Shehaka to his village on the upper Missouri River. Shehaka had gone to Washington, D.C., with Lewis and Clark on their return from the Pacific coast. An attempt to take Shehaka home in 1807 had been stymied by an Arikara attack that left several dead. The Lisa-Chouteau party consisted of 350 men in thirteen barges and boats, James among them. This time the effort was successful.

This western adventure among the traders and Indians of the northwest had given James a thorough seasoning in frontier life before he returned to St. Louis in August 1810. James operated a keelboat on the Ohio

Thomas James. (Frank Everett Stevens, *The Black Hawk War*)

and Mississippi rivers between Pittsburgh and St. Louis, freighting goods for profit until 1815. Then he purchased the mercantile store of John McKnight and his partner in Harrisonville, Illinois. But hard times set in during 1818, and by 1820 James was facing bankruptcy and financial ruin.[2]

At this time he was approached by McKnight, whose brother Robert had not returned from Mexico after having gone there with a trading caravan in 1810. McKnight wished to find his brother and suggested that James could exchange his trade goods in Santa Fe for a high profit. James agreed, despite the risk of being taken prisoner by Mexican authorities. Loading his keelboat with $10,000 in biscuits, whiskey, flour, lead, and powder, he left St. Louis in May 1821 and descended the Mississippi to Arkansas Post. From there he turned up the Arkansas River to Little Rock, where he procured a license to trade with Indians on the Arkansas and its tributaries.[3]

At Fort Smith James was told erroneously that the Arkansas was navigable to within sixty miles of Taos, New Mexico. Proceeding upriver, he reached Three Forks. From there he pushed on as far as thirty miles below the mouth of the Cimarron, passing the site of present-day Tulsa, Oklahoma. When his boat became grounded by low water, James returned downriver to a well-worn Indian trail. He sent four of his men up the trail along the Verdigris to Clermont's Osage village. Several days later the men returned with forty Osages and Captain Nathaniel Pryor, a former member of the Lewis and Clark Expedition who was now married to an Osage woman and living among the tribe.

On invitation, James and McKnight took some trade goods to the Osage town. There they met Indian trader Hugh Glenn, whom James had known at Cincinnati, and Captain Henry Barbour, proprietor of a trading post near Three Forks.[4] James realized that he had to leave the river. He purchased twenty-three horses from the Osages. Abandoning the keelboat and caching the heaviest and least portable of his goods, he, McKnight, and nine other men set off to the west. Pryor and a few Osage warriors gave them escort for a short distance, instructing them regarding the salt prairie and the "Shining Mountains" of which Sibley had written— undoubtedly the Glass Mountains of Major County, Oklahoma.[5]

James and his men managed with some difficulty to climb to the top of the tall plateaus, which were covered with grass and a "shining, semi-transparent rock"—mica—that could be cut with a knife. He had no explanation for the buffalo manure he found atop the high surfaces. James wrote of traveling through hills of sand in which his horses sank to their breasts at times—possibly the sand hills of Little Sahara near

Waynoka. The party also may have found the salt mountain sought by Sibley: James described it as "a high hill evidently based upon salt" standing near the Cimarron.[6] The traders broke off large hunks of the salt with their tomahawks.

In southeast Harper County the voyagers met their first band of Plains Indians. It was not a pleasant meeting. Following a night of alarmed barking by the dogs that kept the men awake, they were greeted the next morning by the sight of nearly one hundred Indians attempting to capture the traders' horses a short distance from camp. James displayed the U.S. flag, and the action drew the Indians, a Comanche war party, away from the horses.

On the advice of his interpreter, James met with the Comanches and distributed presents. There were two chiefs in the party: one who was friendly and one who was not. The latter, a man with one eye missing as a result of some warrior encounter of the past, was especially incensed because the traders were riding Osage horses. Fortunately, the friendly chief took their side. He warned James against traveling northward to the Arkansas, saying that One-eye was planning to ambush and kill him and his men. The friendly chief also provided a Mexican guide who led them south to the North Canadian River, which they struck just above the juncture of Beaver Creek and Wolf Creek.

Scarcity of water had become a serious problem. The country was dry, and the ponds were so contaminated with buffalo excrement that the entire party became ill. The horses, too, were beginning to suffer badly. After traveling along Beaver Creek for seven or eight days, the Americans reached a swampy area of the Oklahoma Panhandle that was dried, cracked mud. But by good fortune, they discovered a large, spring-fed pond of fresh water. After refreshing themselves and their animals at this oasis, the traders followed the spring's flow southwest along Palo Duro Creek. Its course led them to the Canadian River in the vicinity of Borger, Texas.[7]

James and his men continued west along the Canadian River for several days before encountering a second group of Comanches. This meeting near the Texas–New Mexico border proved to be even more unpleasant and dangerous than the first. The travelers had gone into camp for the day when a large body of mounted Indians appeared over a rise. At their lead was the friendly chief the traders had met on the Cimarron. His congeniality, however, did not prevent a warrior from grabbing a brass kettle from the camp and riding off with it. Alarmed at this brazen act, James requested protection for his property. The chief said that he could not promise such, but he did leave a guard for the night.

On the following day the white men moved two miles to the Indian camp, which numbered nearly one thousand lodges. Here James was met by a leading chief whose countenance bore little encouragement. "He was a little, vicious-looking old man and eyed us most maliciously," James wrote.[8]

The traders made camp and stacked their goods, covering them with hides. James was immediately surrounded by a swarm of chiefs and warriors who demanded presents. James painfully laid out tobacco, powder, lead, vermilion, calico, and other items amounting close to $1,000 in value. These were soon gone, and the Indians began to break open the bales of cloth and woolens that James had intended for the New Mexico trade. He was trying unsuccessfully to halt this giveaway when another Comanche chief named Big Star appeared on the scene and ordered the others away.

When James and his men attempted to continue on their journey, however, they were stopped from doing so, even though he issued more presents. On the third day of their stay, word came that One-eye and his band had arrived. All of them were painted black for war and were heavily armed. One-eye was reportedly very angry that the party had not shown up for his ambush. Big Star led James to the principal chief's lodge, warning that he would be killed if he did not stay there. Big Star then sent a messenger to One-eye asking what it would take to save the white men.

The one-eyed chief answered with a demand for a large amount of goods—"for each of his men as much cloth as his outstretched arms would measure"⁹—plus a sword of James's that he had seen on the Cimarron. James had already given the sword to Big Star. The chief generously returned it, saying it was the only thing that could save the lives of the traders. James sent the sword to One-eye along with 500 yards of cloth.

Although this offering mollified One-eye, the white men were still not permitted to leave. When six of their horses disappeared, James was warned not to send his men out to look for them. At sunrise fifty chiefs and tribal elders met in a council circle on a rise above the Comanche camp, smoking and delivering harangues. Meanwhile, the Indian families had begun decamping as warriors on horseback and on foot assembled nearby. An ominous feeling of danger prevailed among the white men, particularly when Big Star came to shake their hands and say good-bye. He told them there was nothing more he could do for them now.

The circle of warriors began closing around the embattled eleven, who put on as brave a front as possible. With their trade goods and saddles behind them, the white men stood with their rifles primed and ready across their chests.

Old trapper Jemmy Wilson had no gun; he desperately grasped an ax. Thus the men stood in confrontation for nearly half an hour as the pressing warriors awaited their signal to attack. The dreaded one-eyed chief, his body charcoaled a gruesome black, was at the front of the group. Another chief rode forth to jab his lance threateningly at the white men. He wore the whole of a white bear skin, with its snarling teeth above his own ferocious brow and the bear's foreclaws dangling over his hands. Death seemed so imminent that some of the men begged to break the dreadful suspense and commence the fight.[10] Finally, one of the traders, a man named Kirker, could stand it no longer. He walked into the crowd with his gun over his head to surrender. The others stood fast, ready to fight to the end.

It was then that the cry of "Tabbaho! Tabbaho!" sounded.[11] The attention of the crowd was drawn to the southwest, from which direction six horsemen were approaching at a full gallop. The riders were led by an officer of the New Mexican military. The man quickly interceded on behalf of the traders. When the officer asked the Comanches why they wished to kill the men, they replied that it was because the Spanish government at Santa Fe had requested that they not let Americans pass. The officer then told them that the Mexican Revolution had taken place and that Spain no longer ruled here.

The Mexican military unit of fifty men was encamped twenty miles away. They, along with three hundred Comanche warriors, had just returned from a campaign against the Navajos and were then on a buffalo hunt. While some of the Indians were looking for stray horses, they had met other Comanches who told them of the plan to kill the James party and divide its goods. The news was carried back to the Mexican camp, causing some of the younger warriors to head out for their share of the loot.

But the saving factor for James and his men had been the presence in the Mexican camp of a Comanche chief named Cordaro. This chief had once been to Natchitoches, where he had been treated well by the whites.[12] In turn he had promised his friendship and protection to Americans passing through his country. He immediately reported the intended massacre to the Mexican officer, who then rode to the rescue.

Cordaro, a tall, erect man of seventy years, wore with great dignity the full regimentals of a U.S. Army colonel. His uniform was complete with blue coat, red sash, white pantaloons, epaulets, and sword. His bright, piercing eyes were undimmed by age, and he possessed a "high, noble forehead and Roman nose."[13] The chief carried a note from the U.S. Indian agent at Natchitoches recommending him as a true friend of the United States. Even when the Mexican officer assured the Americans that they would not be imprisoned at Santa Fe under the new regime, Cordaro was suspicious and insisted that he would check to be certain his new friends were unmolested. James now learned that some of the Comanches had thought him to be a Frenchman named Vaugean, the leader of a hunting party of thirty French and Quapaw Indians that had attacked and defeated a group of Comanches on the Canadian River the preceding spring.

At Santa Fe James and his men were well treated. The trader was permitted to sell his goods, while McKnight traveled to Durango, Mexico, to rescue his brother from prison. On February 5, 1822, a celebration of Mexican independence was held at Santa Fe. On that occasion James met Don Facundo Malgares, who since 1818 had been the governor of New Mexico. In April McKnight returned with his brother Robert, who was so bitter against the U.S. government for not trying to help him during his ten years of imprisonment that he later renounced his citizenship and returned to Mexico.

During McKnight's absence, James had learned that Hugh Glenn of Three Forks was in New Mexico. The men later met in Santa Fe. When time came to depart for the United States in early June, James and Glenn consolidated their parties for the risky journey back across the Plains.[14] In an account of the trip, James indicates that he held a strong dislike for Glenn, whom he accused of cheating him financially and showing cowardice on the trail. But then James spoke harshly of many of the well-known men of his day on the frontier. James was not finished in his dealing with the Comanches or travels in Oklahoma. He would return in 1823 as the first Indian trader in western Oklahoma and the first to leave a written account of the region and its inhabitants.

Three Forks served as a jumping-off point for the Hugh Glenn expedition of 1821. Led by Glenn, with Jacob Fowler second in command, this group traveled up the Arkansas River to Colorado and thence to New Mexico.[15] Glenn, a Virginian who had served in the War of 1812, had settled at Cincinnati until 1817, when he contracted to supply several U.S. forts, including Belle Point (Fort Smith). He opened his trading establishment at Three Forks that year. Three Forks trader Nathaniel Pryor was also a member of the Glenn expedition.[16]

Jacob Fowler, a Kentuckian who had formerly been a surveyor, owner of a large estate, and later a government contractor partner with Glenn from 1814 to 1817, proved to be the most significant member of the party in a historical sense because he kept a diary of the expedition. His record of the journey begins with his departure from Fort Smith on September 16, 1821. During the trip upriver, Fowler stopped overnight at Bean and Saunders' salt works near the Illinois River—"one Small Well with a few kittles . . . Been [sic] and Saunders Has permission of the government to Worke the Salt Spring—they Sell the Salt at one dollar per Bushil."[17] From there it was on to Glenn's trading post, where during the next two weeks arrangements were made for the fur-trapping, Indian-trading expedition to the Rocky Mountains and New Mexico.

Five of Fowler's hunters now deserted him and returned to Arkansas, but eventually a party of twenty men was recruited. These included Glenn, Pryor, Fowler, Fowler's brother Robert, two French trappers called Baptiste Roy and Baptiste Peno, fourteen other white trappers and hunters, and Fowler's servant, Paul. As they departed the trading house on the afternoon of September 25, each of the buckskin-and-moccasin-clad men was well mounted and carried an assortment of rifles, pistols, knives, and hatchets. Seventeen of their horses and mules were loaded with traps and goods for the Indian trade. Several hunting hounds trailed alongside.[18]

Taking the road leading up the Verdigris to the Osage village of the Oaks, the men encountered a hard rain the first night, causing them to pitch their tents and cover their goods with skins to keep them dry. The rain continued for the next two days, holding the men in camp for a time; but the weather cleared on September 29, and the party reached the Osage village. Clermont's town, however, was completely deserted, the entire population having departed on its fall buffalo hunt. After moving north up the Little Verdigris on an old Indian trail, the trappers turned west to strike the Arkansas River near the Oklahoma-Kansas border. Here they found an encampment of Osages from whom they procured supplies of meat, corn, beans, and dried pumpkins. Glenn hired one of the Osages to serve as a guide as the party moved on up the Arkansas to Colorado.

The party spent the winter near the site where Bent's Fort would later be constructed. There they trapped, hunted, fought bears, and dealt with the Indian tribes that frequented the region. In May 1822 the party made its way to Taos, New Mexico. On June 1 the group was joined by the James-McKnight party from Santa Fe and began their return. The route that the Wilkinson-Bell party and they had followed along the Arkansas River from Fort Gibson to Colorado would not become an established road; but it would later serve as a historical connection between the Three Forks region and the Rocky Mountains.

The James-McKnight Expedition of 1823

Thomas James had been home for only a few weeks before he was busy planning a new trip into Comanche country. He remembered Chief Cordaro pleading for a trader among his people, promising James protection if he returned. The chief had also made an eloquent appeal for the Americans to stop trading guns and ammunition to the Osages. He had asked James to write a letter to the military commander at Natchitoches telling how the chief had befriended the Americans. James did so. Cordaro revisited Natchitoches; but, as James would learn later, the chief became ill and died soon after returning home.

James's trip to Santa Fe had been a financial disaster, losing him much of his $12,000 investment in the venture. His many creditors in Illinois were besetting him from every side as he struggled to extricate himself from debt. Despite the dangers involved, James looked to the profits that could be made from Comanche buffalo robes and horses. Teaming up again with his friend John McKnight and McKnight's brother Robert,

James managed to obtain some $5,500 worth of trade goods on credit, a keelboat, and some horses. Recruiting a party of twenty men, he set out in the late fall of 1822 for the mouth of the Canadian River.[1]

The McKnights and eight men left first in the keelboat. James followed behind with twelve men and five packhorses loaded with the trade goods, walking the entire distance from St. Louis to the point of rendezvous on the Arkansas River. In late February 1823 James located the McKnights on the river four miles above the mouth of the Canadian. He found the keelboat locked in ice.

James had not forgotten the keelboat he had left at Three Forks in 1821 or the goods he had cached there. Going upstream thirty miles to Barbour's trading post, he found that the trader was even then heading out for New Orleans in the 1821 keelboat with James's goods. The two men worked out an agreement whereby Barbour would reimburse James when he returned. Barbour died on the trip, however.

Robert McKnight and most of the men took the remaining keelboat, now freed from the ice, to the mouth of the Canadian. James joined them there, as did John McKnight, who had brought the riding horses overland. James and his party passed through, he wrote later, "the best farming country I had ever seen; a beautiful land of prairies and woods in fine proportion."[2] They enjoyed some very good hunting and brought in plenty of fresh meat from the elk, buffalo, deer, wild turkey, and black bear along the river. After five days they reached the North Fork of the Canadian and turned up that winding stream until the keelboat was halted by rapids.

Making the boat fast to trees with stout ropes, they cached their heaviest hardware in a well-concealed hole in the earth. Then, hewing out three pirogues, they continued their ascent of the North Canadian. Game remained plentiful. Black bears were found still hibernating in hollow trees, and twenty or more were killed. While hunting, James and McKnight came onto an elk herd and downed one of the animals. When they returned to camp, they found the others feasting on the meat of a wild horse they had bagged.

During this time the party had been moving through the belt of blackjack forest and underbrush of the Cross Timbers. Quite suddenly the character of the land changed, and the trading party emerged onto the barren plains west of present-day Oklahoma City. James described the scene before them as "one vast plain extending on all sides to the horizon."[3] Almost immediately they began to encounter signs of Indian encampments. One deserted camp, they decided, was that of a large Comanche war party; another of an Osage band returning north after a successful horse-stealing raid.

Now traveling through a country almost destitute of vegetation, the men in the pirogues plied the meandering channel of the stream, while the others followed along the bank with the pack animals. Finally the river channel became too shallow for the boats. James called a halt and put his men to the task of building a fort. The location of this early trading post is uncertain, but it is believed to have been between present-day Geary and Greenfield in Blaine County.[4]

James now proposed that he and two other men go out, locate the Comanches, and bring them in to trade. John McKnight, however, insisted that it would be better for him to go. He was not a family man, and James was needed to superintend the building of the fort. On parting the men agreed that in the event the river should rise and permit the pirogues to go farther upstream into the Comanches' range, the party would abandon this location and advance to another site 100 miles upriver. In such a case, a letter would be secreted in a particular part of the fort to inform McKnight of the move.

Thomas James constructed two trading stockades, probably smaller than this, on the North Canadian River. (Charles Merritt Barnes, *Combats and Conquests of Mortal Heroes*)

McKnight took three men and headed off south in search of the Comanches. Only a few days later a heavy rain brought about the rise in the river that James had hoped for. With the fort only half finished, he gave the order to move on. Loading goods into the pirogues and onto the packhorses, the traders worked their way up the North Fork, as agreed, for another 100 miles. Once again low water halted their progress.

Selecting a site in an area of timber, James put his men to work building a new fort. The location was likely at the juncture of Wolf and Beaver Creeks, the site of present-day Fort Supply, close to where he had enjoined the stream on his march two years earlier. The fort consisted of a "trading house, surrounded by stockades and defended by our swivel, which we mounted on wheels in an angle of the Fort."[5]

Before the post was completed, two of the men who had gone with McKnight arrived at the new location. They had an unfortunate story to relate. Nine days after departing the first fort, McKnight and his companions—Potter, Ivy, and Clark—had met with some Comanches and been escorted to their village. When McKnight tried to talk with the chiefs, he found that Potter was an inadequate interpreter. McKnight was able to explain to the chiefs that he had a good Spanish interpreter, his brother Robert, back in camp. He requested permission to go back for him. The Comanches agreed, but they held the other three men as hostages.[6]

After McKnight had departed, Clark talked sign language with the Indians and, evidently to ensure his own safety, told them that the Americans had many guns and a cannon. This news greatly alarmed the Comanches. On that same day, a party of warriors returned to the camp to say that two of their band had been killed by Osages. That night the village decamped and moved fifteen miles farther south. During the night, the Americans heard much wailing from two of the lodges.

The men were held as prisoners for seven days before Potter and Ivy were permitted to follow McKnight back to the main camp. They were surprised to learn now that McKnight had not been seen. James sent a man back downstream to the old fort, and he returned to report that the letter was still in its hiding place. All agreed that McKnight had likely been killed. There was speculation that perhaps the Comanches had attacked him and that he had killed two of them in the fight.

Accompanied by Potter and Ivy, Robert McKnight returned to the Comanche camp. He stormed furiously at the Indians for killing his brother, but they admitted nothing. Eventually McKnight persuaded them to lead a party of Comanches and Wichitas (whom James knew as Pawnee Picts) back to talk with James, the other three traders being held as hostages. The Indians were led by a Wichita chief. He told James that the Indians were still suspicious that James was aligned with the Osages and would not come to his fort for fear of being attacked.[7]

In response James loaded four pack animals with trade goods and by himself accompanied the Indians back to their village. He was met in friendly fashion by the head chief, who permitted the goods to be deposited in his lodge. The hostages were in good condition, but they gave James some bad news. His old enemy, One-eye, was in camp. Nonetheless, on the following morning James made the customary and expected presents: knives, tobacco, cloth, and so forth. Then the trading began. For each horse, the Indians demanded twelve items. James later commented: "I made four yards of British shrouding at $5.50 per yards and two yards of calico at 62½ cents to count three, and a knife, flint, tobacco, looking glass, and other small articles to make up the complement."[8]

When James had purchased seventeen fine horses "worth at least $100 each in St. Louis," he refused to take the other inferior ones. The Comanche chief was very angry and ordered the Indians to stop trading. Later the chief relented and returned with buffalo and beaver pelts, which James accepted. Now the women brought skins forth to trade; and after a good number of pelts had been traded, the chief again ran the others away. No Indians appeared for the remainder of the day.

That evening the chief came to the lodge where James was staying, bringing five other headmen with him. When they passed the calumet, they did not offer it to James, who realized that he was being chastised. However, he overcame the antagonism of the chiefs by presenting them with tobacco and wampum. He told them that this treatment was much better than they could get from the Spanish and that if they drove him out of the country, no more Americans would come to trade. The bribery and threats worked. The chief went outside the lodge and called out in a loud voice that in the morning the Indians would go to the North Canadian to trade with their white friends, the Tabbyboos.[9]

But all was not yet won. Potter came to James with a gun barrel that One-eye had thrown at his feet with orders to take it to James. It was a warning, and before the matter was done, the trader had given up a silver breastplate, four silver arm bands, two plugs of tobacco, a knife, and wampum in order to pacify the chief. The presents were well spent, however. Later One-eye invited James to his tent to accept him as a brother and make him a gift of his own personal war horse. Moreover, One-eye became a valuable ally in the days ahead.

The Comanche village, and with it some Wichitas, began the march to James's fort. On the way James had a chance to see the efficiency and speed with which the Indians chased, roped, and tamed wild horses. "In twenty-four hours after their capture these horses became tamed and ready for use, and kept near their owners as their only friends."[10]

The Comanches also spent much time becoming good horsemen and fighters. They practiced their skills in mock battles, marching and countermarching, making repeated charges in unison, and performing feats of horsemanship. James was particularly entertained by the Comanche game of placing a plug of tobacco on the ground and then picking it up while riding at a full gallop. If the first of a dozen or so horsemen missed the plug, usually it was retrieved by the second or third man. The winner would go to the back of the line, and the game would continue.[11]

The Comanche camp spread itself for a mile and a half in front of James's fort, and trading operations got under way. Horses, mules, beaver pelts, and buffalo robes were the principal trade items of the tribe. The robes, worth more than $5 in the United States, could be procured for the price of a few strings of beads or a plug of tobacco. One-eye now gave his fierce protection to James, refusing to permit any member of his tribe to bring back an item once a trade had been made.

On one occasion a war party brought in seven American horses, which were shod and branded; a tent; a kettle; an ax; and other articles. James angrily accused the war party of robbing his countrymen. But the Comanches claimed that they had taken the goods from an Osage party that had attacked a Santa Fe–bound trading company. James later found that this was true.

There were many young Mexican captives among the Comanches and Wichitas. James took on one particularly intelligent boy as his interpreter. The boy asked that James purchase him from his master, but an offer of ten horses was rejected. James offered the youngster presents, but the boy told him that it was no use. His master took the presents for himself.

The trading was about to end when a scouting party arrived in camp to report that the Osages were nearby on the Cimarron River. The Comanche chiefs held an excited council and decided to go out and give battle to their old enemies. On the following day the village decamped. The women, children, and old ones were sent upriver, while the warrior force prepared to ride to the northeast. Before departing, some of the chiefs came to James to stress the value of his trade with them. They were particularly concerned that the Americans were trading guns and ammunition to the Osages, who in turn stole the horses of the Comanches and killed their people. The chiefs said that they would like to go to Washington and talk with the Great Father about the matter. However, they did not believe the United States could protect them from the Osages, Cherokees, Choctaws, and other enemies.

Wichita chief Alasares came to see James, saying that his people lived on the headwaters of the Red River near the "three big mounds," which most likely were the Wichita Mountains. He claimed that his tribe owned sixteen thousand horses of better quality than James had procured from the Comanches. As proof of this and to show his friendship for the white people, whose trade he wanted badly, he presented James with his own favorite black war horse. Named Checoba, it was, James insisted, "the best limbed, the best proportioned, the swiftest and the most beautiful I ever saw."[12]

The time had now come for James and his men to depart. The pelts were bundled and packed into the pirogues and onto the pack animals. The pirogues were sent on ahead downriver with instructions to wait for those traveling by land at the unfinished fort. James went with the overland group, which herded the 325 horses and mules taken in the trade. On the second day out, a small herd of buffalo caused over one hundred of the remuda to stampede. James's stock soon became mingled with a wild horse herd, making their recapture extremely difficult.

When James sent a rider out on the speedy Checoba, the war horse suffered a crippling rattlesnake bite that impaired him for life. Later the overland party met a group of Caddo and Wichita warriors who were returning from the north. They had just fought a battle with the Osages, and seven of them were wounded. James dressed their wounds with salve and sticking plaster.[13]

The pirogue contingent was waiting at the abandoned fort, and together the two units moved on down the North Canadian. Passing through the Cross Timbers to the long-grassed prairies to its east, the trading party encountered horseflies so numerous and ravenous that many of the animals wasted away and died. By the time the men reached the mouth of the main Canadian, only seventy-one of the herd remained. Some of these, too, later died from a disease known as the Farcy, which caused a swelling of the horses' breasts and bellies.

Anxious to see his family in Illinois, James hurried on, leaving his goods to be sold for him by two of his men. The pair took the goods to Arkansas Post, their passing downriver being noted by an Arkansas newspaper. The paper reported the arrival of two pirogues laden with buffalo hides and peltries during July.[14] However, according to James, the two absconded with the entire sum realized from the sale of the hides.

James claims to have been the first American trader to venture among the Comanches; so far as we know, he was. But his efforts were financial failures, and he would never return. However, Robert McKnight did go back that same fall. He stopped at Union Mission on Grand River while on his way back to Comanche country to continue the trade. Union Mission records tell of his visit in November 1823 and his recounting of the adventures of the previous expedition. However, no account of his experiences on this sojourn among the Comanches has come to light.[15]

➤ 10

Famous Men at Three Forks

The 1820s in Indian Territory were particularly violent. No new exploring expeditions ventured into the region for the next ten years. Nevertheless, the U.S. presence was made more permanent with the creation of two new forts. In addition to their military value, these posts would become centers of discovery by virtue of both the frontier life that came to them and dragoon detachments that ventured out to explore the surrounding country.

The constant friction between warring tribes; the intrusion of white hunters, travelers, and immigrant tribes; and the competition for territory, horses, and game all contributed to turmoil and conflict. The Osage-Cherokee feud had subsided somewhat from the level of out-and-out tribal war after the Fort Smith treaty, but trouble had not ended by any means. Neither tribe had given up its inclination to do battle, and bloody altercations between the two tribes continued.

Additionally, a serious state of murder, robbery, and violence existed to the south along the Red River. There a band of renegade whites operated distilleries, sold whiskey freely to the Indians, and dealt in a traffic of Indian slaves and stolen horses. The government, realizing it must do something to stop the mayhem, moved to establish closer military oversight in the territory

To obtain better surveillance and control of the Osages and Cherokees, the army issued orders for General Matthew Arbuckle to abandon Fort Smith and take his five companies of Seventh Infantry upriver to Three Forks. By April all of Fort Smith's accoutrements had been loaded aboard keelboats and wagons for transfer to a new site three miles above the Arkansas on the east bank of the Grand River. The military pitched tents there on April 20, 1824, and went to work felling trees and erecting log huts. Arbuckle named the new post Cantonment Gibson in honor of army commissary general George Gibson.[1]

To combat the lawless situation along the Red River and prepare for the arrival of the Choctaws and Chickasaws from Mississippi and Alabama, the army also ordered troops to that area. In May 1824, a month after Gibson was founded, the troops constructed log barracks and surrounded them with a palisade near the mouth of the Kiamichi River. Two companies of Seventh Infantry garrisoned the Red River post that bore the name of Cantonment Towson after the paymaster of the army, Nathan Towson.[2]

Even as the United States established its military presence in the territory, small parties of trappers and traders were making their way into the prairie domain of the Comanches and Pawnee Picts. Robert McKnight returned in 1824; and in May 1825 forty men from Tennessee passed by Fort Smith on horseback, each leading a pack animal, and headed west from there.

During 1826 a trading party under Pierre Menard,[3] a wealthy trader from Kaskaskia, Illinois, headed off into Comanche country with five wagons and twenty pack-horses loaded with Indian trade goods.

Missourians George Nidiver and Alex Sinclair made plans to go up the Canadian River to trade. They intended to build a large cedar log raft and float their goods downriver to New Orleans, where they would sell both the goods and the raft. It took them and their hired crew a year to build the raft. As they came up the Arkansas, the Cherokees tried to seize the vessel. The men succeeded in escaping during the night and set float down the river. However, at the juncture of the Canadian and the Arkansas, the raft hit a sandbar and broke apart. The men were forced to abandon it and give up their trading expedition.[4]

A different kind of exploring party rode out of Cantonment Gibson in September 1826. Led by Nathaniel Pryor, now the Osage subagent, the group consisted of twenty well-armed men. They trailed seven pack mules heavily loaded with food and supplies as well as picks and shovels for gold mining. Among the twenty were a few soldiers from the fort, including Assistant Surgeon John W. Baylor, and civilians from the Gibson and Arkansas areas. One of them was young Cherokee half-blood Jesse Chisholm, who was soon to become a highly regarded frontiersman of Indian Territory and Texas.[5]

The expedition was prompted by rumors that had long abounded of gold on the Arkansas River. The men penetrated as far north as the site of present-day Wichita at the mouth of the Little Arkansas River. But they found no gold. Nevertheless, their venture constituted the first known intrusion into that portion of the river by whites since Lieutenant Wilkinson in 1806.

The U.S. government spent much effort in relocating the southern tribes into Indian Territory. In May 1827 agent David Brearly escorted a party of Creek Indians to Three Forks preparatory to their moving to the area.

The Creeks were taken on a tour up the Arkansas River for sixty miles before cutting southwest to the Canadian and on to Fort Towson. They returned home to give a favorable report on the land, and in February 1828 Brearly brought a party of 280 Creek men, women, and children west. The Indians were resettled around their new agency, which had been set up in a former Chouteau trading post three miles up the east bank of the Verdigris from the Arkansas.

During October and November 1828, a deputation of Chickasaw, Choctaw, and Creek Indians was escorted on a tour of lands where the government hoped to relocate them from their southern homes. Leading the expedition was Captain George H. Kennerly. Lieutenant Washington Hood and John W. Bell served as topographers and Dr. Todson as surgeon. Baptist minister Isaac McCoy kept a daily journal for official record. In addition, there were agents for each of the tribes, interpreters, hired crew members, and servants—in all, forty-two men and sixty mounts and packhorses.[6]

From St. Louis the party moved west across the Kansas border following the Neosho River south past Chouteau's post and Union Mission to the Creek agency near Fort Gibson. From there, the men toured the country around the mouths of the Canadian, North Canadian, and Deep Fork rivers. They returned to Missouri on the same route by which they had come.

The next major group of immigrant Indians to move to Indian Territory were the Western Cherokees, who had settled in Arkansas as early as 1810. In the spring of 1828 the government had induced a delegation visiting Washington, D.C., into signing a treaty exchanging their Arkansas lands for what was known as Lovely's Purchase (now northeastern Oklahoma). During 1829 the Cherokees began moving up the Arkansas River beyond Fort Smith and selecting new homesites.

In 1830 a small advance faction of the Choctaws accepted removal and relocation along the Arkansas near the then-abandoned Fort Smith and on the Red River. Eventually the Jackson administration manipulated chiefs of the Choctaw and Chickasaw tribes into signing away the entirety of their native homelands in the South. In exchange the two tribes accepted a broad strip of land across the southern portion of Indian Territory.

In the spring of 1830 an Arkansas trapping and hunting expedition under Colonel Robert Bean crossed what is now Oklahoma on its way to the Rocky Mountains. Dr. James S. Craig, a member of the party, wrote: "In our route, particularly on the waters of the Red river, and the north fork of the Canadian, we passed through much fine country, and fared sumptuously on buffalo, deer, honey, &c. From which we observed a north course until we struck the Arkansas river, immediately at the mouth of the Little Arkansas."[7]

This same year Congress passed the Indian removal bill, designed to transplant all of the eastern tribes to west of the Mississippi. The U.S. War Department now set out to learn all that it could about Indian Territory—which sections were the best for farms, the water and timber resources, and other pertinent information. Officers and Indian agents interviewed traders and trappers, and military detachments were sent out from the military posts to learn more.

One of these military reconnaissances was conducted by Captain Louis Eulalie de Bonneville from Fort Smith, Arkansas, in September. He was instructed to

———————————————————————→

Explorations of the 1830s *(opposite page)*

1. Bonneville—1830
2. Dawson—1831
3. Albert Pike—1831–32
4. Irving/Ellsworth—1832
5. Many—1833
6. Leavenworth/Dodge—1834
7. Dawson—1834
8. Fort Mason Council—1835
9. Chouteaus—1836–1837
10. Northrop—1838
11. Gregg—1839
12. Hitchcock—1839

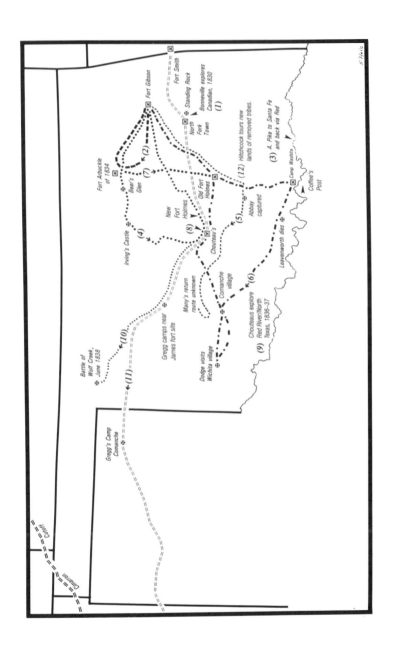

S-746

Fort Gibson

Fort Smith

Standing Rock

Bonneville explores
Canadian, 1830
(1)

North
Fork
Town

Hitchcock tours new
lands of removed tribes.
(12)

A. Pike to Santa Fe
and back via Red
(3)

Camp Washita

Coffee's
Post

(2)

Fort Arbuckle
of 1834

Bear's
Glen

(7)

Old Fort
Holmes

New
Fort
Holmes

Abbay
captured
(5)

Leavenworth dies

Irving's Castle

(4)

(8)

Chouteau's

Comanche
village

(6)

Many's return
route unknown

Chouteaus explore
Red River/North
Texas, 1836-37
(9)

Dodge visits
Wichita village

Battle of
Wolf Creek,
June 1838

Gregg camps near
James fort site

(10)

(11)

Gregg's Camp
Comanche

Cutoff

Cimarron

examine the country adjacent to the Canadian River westward to the Cross Timbers. Bonneville did so, making his report from Cantonment Gibson on November 2, 1830.[8]

Bonneville's detachment surveyed the Canadian as far west as Little River and up the North Fork of the Canadian some twenty-five miles. In passing down the main Canadian, the men witnessed the unique rock seen by the Long party in 1820. Bonneville estimated it to be sixty-five feet high and twenty feet in diameter. "It is a great curiosity and an excellent Land Mark," he observed.[9] He dubbed it Mary's Rock.

Bonneville was not impressed with the country. He saw no place that he thought was suitable for a settlement, no minerals, timber, or arable land. He even reported that he saw but little game — only some fifteen deer, twenty buffalo, two bears, and a herd of elk.

In December 1830 a visiting delegation of Choctaws and Chickasaws was escorted on an inspection tour of southeastern Indian Territory by Lieutenant James L. Dawson. When Dawson marched from Fort Gibson, the Indian delegation was already nearly one hundred miles up the river. He overtook the Indians at Little River. The weather was extremely cold, and it was necessary to cut a path for the horses in crossing the ice-covered Canadian. Led by Dawson's Delaware guide, the combined party now cut southwest across the headwaters of the Boggy and Blue rivers to the Washita. At several points the travelers crossed Roger's Road, a fur-trading trail blazed by men working for trader John Rogers, the founder of the city of Fort Smith, Arkansas.

Dawson found the country of the Boggy, Blue, and Washita rivers "even in winter remarkably picturesque."[10] The region abounded with wild horses, buffalo, antelope, and deer. Occasional parties of Delawares and Cherokees returning from hunting excursions to Washita country were encountered. Two trappers who were met near the mouth of the Blue eventually guided the delegation to Fort Smith.

Dawson conducted a second exploration in October 1831, escorting Reverend Isaac McCoy on an inspection of the country in advance of the planned resettlement of southern tribes. Dawson led McCoy up the Arkansas River to the mouth of the Cimarron, or Red Fork as it was then known. From there the group moved south past the Deep Fork before turning back east toward Gibson. In doing so, the explorers crossed "Osage war Trails, 5 in number abreast of each other, bearing south towards the Canadian."[11]

On October 8, 1832, two outstanding men of American history arrived at Fort Gibson, each on his own and from different directions. Washington Irving, already world famous as an American literary figure, had just returned from Europe, where he had spent the past seventeen years. A chance meeting aboard a Lake Erie steamboat had resulted in an invitation from newly appointed Indian Commissioner Henry L. Ellsworth to accompany him on a trip to see the Indian tribes of the western Plains.

Irving, who would serve as secretary pro tempore on the trip, would have an opportunity to see "the remnants of those great Indian tribes, which are now about to disappear as independent nations."[12] It was an offer of adventure the man of letters could not refuse; and with Ellsworth's small party of five, Irving rode from St. Louis through southeastern Kansas to Fort Gibson by horseback. In his letters to his sister, Irving said he found the trip interesting and invigorating: "I have found sleeping in a tent a very sweet and healthy kind of repose."[13]

The other notable figure to arrive at Fort Gibson on October 8 was Sam Houston, former governor of Tennessee, who came in by steamboat up the Arkansas River. Houston, a resident at Three Forks since 1829, was returning from a visit to Washington, D.C. He, too,

Washington Irving's *Tour of the Praries* first introduced the Indian country to the American reading public. (*Frank Leslie's Illustrated Newspaper*, December 7, 1859)

was filled with plans of a great adventure—that of going south to Texas to lead a rebellion against the Mexican domination of that land and to form a new, independent republic. In doing so, the former governor of Tennessee would forsake his Cherokee wife and his Three Forks trading house known as the Wigwam Neosho.[14]

These two men and Commissioner Ellsworth were received at Fort Gibson by General Arbuckle. The group sat about that evening drinking, smoking, and discussing the events of the day. That night Irving commented in his ever-present notebook on the man

Sam Houston, who once resided in present-day Oklahoma.
(Appleton's Cyclopaedia of American Biography)

who would soon help forge a new destiny for Texas:
"Gov. Houston, tall, large, well formed, fascinating
man—low crowned large brimmed white beaver-boots
with brass eagle spurs—given to grandiloquence. A
large and military mode of expressing himself. Old
General Nix used to say God made him two drinks
scant."[15]

Irving and Ellsworth spent the next day making
arrangements to hurry afield and join a group of
mounted U.S. Rangers under Captain Jesse Bean. The
rangers had departed the fort just three days before on
an exploring jaunt westward into what was then reputed
to be the Pawnee (Pawnee Pict or Wichita) hunting
grounds, now the central area of Oklahoma. On the
morning of October 10, Irving and Ellsworth were
accompanied by Arbuckle and Houston as they forded

the Verdigris River and rode upstream a short distance to Chouteau's trading house, which now served as an agency for the Osages and Creeks.

Irving was a keen observer and a writer with few peers, and his penned sketches of the agency and its potpourri of frontier life challenge the artist's brush:

> A few log houses on the banks of the river . . . men in frocked coats made of green blankets . . . some in sweat-soiled buckskin lounging about on tree stumps or holding rifle matches . . . stately Osages with blankets about their waists and hair shaved to crests with scalp locks dangling behind . . . brightly-garbed Creeks with broad girdles, green or red leggings, beaded moccasins and heads wrapped about with gaudy-print handkerchiefs . . . a muscular Negro shoeing a horse while a curious little cur watched with head cocked and one ear erect . . . a veteran trapper spinning tales of past adventures . . . a pair of half-bloods making iron spoons for melting lead for bullets.[16]

At the agency Irving and Ellsworth rejoined their friends: twenty-one-year-old Count Albert-Alexandre de Pourtalès of Switzerland; his companion and tutor, Charles Joseph Latrobe; and talkative French Creole Antoine Deshetres, or "Tonish," who had been hired as a jack-of-all-things at St. Louis. Having secured horses, trimmed the baggage down to saddlebag and packhorse size, and hired guides—principally the laconic, frontier-wise Frenchman Pierre Beatte[17]—the party set forth in single file up the north bank of the Arkansas River on October 10, passing scattered Creek farmhouses and villages.[18]

On this first day out they crossed an Indian trail that led west, encountering skeletal bowed frames that had once been the lodges of an Osage hunting camp. Later, at an Osage encampment, Ellsworth exercised the duties of his office and made a speech from horseback urging his listeners to make peace with the Wichitas. This peacemaking effort may have had limited value since all of the Osage warriors were gone at the time and Ellsworth's message was heard only by old men, women, and children.

A visit by a small group of Osage warriors to the camp on October 12 gave Irving and the others a chance to see better the human side of the supposedly "stoic" Indians. Irving noted their gossipy laughter, their story-telling mimicry, and their merry fun-making when not inhibited by the presence of white men.[19]

On October 13 at the site of present-day Tulsa, Irving's party overtook the ranger company under Bean. Recruited from the farms and villages of Illinois and Tennessee, the roughly clad, free-spirited group of mostly young adventurers knew only minimum discipline. Bean was himself strongly motivated by his passion for hunting, eventually causing Ellsworth to complain about the captain's propensity to "blunder along" on the march.[20]

Word had been sent ahead by two Creek Indians for the rangers to hold up, and they had spent their time hunting, holding shooting matches, dressing deer skins, gambling at cards, and chopping down trees where bees had stored their troves of honey. Irving's pen skimmed the camp scene: "Jerked venison hanging over coals to dry . . . deer carcasses lying about . . . rifles stacked against trees . . . saddles, bridles and powder horns dangling from the limbs of trees . . . picketed horses scattered through the bushes."[21]

The plan of march was to move up the Arkansas River and then the Cimarron, through the Cross Timbers, and turn south to the Red River. On October 14 the entourage rode the north bank of the Arkansas, bagging deer as well as elk and crowing in pride over each kill as the men feasted around the campfire that night at an idyllic spot dubbed Bear's Glen.[22]

The travelers crossed the Arkansas River a quarter of a mile above the mouth of the Cimarron River on October 15. Here Irving had the unique experience of riding across the river in a buffalo bull-skin boat "atop of about a hundredweight of luggage—an odd way of crossing a river a quarter of a mile wide."[23] The boat was towed by swimmers who whooped and yelled all the way.

While at the mouth of the Cimarron near what is now Coyle, Oklahoma, on October 18 Irving dashed off a letter to his sister:

> We are now on the borders of the Pawnee [Wichita] country, a region untraversed by white men, except by solitary trappers. We are leading a wild life, depending upon game, such as deer, elk, bear, for food, encamping on the borders of brooks, and sleeping in the open air under trees, with outposts stationed to guard us against any surprise by the Indians. . . . Two or three days will bring us into the buffalo range, where we shall have grand sport hunting. We shall also be in the range of wild horses. . . . I was never in finer health, or enjoyed myself more, and the idea of exploring a wild country of this magnificent character is very exciting. . . . We are far beyond any civilized habitation, or even an Indian village.[24]

Downstream he could see the rangers crossing from one bank to the other in a long, oblique line on horseback. Now the expedition took on a more serious tone because of the potential danger of lurking Pawnees who came this way to vie with the Osages for hunting rights in the region. Beatte, who understood the danger better than most, was concerned about the careless manner in which some of the rangers, especially one of the older members, wandered off on hunting sprees. "Dat old man will have his brains knocked out by de

Pawnee yet," he observed. "He tink he know every'ting, but he don't know Pawnees, anyhow."[25]

The distant glow of a prairie fire only increased the foreboding of hostile war parties, as did stories of bloody Indian battles told around the campfires at night. The discovery of an old Delaware camp brought concern about meeting a party of that tribe, whose excursions were daring and far reaching.

On October 17 the ranger party was moving west along the Cimarron River on the bank opposite present Oilton, Oklahoma, where Nuttall and his trapper companion had trekked in 1819. Here Bean and others became engaged in an exciting hunting contest with a band of elk, successfully bagging two of them. Now the expedition began to show its first signs of stress: worn horses, more and more stragglers, and illnesses. A spell of rainy weather that made the traveling more difficult doused everyone's spirit of adventure.[26]

Just north of present-day Perkins, the men reached the forest area of the Cross Timbers, which stretched southward toward the Red River. Latrobe, who published his own account of the journey, described the early-day landmark:

> The dark brown horizon which appeared before us as we emerged from the deep bed of the river, was known to be the Cross Timbers, a broad belt of dwarf oak forest, rarely interrupted by prairie, extending across the country, from the Red Fork to the Great Canadian, in the direction of North and South. Its mean breadth, by the report of the Indians, was twelve or fourteen miles. . . . I will never forget that hilly stony region, with its almost impenetrable forest of the closest and hardest growth, whose low, rugged branches, black and hard as iron cost us many a fierce scramble and struggle on our passage.[27]

At one clearing the party had the novel experience of watching from a hilltop as a wolf pack pursued and killed a buck deer. Renewed excitement swept the party, rangers and tourists alike, at the first sign of buffalo. Few of the men had ever been on a buffalo hunt.

During the day's march on October 20, the party sighted a unique rock formation to the left of the march. Irving described it "as a clump of trees, dimly seen in the distance like a ship at sea; the landscape deriving sublimity from its vastness and simplicity. To the southwest, on the summit of a hill, was a singular crest of broken rocks, resembling a fortress. It reminded me of the ruin of some Moorish castle, crowning a height in the midst of a lonely Spanish landscape."[28] Although Irving dubbed the formation Cliff Castle, Ellsworth gave it the name by which it is known today: Irving's Castle.[29] Camp that evening was made near a cloistered spring in a small rock-layered recess that gave the resting spot the name of Fountain Camp.[30]

October 21 would provide another exhilaration. A wild horse had been spotted, and Beatte quietly slipped from camp with a lariat tied to his saddlebow. Late that evening he returned to camp leading a two-year-old wild colt that he had captured in a breakneck chase. Irving and the others had the opportunity to observe the next day as Beatte, with Indianlike skill, somehow turned the rolling-eyed animal into a calm, obedient member of the remuda.[31]

On the following morning the party forded the Cimarron and found itself enmeshed in the blackjack and post oak of the Cross Timbers. The stout limbs of the thick undergrowth switched and cut the men badly and ripped their clothes. The horses became badly bloodied. The frustrated Irving noted that the ordeal was like struggling through a "forest of cast iron."[32] Meanwhile, Latrobe was impressed with the wild life with which the country abounded: deer, antelope, wild horses, buffalo, wolves, beaver, prairie dogs with their companion burrowing owls and rattlesnakes, white cranes, turkeys, and quail being among those he observed.[33]

As they finally emerged into a clear area south of what is now Guthrie, sighting calls of "Buffalo!" sounded. Captain Bean was not to be denied this sport. With the command in camp near what was likely Cottonwood Creek, the ranger went off on foot to search for buffalo. During his absence, a series of events occurred. First, the campfire caught on the dry grass and started a small prairie fire. No sooner had it been doused than the sudden cry of "Pawnees! Pawnees!" went up. Panic swept the camp as word spread that a war party of over three hundred Indians was just beyond the hill. The alarm, however, was false. Someone had overreacted to an order that Bean had called out for the horses to be driven in. While hunting a short distance from camp, he had seen two men on a distant hill and presumed them to be Indians. It turned out that they were two of the party's straggler hunters.[34]

The rangers' course was now southeasterly down Coffee Creek. They struck the Deep Fork near the present site of Arcadia. It was along this small, wooded creek that a young ranger wounded a buck deer and followed him through some thickets into the bed of a dry rivulet. There he came face to face with a very large black bear, which was dragging the carcass of the deer up the creek bed in contest with several snarling wolves. The ranger fired one shot at the bear without effect but quickly decided it was a contest he did not wish to enter.[35]

On October 25 the exploring expedition crossed the dividing ridge between the Deep Fork and the North Canadian. As the expeditioners crested the ridge and viewed the lush tree line of the river, they spotted a band of wild horses grazing on the level plain fronting the stream. A "surround" of the horses was planned, but in the end it was only after a galloping chase that two of the animals were captured—a black mare heavy with foal and a young, cream-colored colt.[36]

At noon the party crossed the North Canadian and moved on southward to the east of present-day Oklahoma City. Here they met their first Indians—friendly Osages, fortunately—who were returning from a hunt. The Osages were still hopeful of taking a few Pawnee scalps if the chance presented itself. Ellsworth duly lectured them on the merits of peace, and the Indians departed, doubtlessly still unconverted.

Rain overtook the party again as it moved southeast parallel to the main Canadian. The soggy weather held the explorers in camp east of present-day Norman for three days. Here another buffalo chase took place. This time Irving took part, he and Ellsworth making their first kills. During the hunt the young Swiss count became separated from the others. There was much concern when he did not make it back to camp by the morning of October 30, and a search party was sent out. Beatte did the tracking, and the frontiersman displayed all the adeptness and perception of a Leatherstocking tale. Count Pourtalès was finally discovered, having spent the night on his saddle in a tree.[37]

The party had now been in the field for twenty days, and the hard-used horses and men alike were badly worn down. The thrill of outdoor adventure and the excitement of the hunt no longer called in the face of constant travel and privations. The young rangers and tourists yearned for the taste of bread, sugar for their coffee, and salt for their meat, though Beatte declared sarcastically that only "boys" needed bread. There were rumbles of dissension among the rangers, and one corporal was arrested for mutinous talk.

The Red River was still far away, and it seemed unwise to push the worn horses so far. Someone suggested that the decimated ranger force would be a poor match, indeed, for a Pawnee war party. By general agreement, the unit began its return march to Fort

Gibson on October 31. As events would later bear out, this was probably a wise decision.

Following the lead of Beatte, who had hunted this region, the bedraggled expedition headed in a direct northeasterly course toward Three Forks. It was a painful week's journey under difficult circumstances before the worn, weary, and famished detachment reached the Creek settlements along the Arkansas River. There the men enjoyed the generous hospitality of a white settler and his smiling black wife, who produced a steaming pot of turnips and beef "and then such magnificent slices of bread and butter."[38]

Irving described the party's arrival back at Fort Gibson after thirty-one days in the wilderness: "Our horses were tired down by the pasturage being withered, and by their having been coursed after buffaloes and wild horses. Some of them had to be left behind; and those of us who brought back our horses to the fort, had to walk, and lead them for the greater part of the three or four last days."[39]

Irving and his friends spent the night of November 8 at the agency building. They found that they were unable to sleep without the company of the open sky and sparkling stars to which they had grown accustomed. On November 10 the writer took advantage of a steamboat departing from Fort Gibson and ended his foray into Oklahoma, the hunting grounds of the Pawnees, and Three Forks. Later that same month Sam Houston left Three Forks mounted on a bobtailed nag and headed for a new destiny in Texas.[40]

Even as Irving was departing Oklahoma, another well-known historical figure was making his way across the wilds of the Red River country of southern Oklahoma. While Irving was aboard the steamboat headed down the Arkansas, Albert Pike—lawyer, poet, and later-to-be commanding general of Confederate troops in Indian Territory—was resting in the Osage hunting camp of Chief Clermont just north of what is

Albert Pike, who explored the Red River. (*Appleton's Cyclopaedia of American Biography*)

now Davis on the Washita. Pike had journeyed to Santa Fe the year before and now was returning via Fort Towson with a small party.[41]

After spending a few days with Clermont's hunting party, Pike and the others moved on down the Washita through the Arbuckle Mountains, meeting a band of Delawares on November 20. On November 24 Pike's group was at the mouth of the Blue River, passing Caddo Hill, where the Choctaws and Caddos had once fought a fierce battle. On November 29 Pike's party met some Choctaws who were engaged in cutting down a honey tree. After a short stay at Fort Towson, Pike went on to Fort Smith. He would later write an extensive narrative describing his journey across the Staked Plains:

> Imagine yourself, kind reader, standing in a plain to which your eye can see no bounds. Not a tree, not a bush, not a shrub, not a tall weed lifts its head above the barren grandeur of the desert; not a stone is to be seen on its hard beaten surface; no undulation, no

abruptness, no break to relieve the monotony; nothing, save here and there a deep narrow track worn into the hard plain by the constant hoof of the buffalo. Imagine then countless herds of buffalo, showing their un-yielding, dark shapes in every direction, as far as the eye can reach, and approaching at times to within forty steps of you; or a herd of wild horses feeding in the distance or hurrying away from the hateful smell of man, with their manes floating, and a trampling like thunder. Imagine here and there a solitary antelope, or, perhaps, a whole herd, fleeting off in the distance, like the scattering of white clouds.[42]

On the heels of the departing Irving and Houston, the son of another famous American arrived at Fort Gibson. This was Captain Nathan Boone, youngest son of Daniel Boone and commander of a company of Missouri-recruited mounted rangers. Earlier, in 1832, Boone and his men had fought Indians in Wisconsin under Colonel Zachary Taylor. Now Boone's company and that of Captain Lemuel Ford established Camp Arbuckle a mile and a half below Fort Gibson on the opposite side of the Arkansas River. These ranger units, which preceded the formation of the U.S. Dragoon Regiment, were to become the first American troops involved in action against the Comanches and Pawnee Picts.[43]

Attacks against white travelers on the Plains were causing concern. An incident occurred in December 1832 when Comanches and Kiowas assaulted a twelve-man party of American traders who were returning from Santa Fe to Missouri. Led by Judge W. C. Carr of St. Louis, the men were crossing the Texas Panhandle when they were surrounded by Indians near present-day Lathrop, Texas. After a thirty-six-hour siege, during which two of the Americans were killed, the traders made their escape. They left behind all of their goods and a considerable amount of Mexican money. Five survivors later stumbled into Fort Gibson in dire condition after a grueling journey across most of present-day Oklahoma.[44]

The Mexican money taken from Judge Carr's party turned up again in April 1833 following an Osage massacre of a Kiowa village near the Arbuckle Mountains. Having failed to reach treaty terms with the government at a Fort Gibson peace council, the Osages had departed three hundred strong for a summer hunt at the Salt Plains. En route they encountered a Kiowa trail leading eastward.

The Osages began back-trailing the Kiowas and were eventually led to what they knew as Rainy Mountain Creek near the Wichita Mountains, finding a Kiowa village completely unprotected, with its warrior force gone. Falling upon the warriorless encampment without mercy, the Osages committed their slaughter, compounding their act by cutting off the heads of all the dead and placing them in brass buckets around the destroyed village.[45]

They also discovered some of the Mexican money in the Kiowa village and carried it back to the Verdigris settlement with them. They brought along over one hundred Kiowa scalps, five captive children, and some four hundred horses. This event became known to the Kiowas as the "summer they cut off their heads."[46]

Concerned already about the threat that the western Indians posed to the eastern tribes and hoping to intimidate the Plains bands against molesting Americans, on May 6, 1833, General Arbuckle issued orders for two companies of Seventh Infantry (mounted) and three companies of rangers to march into Comanche and Pawnee Pict country. If the force met Indians east of the Washita River, it was to drive them westward. If the Indians were encountered on the upper Red River, the unit's commander, Colonel James B. Many, was to treat with them, make gifts of medals and flags to their chiefs, and invite the tribes to come to Fort Gibson for talks.[47]

Boone's rangers were a part of the unit that left Fort Gibson and moved southwestward to the Blue River. It was here on June 2 that one of Boone's men, George B. Abbay of Missouri, went off hunting alone some mile and a half from camp. Just as Beatte had warned the rangers under Bean the year before, the man was seized by Indians and carried off. A detachment was sent to look for Abbay, but night fell before much could be determined. When daylight broke the next day, guides picked up the trail of a large band of Indians that had been camped nearby.[48]

The Indians, estimated at from 150 to 200 and thought to be Pawnee Picts, had fled west in such a hurry that they had left behind a trail of saddles, robes, bows and arrows, and horses. Many's command set off in pursuit and after a march of some twenty-six miles reached the Washita. The river was in such a flooded stage from recent rains that the troops could not cross. Colonel Many continued up the north bank of the Washita, hoping to encounter the Indians or to locate their village; but he was luckless on both counts.

After twelve days of fruitless scouring of the country, the command began to run out of provisions. The officers decided to drive on farther west into the buffalo range where meat could be procured. This took them thirty miles deeper into Comanche–Pawnee Pict country to the vicinity of the Wichita Mountains. Although game was plentiful, the troops were now becoming ill and the horses badly exhausted. The weary command turned about and headed back to Gibson, arriving there in early July after having lost one man and contacted no Indians.[49]

The government was not finished with the matter, however. Organization of the ten-company First Regiment of U.S. Dragoons was under way. Nathan Boone, who had conducted a survey of the Cherokee-Creek boundary during March and April 1833, returned to Missouri that fall to recruit a company composed entirely of Missourians. In 1834 this unit became Company H, First Dragoon Regiment, stationed at Fort Gibson. Among the officers to serve with the dragoons at Gibson were such famous names as Stephen Watts Kearny, Philip St. George Cooke, and Jefferson Davis.

Yet another incident took place in May between the Blue and the Washita rivers. Judge Gabriel N. Martin, who resided in present-day eastern Oklahoma along the Red River (then Miller County, Arkansas), had taken his son and some servants on a hunt to the west. There they were attacked by Indians. The judge and a black servant were killed, and the boy, nine-year-old Matthew Wright Martin, and another slave were captured.[50]

Lieutenant Dawson made a second excursion up the Arkansas River in June 1834, this time under orders to locate a site for a new military post near the mouth of the Cimarron River. Dawson's recommendation resulted in the erection of another short-lived Camp Arbuckle, it consisting of a blockhouse and defensive works. From there Dawson surveyed a road leading south to the mouth of Little River, where Fort Holmes was being erected. He marked the route with mounds of earth, stakes, and blazed trees.[51] While Dawson was thus engaged, the remainder of the dragoon regiment was making ready for a historic military expedition into the heart of the Comanche-Wichita domain.

The Leavenworth-Dodge Expedition

Brigadier General Henry Leavenworth lay on the cot in his tent, his long, thin form racked with a high fever that was agitated by the scorching, breezeless heat of early July. Artist George Catlin, who shared the general's tent, described Leavenworth's agony in a letter to his brother.[1] The fanning efforts of a dragoon orderly had no effect in easing the labored breathing of the affable officer who was held in such high esteem by his officers and men alike. "All love him," a soldier of the First Regiment of U.S. Dragoons once wrote, "for all have access to him, and none that know him can help but love him."[2]

Throughout this encampment at the mouth of the Washita River, both men and horses of the expedition had been stricken with a mysterious, deadly epidemic of bilious fever. Nearly half of the 500 dragoons who had departed Fort Gibson on June 20, 1834, were likewise disabled. Men and horses alike were falling incapacitated daily.

Henry Leavenworth. (Kansas State Historical Society)

As Catlin watched the gasping general, he recalled an incident of a few days before when the long, winding columns of mounted dragoons and wagons were crossing the Blue River. At that time the kindly general, Catlin, and several of the unit's officers had indulged in a wild chase after a herd of buffalo. The general and Colonel Henry Dodge bagged a fat cow, but Leavenworth after-

George Catlin, artist. (*Catlin's Notes of Eight Years' Travel*)

ward commented wearily that he was ready to leave this sport to the younger men.

But even as he had spoken, riding at the lead of the group of hunters, the general topped a rise and suddenly wheeled his horse about to whisper the news that a small band of buffalo grazed just beyond. Forgetting his thought of retirement, Leavenworth quickly laid plans for a coordinated charge—Lieutenant Thompson B. Wheelock to the left, Catlin to the right, and himself and Dodge to the center. Catlin later recalled "the waving grass . . . the trampling hooves . . . the blackened throng . . . the darting steeds . . . the flashing of guns . . ." all of which blurred in his excited vision when a tree limb wiped him from his saddle.[3]

Henry Dodge. (*National Cyclopaedia of American Biography*)

Dazed but unhurt, Catlin rose, steadied his legs, and recovered his horse. The general came riding up to see if the artist was injured and, finding he was not, quickly galloped off in chase of a buffalo calf he had spied. Catlin followed to a hilltop where he could watch the chase. The frightened calf adeptly dodged the charge of the general's horse, which lost its footing and fell, dumping its rider headlong onto the prairie. Catlin hurried forward to find the general struggling to his hands and knees. Leavenworth insisted that he was not hurt, but then fainted. With no water available, Catlin turned to the popular remedy of the day. He took out his pocket knife and attempted to open a vein in the officer's arm for bleeding.

The general revived and protested that the operation was unnecessary. With Catlin's help, he remounted his horse, and the two men rode on to join the regiment. But from that time on, the fifty-one-year-old general had appeared pale and feeble and suffered from a bad cough. Privately he told Catlin that he feared he had been injured much worse than he had first thought. Now observing the man burning away with fever, the artist held the fear that Leavenworth might well be on his deathbed.

The Leavenworth-commanded expedition into the Comanche–Pawnee Pict domain of southwestern Oklahoma in 1834 was of special significance in several ways. It was the first American military thrust into this section of the American western wilderness beyond the Wichita Mountains, and it resulted in the first formal U.S. contact with the Comanches and Wichitas. Its purpose was to establish good relations with those and other warring Plains tribes not only to protect U.S. citizens who came into the region but also to ease the fears of eastern tribes that were being removed to Indian Territory.

The expedition also provided the general public with a descriptive view of the area, one that was enhanced through the presence of George Catlin. Both Catlin's scenes and narratives of the two tribes contributed much to the persona of the early West. And the mysterious illness that swept through and decimated the dragoon regiment intensified the danger and drama of the expedition.

Leavenworth had succeeded Arbuckle in command of the southern wing of the Western Department of the Army with headquarters at Fort Towson in January 1834. He immediately proceeded with the laying out of a road between Towson and Gibson and another from Towson westward along the Red River to the Washita. In April he moved his headquarters to Fort Gibson, where in May the Seventh Infantry had been reinforced

The stone fireplace where Confederacy president Jefferson Davis once served as adjutant of the First Dragoons stands beside the restored buildings of old Fort Gibson. (Author photo)

with nine companies of First Dragoons from Jefferson Barracks, Missouri. The general also ordered that roads be laid out and marked from Fort Gibson to the mouth of the Washita for the establishment of a military post at that point. Another post was to be established at the mouth of Little River on the Canadian.[4]

There were several reasons for an expedition to the prairie. The government wished to soothe relations among the eastern tribes it had recently removed to Indian Territory. Also, officials wished to impress the Comanches and others with the military might of the United States. Furthermore, there was hope that ranger George Abbay and the other kidnap victims could be found and rescued.

On April 30 a military review of the garrison was held at Fort Gibson. The dragoons, dressed in their black jackets and hats with long black plumes waving behind as they rode, went through military maneuvers of charge and repulse before a large audience of Indians who had come to observe the event. The horses of each company had been selected by color: one of bays, one of blacks, one of whites, one of sorrels, one of cream coloreds, and so on.[5]

Among the leading officers of the expedition were second-in-command Colonel Henry Dodge, Lieutenant Colonel Stephen W. Kearny, Major Richard B. Mason, and Captain Edwin V. Sumner, all of whom would become well-known figures of the West. Another officer was Lieutenant Jefferson Davis, one day to become famous as secretary of war and, more notably, as president of the Confederacy during the Civil War. Lieutenant Wheelock was assigned the task of keeping a journal of the expedition.

A number of Indians were recruited as scouts, guides, and interpreters—Osages, Cherokees, Delawares, and Senecas. A Wichita girl and a Kiowa sister and brother, captured at Rainey Mountain Creek, had been purchased from the Osages to serve as tokens of friendship in meeting their tribes. The boy, however, was tragically killed by a ram at Fort Gibson prior to departure of the expedition. Notable among the Indians were the Cherokee warrior and chief Dutch; Jesse Chisholm, later to be famous as namesake of the Chisholm Cattle Trail; and the frontier-wise Beatte, whom Washington Irving had praised so highly.[6]

George Catlin, whose drawings and narratives of adventures among the Indians of the West had already established his fame, had arrived at Gibson two months earlier. He had spent his time painting and studying the Osages, a band of which still resided north of Fort Gibson on the Verdigris and was constantly at the post to conduct trade. The artist painted many of the Osages, including Clermont III. The Osage had inherited the chief's role when his father, Clermont II, had died in 1828.[7] Catlin also made portraits of Clermont's

Stephen W. Kearny. (*Appleton's Cyclopaedia of American Biography*)

Edwin V. Sumner. (*Appleton's Cyclopaedia of American Biography*)

Jefferson Davis. (*National Cyclopaedia of American Biography*)

wife and child and the giant one-eyed Osage chief Black Dog, whom Catlin estimated to stand nearly seven feet tall and weigh between 250 and 300 pounds.

Even before the expedition departed from Camp Rendezvous, eighteen miles west of Fort Gibson, twenty-three of the men had been declared too ill to travel and were sent back to the fort. Nevertheless, on June 21 the unit moved southwest in good spirits, 500 strong with supply wagons and seventy head of beef cattle on which the small army would feed.

The expedition camped the first night on the south bank of Little River. Lieutenant Theophilus H. Holmes, Seventh Infantry, was busy erecting a fort and quarters to accommodate two companies of troops at the site. Twenty-seven men, stricken with high fever, were left there as the command crossed the Canadian and proceeded west toward the conflux of the Washita and Red rivers. En route the expedition came onto Black Dog's village of Osages heading out to the prairie in search of buffalo. It was on the Blue River that Leavenworth and his officers conducted their hunt.[8]

It had been prearranged that two Third Infantry companies from Fort Towson would meet them at the mouth of the Washita, where a military post was being constructed. As scouting detachments and straggler elements of the march arrived, the expedition went into camp to rest, regroup, and reshoe horses. But now the strange illness of men and animals alike began to take a heavy toll. On July 1 three officers, including the general, and forty-five men were reported ill. Seventy-five of the horses and mules were disabled. The surgeon blamed the oppressive 103–107 degree heat and the rapid marches.[9]

On July 3 rafts were constructed and other preparations were undertaken for crossing the Washita. This stream was considered to be a "Rubicon" entry to the sacred soil of the Indian. Although not wide, the Washita ran deep, and its high, miry banks made the crossing difficult. Several horses were lost in the operation, but by the evening of July 4 the command was safely across the river. Camp Leavenworth was established on the west bank.

General Leavenworth was now so ill that he had to abandon his plan to personally lead the command to the Wichita villages. Colonel Dodge was placed in charge, and the reduced expedition—now consisting of six companies of 42 men each and a total complement of around 250 men—moved westward.[10] Wagons were left behind; Indian scouts rode in advance. "All seemed gay and buoyant and the fresh start," Catlin wrote, "which all trusted was to liberate us from the fatal miasma which we conceived was hovering about the mouth of the False Washita."[11]

But hopes that they had escaped the sickness soon vanished. Men were becoming so ill that they had to be carried on litters between horses. The already jittery command went into near panic on the night of July 7 when a raw recruit on sentinel duty spied a dark form moving toward him in the bushes. The form did not answer his challenge to advance and give the counter-sign, so the recruit aimed his carbine and fired.

The blast of the gun in the night stillness set off a turmoil of horses and mules screaming and men yelling that the Indians were attacking. The frightened animals stampeded into the darkness, and it was hours before calm was restored. At morning's light the camp discovered that the form seen by the sentry was a dragoon's mount that had been lost and was returning to camp. It lay dead with a bullet through its heart. The next day was spent rounding up the stampeded stock, though fifteen to twenty escaped to join the wild bands of mustangs on the prairie and were never recovered.[12]

Moving on a northwesterly course, Dodge's command passed through country that teemed with large herds of wild horses and immense numbers of buffalo. Indian signs became more and more pronounced, and on July 14 a Comanche war party was sighted on a distant hill. The warriors' lances gleamed in the sun so brightly that at first Dodge's command thought that they were Spanish troops. Dodge's force advanced toward the Indians, who would disappear behind a hill and reappear again in a different direction. After several instances of this maneuver, Dodge and a few of his officers rode forward with a white flag.

The Indians responded with a single warrior, who met them on a milk-white pony with a flowing mane. The man had a war shield on his back, a rifle mounted in a handsome buckskin case, and a bow in one hand and a lance in the other. A piece of white buffalo skin was tied to the lance tip.

The warrior came forward in the zig-zag motion that on the prairie signified "peace." Finally he galloped up to the dragoon holding the white flag, touched his lance to it, then wheeled about to shake hands with Dodge and the others. This done, the rest of the Comanche party of eighty to ninety warriors came forward to shake hands. All then dismounted, a pipe was passed about, and a talk was conducted in Spanish.

Dodge explained that he had been sent by the president of the United States to meet the chiefs of the Comanches and Wichitas, make peace with them, and establish trade relations. The Comanches agreed to lead the dragoon regiment to their village and joined the march. Both the dragoons and Indians hunted buffalo and chased wild horses as they went.[13]

The two parties reached the Comanche village on July 16. Several hundred conical lodges with smoke curling above sat nestled in a serene valley backed by a lofty mountain range to the southwest. A small stream cut through the encampment valley, which was speckled with an estimated three thousand horses and mules. As the dragoons approached the village, they could see figures dashing about to catch horses. Dodge ordered his command into a three-column formation, with a fronting line composed of himself and his staff. Catlin, who was permitted a place in the forward reception, watched with admiration as the Comanches dashed their ponies forward and wheeled into a well-dressed formation equal to a disciplined cavalry.

The dragoon line was centered by a white flag connoting peaceful intentions. A warrior galloped forward on his pony and planted an emblem of white buffalo skin. The Comanches, who were largely minus their war paraphernalia, showed no signs of hostility. The two lines faced each other at twenty to thirty yards' distance for nearly half an hour before the head chief of the village galloped up to Colonel Dodge and shook his hand. The chief then proceeded to shake hands with every single man in the dragoon regiment. Several other principal men and warriors followed suit. This welcoming procedure took nearly an hour, after which the expedition was escorted to the banks of a clear stream with a good spring a half mile from the village. There Dodge established Camp Comanche.[14]

Catlin, though ill himself, continued to be an astute observer of Indian life. He strolled about the Comanche town, making quick sketches and studying the habits and interesting facets of Comanche life. He found that the Comanche warrior was an incessant horseman, spending most of his time playing games of war astride his horse. "I am ready, without hesitation," Catlin declared, "to pronounce the Comanches the most extraordinary horsemen that I have seen yet in all my travels, and I doubt very much whether any people in the world can surpass them."[15]

He was particularly amazed at the ability of the warriors to fall to one side of their animals while at a full gallop. They seemed to support themselves only by hooking a heel on the horse's spine while shooting their arrows or throwing their lances with ease from that position. Determined to discover the secret to this defiance of gravity, Catlin bribed a young warrior with a few plugs of tobacco to explain the feat. The Indians, he discovered, employed a short hair halter that was braided into the horse's mane and hung down as an arm support against the animal's breast. By hooking the middle of their upper arms in this loop, the warriors could support themselves and at the same time have both hands free for combat.[16]

Beatte impressed Catlin, as he had Irving, with his Indian-taught ability to capture and tame the wild mustangs. The artist finally learned the missing clue to the magical taming of wild horses. After lassoing the wild horse and hobbling its forefeet, Beatte would throw a noose about the animal's lower jaw. Working his way slowly up the lasso, he placed his hand over the horse's nose and then over his eyes; finally, by breathing into the horse's nostrils, Beatte rendered it conquered and obedient to his control![17]

Through drawings and narrative sketches, Catlin portrayed a number of Comanche leaders: the mild-mannered, unpretentious head chief Ee-shah-ko-nee, or the Bow and Quiver; the obese and bearded second chief Ta-wah-que-nah, or the Mountain of Rocks; and the adopted Mexican captive warrior, the Spaniard, who endeared himself to Catlin and the dragoons by helping to carry the litters of sick men across the river. The Spaniard even offered to carry Catlin on his back. Catlin preferred to ride his horse across, but the muscular little warrior still insisted on leading the mount by the bridle for safety. Catlin rewarded him with the gift of a knife, which pleased the man very much.[18]

Dodge spent only a short time at the Comanche village before heading on for the Wichita (Tayosh or Taovaya) village on the North Fork of the Red River. A council was planned with that tribe as well as with the Comanches and Kiowas. With more of the dragoons falling ill each day, some ten miles from the Comanche camp Dodge decided to disencumber the march by leaving the sick behind. A brush arbor was erected near a stream to shield the men from the fierce heat, and a guard was left with them. Catlin was one of those too ill to proceed. He gave his sketch pads and notebooks to a friend and asked him to fill in.[19]

A three-day, seventy-mile march westward, skirting to the south of the mountains, was required to reach the North Fork. Here the dragoons found the Wichita village on the bank of the river beneath a towering granite bluff. Well cultivated and fenced fields of corn, melons, and squash surrounded the two hundred or more thatched huts. A large party of Wichitas met the dragoons and escorted them to their village. Dodge ordered the troops into camp a mile from the settlement. The next day he held a conference, conducted by the interpreters in the Caddo language, with the elderly but eloquent chief We-ter-rah-sah-so.

When Dodge pressed the Wichita chief on the subject of the Martin murder and the 1833 abduction of ranger Abbay, the headman denied any knowledge of either. It was only when a black man discovered in the camp was brought forth that the presence of young Martin was acknowledged. Dodge refused to conduct any further talks until the boy was produced. After the Wichitas consulted among themselves, they brought the boy forth, entirely naked, from where he had been hidden in a cornfield. When asked his name, he promptly replied, "My name is Matthew Wright Martin."[20]

Dodge responded by presenting the Wichita girl to her family. The parents embraced the girl with tears of gratitude. The old chief was also very grateful, but he still insisted that ranger Abbay had been captured and murdered by Texas Indians—Lipan Apaches—residing near San Antonio.[21]

The Comanches had followed the dragoons to the village, and Dodge talked with their chiefs there. He indicated the desire of the United States for friendship and promised to send traders to their nation. Even as these talks were taking place, a band of thirty to forty Kiowas charged into the camp, creating a furor of excitement and sending tribespeople scurrying for safety. The Kiowas had learned that Osages were there, and they came to avenge the massacre of their village the year before. Dodge was able to calm them and win their friendship by presenting the Kiowa girl rescued from the Osages. "The gratitude of the Kioways was unbounded when Colonel Dodge gave up to her nation our Kioway prisoner. Her uncle, who was chief, made a most animated address to his people upon the occasion; he told them that the man who had travelled so far to restore to them their lost daughter, must be a very great and a very good man; and that he longed to embrace him with the arms of friendship and love."[22]

The brush and pen of Catlin's "friend Joe" and the log of Lieutenant Wheelock cataloged items of interest regarding the Indians and their leaders. The Kiowas, taller and more graceful afoot than the other Indians, were seen by Wheelock as combatants of chivalric mold reminiscent of the Scottish Highlanders. Their chief Teh-toot-sah (Tiche-totche-cha) was a "very gentlemanly and high-minded man, who treated the dragoons and officers with great kindness."[23] The Wichitas and Comanches still held to their long alliance; but even as in the days of Spanish rule a century before, the Wichitas resented the manner in which the Comanches often cheated them in trade.[24]

A council was held with the chiefs at the dragoon encampment amid the presence of some three thousand warriors. Speeches were made by leaders of both the Plains tribes and representatives of the immigrant tribes. The talks went well, and Dodge persuaded a number of the Indians to return with him to Fort Gibson for the purpose of making peace among the tribes.

The Kiowa chief and fifteen of his warriors were the first to agree. They were followed reluctantly by the Comanche chief and four men, a woman, and the Spaniard. The elderly Wichita chief and two of his men finally agreed to make the journey, as did a Waco chief. They expressed fears, however, that they would be killed while traveling through timber country.[25]

Returning to the sick camp where the invalid men had been left, Dodge regrouped his command. A servant to Lieutenant Wheelock died. The lone Comanche woman became sick, causing the chief and all of his party except the Spaniard to turn back. Dodge, concerned because he had not heard from General Leavenworth or received wagons that were supposed to have been sent, dispatched a courier to make contact with Leavenworth and report on the progress of his command. The heat of late July remained overpowering, and fresh meat remained scarce. The only water was that of stagnating, buffalo-wallow pools that were contaminated with urine. "Many of us are now sick and unable to ride," Catlin wrote, "and are carried on litters between two horses. Nearly every tent belonging to the officers has been converted to hospitals for the sick; and sighs and groaning are heard in all directions."[26]

Moving east by north, the dragoons crossed the Washita on July 30, now finding fresh water and an abundance of buffalo. They reached the Canadian River on August 1, and the men indulged in an orgy of buffalo hunting. The expedition moved on down the river and was taking a rest on August 5 when word arrived that Leavenworth was dead. Despite his grave condition, the elderly officer had attempted to bring the wagons on beyond the camp at the mouth of the Washita. He had passed beyond the Cross Timbers some fifty to sixty miles when he died.[27]

Dodge's force arrived at the mouth of Little River to find that Lieutenant Holmes had finished erecting a blockhouse and quarters for one company of troops at what would be known for a short time as Camp Holmes. Several soldiers had died and were buried there. On August 15 the decimated, ragged, and totally fatigued regiment of First Dragoons reached the banks of the Arkansas River across from Fort Gibson.

Catlin had made much of the return trip in a baggage wagon with several sick soldiers. The jarring and jolting against the hard boards had rubbed his elbows and knees raw. A number of the command had succumbed on the prairie. Some had been buried there, some were brought into the fort for burial, and others died after returning.[28]

> What the regiment of Dragoons has suffered from sickness since they started on their summer's campaign, is unexampled in this country, and almost incredible. When we started from this place, ten or fifteen were sent back the first day too sick to proceed; and so afterwards our numbers were daily diminished, and at the distance of 200 miles from this place we could muster, out of the whole regiment, but 250 men who were able to proceed. . . . Since our return, the sick have been brought in by the dozens and scores from the points where they had been left. . . . The Dragoons well enough to leave have all marched off . . . [leaving] at this place 140 or 50 sick, who are burying two to three and four per day.[29]

As Catlin recuperated in his quarters at Fort Gibson, he could hear the mournful sound of a muffled drum several times a day as burial processions made their way to the Fort Gibson graveyard. Among those buried there was the Prussian botanist Monsieur Beyrick, who had accompanied the expedition in a Dearborn wagon. He had driven the wagon from St. Louis to Gibson and on with the dragoons, collecting samples of plant and animal life during the whole of the march to the Washita and the Cross Timbers. The botanist made it back to the fort; but only a few days after his young assistant had died, so did Monsieur Beyrick. It was estimated that at least one-third of the 450 men who began the expedition perished.[30]

With a few days' rest, most of the men began to recover. The deadly disease subsided enough that Dodge could call a council, so that the Indian tribes in the region could talk with the visitors from the prairies. Runners were sent to seven or eight tribes early in September, and soon huge numbers of Indians began arriving at Three Forks. They camped their villages, shook hands all around, smoked the calumet, and made vows of lasting peace and friendship. But despite all of the oratory that flowed forth, many had doubts that the great rivalries between the prairie tribes and the intruders on their land—white and eastern immigrant Indians alike—would be ended. Even before Catlin departed Three Forks, a company of eighty men was being outfitted at Gibson for the purpose of entering Comanche country to trap, hunt, and perhaps even build a fort among them.[31]

➤ 12

The Treaty of
Camp Holmes

As the hot days of July burned away, the Comanches, Kiowas, and Wichitas were becoming more and more annoyed and angry. They had been promised that the white chief would come to these council grounds with presents and food. But the days lingered one into another, and the white chiefs did not appear. For a time there was buffalo to hunt and eat, but not nearly enough to feed the seven thousand or so tribespeople whose lodges were scattered for several miles along the banks of the Canadian River and Chouteau Creek.

The situation was growing more and more precarious. The Osages, who had come there with the advance troops, reported that the Comanche third chief, the battle-scarred Tabaqueena, or Big Eagle, was stirring up trouble. He was trying to get other bands to join him in wiping out the small force of dragoons camped nearby on the edge of the Cross Timbers and take their horses.

Major Richard B. Mason, the dragoon commander, had sent an urgent call for reinforcements back to Fort

Gibson by Osage scouts. But Gibson was a week's march away at the very least. The situation seemed desperate for the greatly outnumbered soldiers. The day was saved by the Comanche chief Ichacoly, or the Wolf, who persuaded the tribes to be patient a while longer. Nevertheless, with their people facing starvation, the Kiowas and many of the Comanche and Wichita bands broke their camps and disappeared westward into the prairie where they could find buffalo.[1]

The talks that had been held at Fort Gibson in the fall of 1834 precluded the government's efforts to establish its sovereignty over the prairie tribes with a formal pact. At that time officials had promised that a treaty council would be concluded "when the grass next grows after the snows shall have melted away."[2] And in March 1835 Indian trader Holland Coffee, who operated a trading post across the Red River from the mouth of the Washita, arrived at Fort Gibson to report that the Indians were anxious to know when the treaty council would be held. The tribes had also stated their desire to hold the meeting on the prairie, perhaps near Coffee's place, where there were plenty of buffalo.[3]

On March 27 the secretary of war appointed a three-man peace commission and assigned $11,000 for the purpose of conducting treaty talks with the Comanche, "Caiaway," and other nations of the southwestern frontier. Congress having passed the Indian removal bill, treaties were being initiated with the large tribes of the South for their removal to Indian Territory. Accordingly, for both the good of the removed tribes and the United States itself, the government sought to establish peaceful relations with the warring prairie Indians.

The three commissioners appointed to the task were Brevet Brigadier General Matthew Arbuckle, commanding Fort Gibson; former governor of North Carolina Montford Stokes; and Major Francis W. Armstrong, agent for the Choctaws. The commission was instructed that its prime goal was to establish amiable relations between the eastern immigrant tribes and those of the western prairie. Armstrong, however, was too ill to come to Fort Gibson from his agency post near present-day Spiro, Oklahoma.[4]

In the meantime, three prairie Indians—two Wichitas and a Waco—arrived at Fort Gibson to inquire into the matter of the peace council. Because of the lack of an interpreter, however, it was several weeks before an interview with them could be held. When talks were finally arranged on May 14, the commission learned that the Comanches would be detained for a time. They were busy with their raids into the Mexican province of Texas; afterward they would hold their summer buffalo hunt. They would return north when it was time for the green corn feast held annually by the Wichitas.[5]

The commission decided that it would send a party of First Dragoons under Major Mason, who had been with the Leavenworth expedition, to the head of Little River to locate a suitable place for a peace council. A preliminary meeting was held with the Osages to seek their support in this peace effort. Clermont, Black Dog (Shonetashba), and other Osage leaders, displeased at being offered only a few plugs of tobacco as presents, expressed indifference to the peace effort. They said they could get more from taking Comanche horses and hunting on the prairie than they could from a treaty. However, when Chief Black Dog was given a keg of powder for his band, he gave in and said he would attend the affair.[6] The Osages agreed to send a small party of warriors with Mason. They also gave up two captive Wichita girls.

The commissioners were concerned about reports that Mexican officials in Texas were outfitting a war party of south Texas Indians to raid Coffee's post and attack the Comanches. Mason was ordered to be on guard against this threat as he departed Fort Gibson on June 10 accompanied by the Osages, the two captives, and trader Colonel Auguste Pierre Chouteau.

Mason located a site for the proposed council on Chouteau Creek at the western edge of the Cross Timbers not far from the Canadian River near present-day Lexington, Oklahoma. Here, along a spring-fed rivulet with a stand of timber to the east and open prairie to the west, Mason established a new Camp Holmes, replacing the post now abandoned at the mouth of Little River.[7]

At the same time, a detachment of Seventh Infantry soldiers under Lieutenant Augustine F. Seaton had been assigned the task of constructing a road westward from Fort Gibson to the new site. Seaton's group departed Gibson on June 17 in breathless heat; both men and horses were tormented to the extreme by swarms of flies. The weather soon cooled, but a torrential rain made traveling even more difficult and painful. Ravines and creeks were either flooded or so steep that their banks had to be dug out to permit wagons to cross. On June 25 the group reached Little River and went into camp with everyone soaked to the skin.[8]

For several days the road builders were marooned on a narrow ridge two yards by fifty in dimension, sharing their perch with tarantulas, scorpions, lizards, centipedes, and snakes that had been driven there by the rising water. Unable to cross the flooded river and with rain continuing intermittently, several of the men, including Seaton (who died the following November from this exposure), became ill. On July 2 a pirogue was made from a felled tree. Completed on July 4, the boat was dubbed the Independence. Word arrived from Mason ordering the road builders to push on to the council grounds as quickly as possible. The detachment crossed Little River in the pirogue and resumed the march.

Seaton and his men reached Camp Holmes on July 11 with a number of them ill, among them Assistant Surgeon Leonard C. McPhail. He had maintained a diary of the trying journey until he became so sick that he ceased his entries for a time. Nevertheless, his account of the Camp Holmes meeting provides colorful behind-the-scenes details of this first U.S. treaty council to be held with the Plains Indians in present-day Oklahoma.

Opposition by Comanche chief Tabaqueena subsided with the arrival of Seventh Infantry reinforcements under Captain Frances Lee, who brought along an artillery field piece. Also contributing much to the harmony of the meeting was the appearance of Comanche head chief Ichacoly. He was a handsome man whose pretty daughter caught the attention of the male-abundant camp. Dressed in deerskins fringed with elk's teeth, bedecked with bracelets, and with the part in her dark hair, her eyelids, and her lips painted with vermilion, the girl was the belle of the camp.[9]

Many of the Indians, McPhail noted, were taking down their lodges, packing their buffalo-hide covers onto travois, and heading back to the prairie. Partly this was because the supply of buffalo had run out and partly it was because the increased number of soldiers raised distrust among the Indians. But still another reason came to light.

An Osage had recently stolen a Comanche's horses, and a Comanche delegation had gone to Clermont's village to retrieve it. While the Comanches were there, Clermont had encouraged them to continue their summer buffalo hunt and ignore the peace council. Clermont had told them that Mason and the other officers were not chiefs and were of no importance—"as useless as the dead grass of the prairie."[10] This talk was opposed by Chief Black Dog, however, who had been encouraging the Indians to remain at the council site. He openly hoped that the white chiefs would arrive soon, so that he would not appear a liar.

Everyone awaited the arrival of the commissioners. Time was spent in wrestling and foot-racing contests between the soldiers and the Osages. When a buffalo herd appeared in the area, Mason, an avid sportsman, joined in the hunt. In a letter to a friend, he told how one Osage hunter had driven an arrow completely through a buffalo. He also recounted how another Indian had shot a buffalo on a dead run, the arrow penetrating to within two inches of the feathered end of the shaft. When the buffalo did not fall, the Indian jerked out the arrow while still riding at a breakneck gallop and shot the animal a second time, this time killing it in its tracks. Mason exulted that he himself had bagged some buffalo, along with bear, deer, and turkey.[11]

McPhail recorded several incidents of interest. On one occasion a sentry attempted to use a gun butt to shove away an Indian who was washing his feet in the camp spring. The Indian grabbed the rifle, which discharged and sent a bullet through the palm of the soldier's hand. McPhail was forced to amputate the hand at the wrist.[12]

An infantryman who had become lost from Captain Lee's company during its march to the council grounds had not been found by several search parties sent to look for him. On July 17 an Osage came into camp with a musket he had found near the body of a dead man. A detachment was sent to investigate. It found the remains of the missing soldier, who had been dead for about two weeks only three miles from camp.[13]

A din of wailing awakened the camp one night. It came from the Wichita camp, where tribespeople had just learned that one of their war parties had suffered the loss of a number of warriors in a fight with whites at a Texas settlement. McPhail was also witness to a Comanche man in mourning over the loss of a daughter. The Indian painted himself black, and about his neck he wore the trinkets that had belonged to his child. Among them was a little buckskin doll whose head was covered with a lock of the dead girl's hair.[14]

On another occasion a Comanche and the wife of another man ran off together. The two were caught a few days later and brought back to be punished. Their faces and bodies were slashed, and then charcoal was rubbed into the wounds to leave permanent evidence of their crimes.

McPhail, who treated several wounded Indians while at Camp Holmes, observed a method used by the Indians to treat skin diseases. After scarifying the surface with a flint, they applied suction through a buffalo horn—the "cupping" often used in early medicine. For pains in the neck, spine, or other parts of the body, the Indians used live coals to burn the skin. The surgeon, who treated his own illness by having himself "blooded freely," had opium and ipecac for use against malaria and dysentery.[15]

Flies were so bothersome to the horses at Camp Holmes that it became necessary to graze them at night and hold them in camp during the day, so that smokey fires could be used to drive off the pests. The men suffered badly from a nettle rash, which McPhail thought was caused from eating meat of buffalo that had fed on a white flowering nettle in the area.

When the dragoons learned that the Kiowas had departed, a detachment was sent out to locate and bring them back. The other Indians had their doubts that it could be done. The Kiowas were like wolves, they said, difficult to find. Indeed, the search party had no success, though a Kiowa and his wife did appear in camp on August 9.

McPhail entertained himself with a bit of exploring, crossing the Canadian River to a hill that bordered the river and stood some one hundred feet above the level of the prairie. The eminence offered him a commanding view of the surrounding countryside.[16]

At Fort Gibson the commission had been delayed by preparations and by illness. Major Armstrong still lay ill at his agency. On August 2 the commission received a letter from Armstrong's physician stating that the agent was in such condition that a trip to the treaty grounds would endanger his life. The seventy-five-year-old Stokes was ailing also, and word was sent to Mason to hold the Indians at the council site until August 20. Finally, however, the commission party departed for Camp Holmes, taking with it a wagon train loaded with over $6,000 in treaty presents. On the same day Major Armstrong died in his agency home.[17]

The commission caravan was accompanied by delegations of Indians representing the Creeks, Osages, Senecas, and Quapaws, while others from the Cherokees, Choctaws, and Delawares were set to follow. The thirteen-day journey to the council site was a hot and punishing one, particularly so for the indisposed Stokes. The entourage of commissioners, clerks, soldiers, interpreters, Indians, teamsters, and traders arrived on August 19. But many of the Indians were gone. "The promises held out to the Indians should never be broken," McPhail noted, "They were to be met when the grass was in *blade* and not in the *leaf*."[18]

The chiefs who were still present insisted that they had been left there to make a peace treaty that would stand good for their nation as well as for the Kiowas. A large brush arbor was erected, with seats made of split logs. On August 22 the council finally assembled for talks. First Lieutenant Washington Seawell, Seventh Infantry, served as secretary and recorded the speeches of the commissioners and Indians alike.

Stokes spoke first, but only briefly because of his poor health. He stressed that all the Great Father wished was for the Indians to be at peace with white people and other Indian nations alike. This same theme was stressed by Arbuckle, who promised U.S. protection for all tribes that made treaties with the government.[19]

This promise was spurious at best; the United States was in no position to exercise military force on the Plains. Equally as questionable was a commitment by the commission that the government would pay for stock stolen from the prairie tribes by U.S. citizens.

Other stipulations of the pact were entirely unrealistic. One article called for "every injury or act of hostility by one or either of the contracting parties on the other shall be mutually forgiven and forever forgot."[20] Yet another clause required the prairie tribes to repay the full value of any injury or loss of property made upon U.S. citizens while passing through their country. There was no clue given as to just how the moneyless prairie Indians would do this.

But the clause in the treaty that most concerned Wichita chief Koshawka was the one calling on his tribe to live in peace with the Republic of Mexico and its province of Texas. "The Spaniards have attacked us three times," the chief complained. "They have killed three of my children, and two of my warriors."[21] He wanted to know if the Americans would make war on the Wichitas if they went to war with the Spaniards. The commissioners assured him that the treaty did not bind his tribe to keep peace with the Republic of Mexico and that the United States would not make war on the Wichitas if they did have trouble.

Significantly the treaty proclaimed that immigrant Indians as well as whites would be freely permitted to come onto the lands of the prairie Indians and hunt at will. This unrealistic stipulation would prove to be the greatest weakness of the Treaty of Camp Holmes.

Ichacoly of the Comanches, also ill, made only a brief talk. "Half of my body belongs to the Osages and half to the Comanches," he said, indicating his willingness to make peace.[22]

On August 24 the treaty was signed by all of the tribes present, and on the following day final speeches were made and gifts were issued to the prairie chiefs by several of the eastern chiefs. "Brothers," Chief Rolly McIntosh of the Creeks said, "we have now established the road for us all. Some of my people are going home with you, and when they return I hope they will bring us a favorable account."[23] "If there be any killing," said

Mushalatubee, or the Mankiller, of the Choctaws, "let it be by the falling of limbs of trees."[24] Black Dog of the Osages; Thomas Brant of the Senecas; and Hekatoo, or the Dry Man, of the Quapaws all said a few words. "There must not be any blood on that road unless it be the blood of the buffalo," Hekatoo insisted.[25]

On August 26 the presents were distributed to the Wichitas and Comanches. Soon after they began the business of taking down their lodges, loading their camp equipage onto their horses and travois, and making their mass departure for the prairie. With heavy rains returning, the commissioners and others wasted no time in heading out also.

The commissioners returned home satisfied that a treaty had been consummated. But it had been with only a small representation of the prairie Indians and with negative feelings on the part of those who had left early. Not long after the treaty council, Colonel A. P. Chouteau erected a small picket fort a short distance from the council site and opened trading operations with the prairie bands. Although Camp Holmes was never more than a temporary military position, Chouteau's post became a center of trading activity for a time.

In December 1835 a Kiowa Indian in the company of a Wichita chief appeared at Fort Gibson to inquire about his people's being included in the government's consideration. He said the Kiowas wished to treat, but their horses were poor, and the tribe would be engaged in hunting until spring. They could not come to Fort Gibson to talk until then. The commissioners immediately assigned Major Paul L. Chouteau, brother of Colonel Chouteau, to the task of locating the Kiowas and bringing them in. The trader left in December to do this, but he soon learned that the Kiowas were, indeed, difficult to find.[26]

Chouteau went first to Coffee's trading house. Learning nothing of the Kiowas there, he rode on westward some sixty-five miles to Cache Creek. Again, he had no luck. Two days' travel brought him in contact with a band of Tawakonis and Wacos who directed him to a Wichita village. The Wichitas said that the Kiowas could be found on the Colorado River in Texas.

Dutifully, at midwinter Chouteau continued to scour the headwaters of the Colorado. His horses were almost worn out when he finally stumbled onto a combined encampment of Comanches, Kiowas, and Plains Apaches. Having conducted raids against the Texans and Mexicans, they were just preparing to begin their seasonal movement northward to the buffalo grounds.[27]

Chouteau moved north to Cache Creek with them and held interviews with their headmen. The chiefs were skeptical of Chouteau and his mission, but they finally agreed to send representatives to Fort Gibson. It was April 1836 before Chouteau returned to Fort Gibson to report to Stokes and Arbuckle and voice his appreciation for the hospitality shown him by the Indians. The delegation did not appear at the fort as promised, however. Instead the tribes continued their warring to the south and with their enemy tribes.

During the following winter, Edward Chouteau, son of Major Paul Chouteau, and four others set out to contact the Comanches and Kiowas in their winter camps south of the Red River. The men returned in January to report that the Comanches, now realizing that the treaty had given the eastern tribes the right to enter their hunting grounds, were very angry and hostile. The Indians had, in fact, burned their copy of the treaty. Chief Ee-shah-ko-nee had threatened to attack Camp Holmes and destroy it. Because of this, the eastern tribes were warned against the danger of venturing west.[28]

During the spring of 1837 the Comanches and their allies continued to carry on a steady campaign of depredations against the Texas settlements, which then barely extended beyond San Antonio. The raiders killed settlers, stole their horses, and took women and children captive. The Kiowas and Wichitas held several prisoners, but the Comanches had the most—an estimated thirty to forty captives.

A Comanche war party brought three white prisoners into Camp Holmes in May. Among the Comanche captives was Cynthia Ann Parker, who two years earlier at the age of twelve had been abducted from her home on the Navasota River of Texas. Jack Ivey, a frontiersman who had been with the James trading expeditions, purchased a white woman and a two-year-old girl from the Wacos and brought them to Coffee's trading house.[29]

The activity of Mexican agents working among the Indians to incite them against both the Republic of Texas (after its independence in 1836) and the United States further complicated the Plains Indian problem for the U.S. Army. With most of its forces fighting the Seminoles in Florida, there was little the army could do on the prairie. In April 1837 Colonel Chouteau was prevailed upon to go out among the Plains tribes in an effort to make new agreements with them. He returned to Fort Gibson in May with a delegation of chiefs from the Kiowas, Plains Apaches, Tawakonis, and other tribes. A treaty similar to the Camp Holmes pact was initiated with them.[30]

Nevertheless, government officials decided that the Indians needed to be shown that the strength of the United States was far greater than what they could see on the frontier. Colonel Chouteau spent the winter of 1837–1838 at Camp Holmes conducting talks with the Indians. He persuaded some of the chiefs to accompany him on a trip to Washington, where they could meet the Great White Father, the president. The plans fell through, however, when government officials decided to postpone the visitation.

During the spring of 1838 new players entered into the drama of the southern Plains. Like the Pawnees of

the Loup River and the Osages, war parties of Cheyennes and Arapahos had been coming down from north
of the Arkansas River to raid the horse herds of the
Comanches, Kiowas, and Wichitas. When Chouteau
learned that the Comanches and others were planning
to go to war with the two northern tribes, he attempted
to dissuade them. But events had already been set in
motion for a conflict.

In 1836 a party of Cheyenne Bowstring soldiers,
coming south on foot to steal horses, had been caught
by the Kiowas and killed to the man. When the Chey-
enees learned that the Kiowas had "danced their scalps,"
the Cheyennes were determined to have revenge. In
June 1838 a large consolidated Cheyenne and Arapaho
war party attacked and massacred a Comanche-Kiowa
camp on Wolf Creek.[31] It so happened that a detachment from Camp Holmes under Lieutenant Lucius B.
Northrop was on its way to the area when the fight
took place. Northrop reported back to Chouteau:

> As the Cheyennes advanced to attack their enemies,
> they were met by the latter about a mile from the
> encampment. The latter were slowly beaten back into
> their encampment, though disputing every inch of
> ground. The whole scene was in an open prairie. The
> women dug holes in the earth, in which to hide them-
> selves and their children. The Cheyenne continued to
> make dreadful havoc of their wretched enemies, and
> would have reduced the whole to a heap of corpses,
> when a messenger from camp mounted a horse and set
> off to meet the detachment of dragoons to solicit
> assistance. . . . The Cheyennes instantly retired, leaving
> fourteen dead on the ground. Fifty-eight of the Kiowas
> and Comanches were killed. More than one hundred
> horses lay dead on the ground, chiefly within the
> encampment.[32]

In October Colonel Chouteau, who had been badly
injured in a horse fall, returned to Fort Gibson. He died

there on December 25, 1838.[33] His good friend Clermont had died earlier that summer. The loss of these two influential men—along with the flood of immigrant southern Indians removed to Indian Territory—brought new instability to the already unsettled region.

➤ 13

On the Prairie

During the five-year period encompassing 1839 through 1843, the prairie wilderness of Oklahoma was crossed or explored by several interesting parties. One was a merchant who wrote a classic book on the West; another, an observing French medical student who toured the Plains with an Osage hunting party; a third, a soldier who conducted a military reconnaissance through the central portion of the state; and still another, a former governor of South Carolina who held a peace council with the Comanches on the Red River. The accounts of these men who ventured onto the prairie add much to the picture of the American frontier beyond Fort Gibson as it was in the decade before the mid-nineteenth century.

These explorations were made during a time of great turmoil among the Indian tribes of the region. In July 1839 the Texas army attacked the Texas Cherokees on the Neches River; killed many of them, including Chief Bowles; and drove them north of the Red River into Indian Territory. Then in 1840 the Texans massacred a number of leading Comanche chiefs during a council in San Antonio. The incident created fear of and a burning hatred for the Texans among both the Comanches and Kiowas. Search-and-destroy forays by the Texas Rangers forced the Comanches, as well as the Wichitas, Caddos, Wacos, Tawakonis, and others, to move their home camps northward toward the Red River and beyond.

The situation on the Plains for white travelers was tenuous. Wagon trains on the Santa Fe Trail in Kansas often came under Indian attack. Little was yet known of a potential route between Arkansas and New Mexico across Indian Territory. It was generally assumed to be very dangerous. Nonetheless, in the spring of 1839 a Santa Fe trading caravan was organized at Van Buren, Arkansas, by an enterprising trader named Josiah Gregg.

Having four times crossed the Kansas prairies with trading caravans, originally for health reasons, the Missouri farm boy had become a veteran of trail commerce. With the French at the time blockading the seaports of Mexico that serviced New Mexican trade, Gregg saw the advantage of reaching Santa Fe at an earlier date than competitors using the northern routes. This, he reasoned, would be possible by the month-earlier pasturage available along the Canadian River route through Indian Territory.

Gregg and his brother John departed the new settlement of Van Buren on April 21 with fourteen wagons, half of them drawn by mules and half by oxen; one carriage; one Jersey wagon; and a party of thirty-four men. In awareness of the dangers from hostile tribesmen on the prairie, members were well armed with pistols and Colt repeating rifles. Two wheel-mounted, swivel howitzers supported the security of the caravan.[1]

On April 28 the traders crossed the Arkansas River a few miles above the mouth of the Canadian, reaching

Josiah Gregg, author of *Commerce of the Praires*. (Josiah Gregg, *Commerce of the Prairies*)

the North Fork of the Canadian on May 2. Because of difficulties among the Cherokees, General Arbuckle at Fort Gibson could not immediately furnish the dragoon escort he had promised earlier. However, the trading caravan moved over a ravine-slashed road without incident to the far edge of the Cross Timbers, going into camp at the now-abandoned site of Chouteau's trading post. At this point the traders were joined by a company of dragoons from Gibson under the command of Lieutenant James M. Bowman.[2]

While encamped at this "wild romantic spot," they were met by Comanche chief Tabaqueena with a party of Comanche and Kiowa families, about sixty members in all. The Indians were on their way to visit the "Capitán Grande" at Fort Gibson. On seeing the Gregg train, they had supposed it to be Colonel Chouteau bringing fresh goods and presents. They were disappointed and much grieved to learn that Chouteau had died the previous winter. At Gregg's request, Tabaqueena was provided a sheet of paper upon which he drew a map of the prairie, reflecting his thorough knowledge of the whole Mexican frontier as it bordered the United States.[3]

Tabaqueena went on with his entourage toward Fort Gibson, but he later turned back with a small party and rejoined Gregg's caravan for a time as it moved westward on the dividing ridge between the main Canadian and the North Canadian. Eighty miles west of Fort Holmes the travelers reached an area of "numerous spring-fed rills and gurgling pools" filled with fish.[4] Gregg believed this location, which he named Spring Valley, was near the site of the James-McKnight unfinished fort of 1823.

The travelers were now encountering buffalo, which provided them with fresh meat, along with deer, turkey, and grouse in bountiful numbers as the caravan continued on between the two rivers to the big northward bend of the Canadian near what is now Taloga. During this part of the trip they met with a Kiowa who was living in the brush with another man's wife; the traders were threatened by a large prairie fire. Tabaqueena having departed, the traders headed west on a course that ran through the sandy shin-oak country south of present-day Arnett and crossed the 100th meridian boundary between the United States and Mexico near Shattuck.[5]

In the vicinity of Lipscomb, Texas, Gregg and his companions met a friendly party of Comanches on June 5. With the Canadian to the south and Wolf Creek to the north, the Americans established a camp and held a talk with a Comanche principal chief and nine others. The principal chief was a man of about fifty, small in stature. He wore a pair of long, white cotton hose and a tall, red feather that marked his status as the headman of the tribe. Gregg did not give his name.

The Comanches refused to smoke the calumet. However, once they learned that the white men were Americans and not Texans or Mexicans, they were persuaded to take a few puffs from a Mexican cigar. Gregg presented gifts of scarlet cloth, vermilion, tobacco, and beads to the chief. The Comanches indicated their desire to establish trading relations with the Americans.[6]

Josiah Gregg's Camp Comanche in the northeastern corner of the Texas Panhandle. (Josiah Gregg, *Commerce of the Prairies*

The Indians departed "Camp Comanche" on the following morning. Lieutenant Bowman also concluded that he and his men were beyond the limits of their jurisdiction and were required to return to Fort Gibson. The dragoons shouted their farewells and began their march back to the east. Gregg and the others could not have realized that within a few weeks the likable young officer would die at Fort Gibson.

More Comanches were met shortly. Among them was a woman of Mexican appearance. Addressing her in Spanish, Gregg learned that she had been captured by the Comanches in the area of Matamoros. She was now married to a Comanche man and had no desire to return to her people. Another Mexican captive, a boy of ten to twelve years of age, was also interviewed. He had been captured four years before; and he, too, showed no interest in being ransomed from his owner, who, the boy knew, would not sell him. Gregg believed that the youngster had been taken during a raid by some three hundred Comanches on the Mexican city of Parral in

1835. The Comanches had killed a large number of people and carried off many captives at that time.[7]

To conduct trade with the prairie tribes, Gregg noted, Mexican traders and hunters—Comanchéros—had only one route from Santa Fe. That was across the flat, arid region of the Texas Panhandle, which was particularly difficult to travel during the dry season. Watering holes were often fifty to eighty miles apart and hard to find. "Hence the Mexican traders and hunters, that they might not lose their way and perish from thirst, once staked out this route across the plain, it is said; whence it has received the name of *El Llano Estacado*, or the Staked Plain."[8]

Gregg and his trading party reached Santa Fe without further incident. He continued on from there to Chihuahua, Mexico, where he spent the winter of 1839–1840. On February 25, 1840, he set out from Santa Fe for the United States with twenty-eight wagons, forty-seven men, and a Comanche who served as a guide. They also drove a herd of some two hundred mules and three hundred sheep and goats. On this return trip, Gregg hoped to blaze a new trail south of the Canadian River.

On March 23 the caravan crossed the 100th meridian and camped just east of Antelope Hills, which Gregg called the Boundary Mountains. By March 29 they were in the vicinity of Spring Valley again, and on April 22 they reached Van Buren. This was Gregg's last trip to New Mexico, though he made another excursion to the prairies the following summer and visited among the Comanches and other tribes.[9]

Five years after his journey, Gregg published his book *Commerce of the Prairies*. It not only offered excellent descriptions of the Plains and New Mexican cultures of that day, but it also was filled with observations on natural science, human nature, and the difficulties of wagon-train travel across the prairie. The book would serve as an invaluable guide for many westward travelers in the years to come.[10]

Capitalizing, perhaps, on Gregg's reopening of the Canadian River route to Santa Fe, a party headed by Jesse Chisholm used the road to journey to far-off California in the fall of 1839. Chisholm traveled with a passport issued to him by General Arbuckle at Fort Gibson. On the return trip, Chisholm purchased a Negro slave boy from the Comanches, taking him back to Edwards's trading post at the mouth of Little River.[11]

During the summer of 1840 Victor Tixier, a twenty-five-year-old Frenchman who was vacationing from his medical studies in Paris, joined an Osage caravan in Missouri for a hunting tour into western Kansas and Indian Territory. His account of the experience is perhaps the most detailed and authentic of any writer to visit this part of the early West. Nowhere is there to be found a fuller view of the Osage Indians or the mode of frontier life of the time.[12]

Traveling with Tixier were two other Frenchmen as well as James Trudeau of St. Louis; Pierre Papin, agent for the American Fur Company, who resided among the Osages; and two half-blood brothers, Baptiste and Joseph Mongrain. The party set forth from the Osage village of Nion-Chou in southwest Missouri on June 4, joining a large entourage of mounted Grand Osage warriors, women, and children. The Indians drove with them a herd, by Tixier's estimate, of some three thousand horses and were accompanied by some fifteen hundred dogs.

Their route was to the Verdigris River of southeastern Kansas, where a hunting camp was established. From there the expedition headed due west on the Osage war road that led to the Arkansas River. Although Tixier is not precise on the route of the march, the Osage trail is believed to have intersected the Arkansas in the vicinity of present-day Wichita.

After a short stay in a temporary camp, the Osages forded the river to the prairie beyond. A vanguard of warriors preceded the long file of elders, women, and children on horseback. In travois fashion, packhorses dragged the arches and poles needed for construction of brush lodges on the treeless plains. As the march continued westward, the discovery of buffalo carcasses indicated that the Little Osages were hunting just ahead. Soon, however, the Osage trailed off to the north, and Tixier's party continued on westward where the herds were yet undisturbed.

During the trip Tixier, who made every attempt himself to be "Osage" while on the prairie, was recording a narrative picture of the Osages in full: their hunting grounds milieu, customs, amusements, attitudes, and social mores. He described the Osage reverence for the dead, the servitude of their women, the hunting expertise and horsemanship of their warriors, the ever-hungry wolf-dogs of the tribe, the male penchant for self-decoration, the organization of Osage war parties under partisan leaders, sexual and marital habits, the enormous dependency of the tribe on the horse, and colorful accounts of the Osage hunting village on the move.

Well beyond the Arkansas, the Osages encountered a Kansa hunting camp and for a time joined that tribe, with which the Osages were now allied. It gave Tixier a chance to observe the pretty Kansa girls, who displayed little modesty while bathing in the river alongside the men. Joining in a smoke with the Kansa chief, White Feather, Tixier enjoyed a meal of broiled beef and a dish of dried pumpkin mixed with beans, plus a cup of coffee that had been mixed with roasted acorns

───➤

Explorations of the 1840s *(opposite page)*

1. Tixier—1840	6. Gilpin—1848
2. Boone—1843	7. Buford—1848
3. Eldredge—1843	8. Marcy—1849
4. Butler/Stanley—1843	9. Michler—1849
5. Abert—1845	

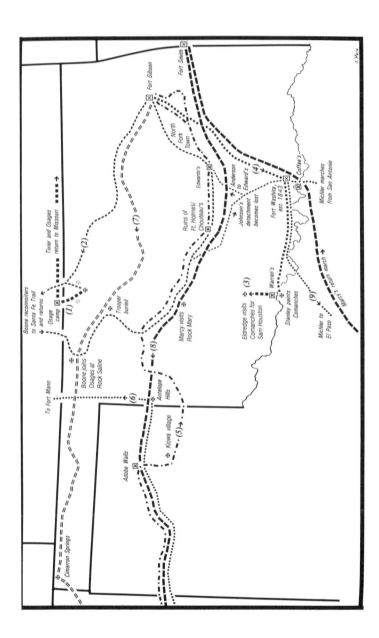

S. Heis

Fort Smith

Fort Gibson

North
Fork
Town

Edwards'

Ruins of
Ft. Holmes/
Chouteau's

Anderson
to
Edwards'   (4)

Johnson's
detachment
becomes lost

Coffee's

Fort Washita,
est. 1843

Michler marches
from San Antonio

Tixier and Osages
return to Missouri

(2)

(7)

Warren's

Eldredge visits
Comanches for
Sam Houston   (3)

Stanley paints
Comanches

Michler to
El Paso   (9)

Marcy's return march

Boone reconnoiters
to Santa Fe Trail
and returns

Osage
camp

(1)

Trooper
buried

Marcy visits
Rock Mary

(8)

To Fort Mann

Boone joins
Osages at
Rock Saline

(6)

Antelope
Hills

Kiowa village

(5)

Adobe Walls

Cimarron Springs

and sweetened with maple syrup. One of the chief's two wives was a woman of such distinction that Tixier drew a sketch of her.

The French tourists also had the chance to take part in a buffalo hunt. When scouts sighted a large herd, the order went out in the camp that no one would fire a gun. The penalty would be a flogging by one of the camp "soldiers," who carried long whips. Under the lead of the Partisan, the Osage village moved off at dawn in good order. Three stray buffalo were left untouched for fear of frightening the main herd. Now the village was sent aside to camp on an out-of-the-way stream while the hunters mounted their horses bareback and rode off in a line behind the soldiers and the commanding Partisan.

When the main herd spotted the hunters, it began moving off. Now the Partisan sounded his war cry, and the charge was on. The hunters galloped after the buffalo in a mad chase, bowmen and riflemen to the right of the animals, those with spears or pistols to the left. Even when the enraged buffalo bull would turn to fight, his tail risen and bent stiffly in brutish defiance, the Indian hunter never hesitated. He depended on his well-trained horse to evade the bull's horns. Seldom was more than one arrow needed for a kill, while generally several bullets were required.

By the end of June the Osage hunters were well out onto the prairies of southwestern Kansas. Now tribal leaders decided that the tribes would head southeast for the Grand Saline. A howling set up by the camp dogs one night caused much concern that a Pawnee war party might be in the area. Tixier was witness to the Osage ritual of "striking the post," a ceremony in which each warrior came forward to a red post that had been set up in camp and struck it with his tomahawk. After doing so, the warrior extended his hands toward the post and recounted his previous acts of courage and his hatred for the Pawnees.

The warriors appeared before a war leader, who selected from among them the ones he wanted for a war party. The chosen warriors then went to their lodges and painted their entire bodies with charcoal. They bedecked themselves with costumes of crow's beaks, swan's down, eagle feathers, buffalo tails, gourds filled with pebbles, skins of white animals, wings of birds, small bells, and other paraphernalia. Thus prepared, the warriors faced off in two lines and began their gyrating war dance to the accompaniment of beating drums, reed flutes, and singing.

The war dancing over, the Osages moved south, leaving the broad prairie country and entering a desolate area of ragged hills and deep ravines. From here a party of thirty warriors was dispatched to scout the Rock Saline on the Cimarron. They returned a few nights later with big lumps of rock salt hanging from their pommels. Tixier wrote of the salines: "The salines cause much trouble among the red tribes. Each one claims it has the right to them. . . . Near the latter [Rock Saline] is a huge red cedar which the Pawnee worship fervently. The warriors frequently bring all kinds of offerings, and even make sacrifices to it. This tree doubtless is for the Pawnee the manitou of the saline. This is the one place where the Osage go most frequently."[13]

After taking time to chase the numerous wild horses that ranged in the region and capturing many, the Osages moved on toward the Grand Saline. Now at mid-July the expedition feasted on the abundant supply of wild sand plums. On July 20 the Osages encamped on Medicine Lodge Creek near the Kansas-Oklahoma border some twenty-five miles from Grand Saline. Tixier described the location in great detail: "the prairie arid and rolling . . . the horizon bordered by very high ridges . . . several rivers winding between the hills . . . dried salt marshes with a white crust that the horses licked while walking . . . an abundance of antelope, elk, buffalo, deer, black bears, and grizzlies."[14]

For several days the Osages waited for the sign of smoke from the saline that would foretell the presence of the Comanches. Finally when no smoke signal was seen, the Osages themselves set fire to the prairie to herald their own presence. With the main camp remaining there, Tixier and a party of fifty to sixty horsemen, each carrying skin bags for gathering the salt, departed two hours before sunrise to make a one-day visit to Grand Saline.

A stint of dry weather had crystallized the salt into layers sometimes four inches thick and made the conditions ideal for gathering. As they approached the saline, a heavy mist and the rising sun produced mirages where even small piles of buffalo dung were thought to be buffalo herds grazing in the distance. While some sacked salt, others hunted buffalo. After a steak feast, the party galloped home, stopping only to top the meal at a stand of tasty wild plums.

In camp the Osage women cleaned the salt by boiling it in large basins. Plagued by heavy, frightening storms, the Osages decided to return to Missouri. En route they hunted buffalo and wild turkey along Bluff Creek. Bloody battles between the Osages and Comanches had occurred there in earlier times, Tixier was told. During one such battle in 1830, the great Osage warrior Bahabeh had been killed, and the tribe knew the stream by his name. During still another fight, many men of both nations had been left unburied on the ground. Tixier had hoped to visit the site and gather up skulls; but the Osages were moving on, and there was not enough time.

Crossing the flooded Arkansas was particularly difficult. Boats made of the buffalo-skin lodge coverings were constructed, and the children, puppies, and luggage were towed across. Some, like Tixier, forded the swollen stream on horseback, but others—men, women, horses, and dogs—were obliged to swim. The expedition reached Nion-Chou in early August. Tixier and his companions were back in Paris, France, by October 24, possessors of the rare experience of having lived the life of an Osage Indian on the western prairies of North America.

During the winter of 1841–1842 the eastern portion of Indian Territory was toured by Major Ethan Allen Hitchcock.[15] He had been instructed to report on the condition of the Indian tribes that had recently been removed to the territory. Arriving at Fort Smith on November 22, 1841, Hitchcock began an investigation that took him through the Cherokee, Creek, and Choctaw-Chickasaw Nations. His scathing report not only provides evidence on the scandalous treatment and conditions of the immigrant tribes but also records much detail of the region and its inhabitants.

During the spring of 1842 the Cache Creek region was visited by a man whose fame would outlast most others of his day. This was Sequoyah, inventor of the Cherokee alphabet. Guided by his son Teesee and a Cherokee named Oo-chee-ah, or the Worm, Sequoyah was on a pilgrimage to Mexico, where he wished to persuade dissident Cherokees to return to their Nation in Indian Territory. Having become ill, the elderly Sequoyah was taken in by a benevolent Keechi chief, who fed and comforted him. After a brief rest, Sequoyah continued on to Mexico, where he soon died.[16]

North-central Oklahoma was explored once again during the summer of 1843, this time by an American military expedition under Captain Nathan Boone. Brigadier General Zachary Taylor, commanding the Second Military Department at Fort Smith, wished to establish better control between the Arkansas and Red rivers and to investigate the potentially valuable salines. Boone's resulting reconnaissance would extend from Fort Gibson northward to the Santa Fe Trail in Kansas and back through western Oklahoma.[17]

Boone and his brother Daniel had once operated a saline in Missouri at what became known as Boone's

Lick. This background supported his choice as leader of such an exploration. Taylor further ordered him to be on the lookout for renegade white marauders from Texas who were attacking and ravaging trading caravans on the Santa Fe Trail.[18]

On leaving Fort Gibson, Boone's detachment consisted of sixty dragoon regulars and two other officers. One of the officers was Lieutenant Abraham Buford, who authored the expedition's journal.[19] Some seventy-five miles up the Arkansas, they were joined by Lieutenant Abraham R. Johnston, Lieutenant Richard H. Anderson, Assistant Surgeon Josiah Simpson, and twenty-seven men.

Departing Fort Gibson on May 14, 1843, Boone's command marched northwest up the Arkansas River. Pushing on through the southern tip of Osage County, the detachment crossed the Arkansas to its west bank and moved on an Indian trail across the Black Bear, Red Fork, and Salt Fork rivers. The dragoons witnessed numerous deer and antelope but saw no buffalo, despite the presence of numerous old buffalo wallows and bones bleaching on the prairie. The disappearance of the buffalo from this grazing area caused Buford to comment portentiously on the extinction of the American bison: "In a few years they will be known as a rare species."[20]

On May 26 the dragoons passed near present-day Ponca City before swinging to the west along the north bank of the Salt Fork. Passing the sites of present-day Tonkawa and Lamont, they encountered the carcasses of buffalo southwest of the Medford area. Scouts thought that the late spring of that year had caused the animals to starve. Turning northward, Boone crossed the Kansas border near Manchester on May 29. On this day he met his first Indians of the trip, an Osage hunting party that had just killed twenty-five buffalo in the area.

Upon being told by the Indians that the Salt Plains were near, Boone decided to encamp on Bluff Creek and procured an Osage guide to lead him there. But during the night the picket ropes of ten horses and two mules were cut and the animals stolen. The Osages said that they, too, had had some ponies stolen and blamed the Pawnees.

Boone took two officers and thirty men and followed the trail of the animals at a hard gallop for some thirty miles before losing it in a sandy area grazed by a herd of buffalo. The dragoons suspected that it was really the Osages who had taken the stock. Boone confronted the Indians, saying that they would not be permitted to go on with their hunt until the animals had been returned. The Osages responded by taking him to find the Pawnee trail, but the one found was made by shod horses and was considered a false lead.

With the command in camp on Bluff Creek, Boone with another officer and two guides rode southwest to a butte from which they could view the Salt Plains in the distance. Fearing Comanches, they returned without visiting the region. On the following day Boone led a large portion of his unit back to the saline. There he and his men experienced the effects of mirages that made buffalo bones appear as large, white animals and caused the men to see nonexistent buffalo standing in pools of water.

Returning to the Bluff Creek camp and moving on from there, Boone surprised a small party of Osages, one of whom was riding one of the stolen mules. Although Boone took away all of their guns, bows, arrows, and ponies, the Osages refused to divulge the location of their camp or promise to bring in the other animals. The Indians finally departed on foot to the south, while the dragoons continued on their northerly course, crossing the Arkansas River at the site of Hutchison, Kansas. On June 5 they reached the Little Arkansas junction of the Santa Fe Trail.

This was the place where New Mexican merchant Don Joe Antonio Chavez had been robbed and killed the year before. Chavez was captured by a band of Texas border ruffians while traveling to St. Louis with a load of valuable furs in two wagons and carrying between $10,000 and $12,000 in specie and bullion. He and his five servants were murdered in cold blood and their money and goods taken. The Texans, led by John McDaniel and his brother, had come north to join others in attacking Mexican traders on the Santa Fe Trail. Eventually the McDaniels were captured and hanged.

Now turning to the west, Boone recrossed the Arkansas River and moved along the south bank through country heavy with buffalo and elk. The dragoons enjoyed some excellent hunting near Great Bend. However, misfortune struck during a buffalo chase. Lieutenant Johnston's rifle, which was slung to the side of his saddle, accidentally discharged and shot the officer in the foot. The command lay in camp at Great Bend from June 13 to June 21.

During this time the party was met by another dragoon command from Fort Leavenworth under Captain Philip St. George Cooke. The dragoons were escorting a forty-seven unit wagon train in protection against both Texas marauders and Indians. Boone and his men also encountered a wagon train under William Bent, operator of Bent's Fort on the upper Arkansas River. The trader was taking a load of furs and robes and a herd of cattle from his fort near the mountains to market in Missouri.

Carrying the wounded Johnston in a wagon along with a private named Bean who suffered "illness of the brain," Boone turned southward on June 22 with the intention of locating Salt Rock. In passing through present Pratt County, Kansas, they met a large party of Osages under Chief Black Dog. The Indians were friendly and offered to accompany the dragoons to Salt Rock. But Boone was suspicious of them and went his own way. On June 29 the dragoons camped among the sand dunes and gypsum hills just north of present-day Freedom, Oklahoma.

The detachment marched to Rock Saline the next morning and made camp nearby. Boone and his men spent the next two days exploring the site. A clean, white salt crust, often an inch thick, covered the surface of a riverbed a mile in width. On Sunday July 2 search parties went looking for the salt rock, but found nothing that matched their expectations. The most interesting formation was a cave that "appeared to be one immense salt spring of water so much concentrated that as soon as it reaches the point of breaking forth it begins depositing salt."[21] Osage Chief Talle, whose band arrived and camped with the dragoons, confirmed what Sibley had been told in 1811—that rain usually washed away the crystallized salt but that the sun would bring it back in a few days.

The dragoons, uncomfortable with the Indians as the Indians were with them, broke camp on July 3 and marched down the north bank of the Cimarron. They took time out to stop and celebrate the Fourth of July by roasting and curing buffalo meat and resting in camp east of present-day Waynoka. On July 6 at a camp on the west bank of the Cimarron northeast of present Fairview, Private Bean died. He was buried at the foot of a cottonwood tree on which his name was cut. A small creek nearby was named Dragoon Creek in his honor.

Pushing across the North Canadian to the main Canadian, Boone explored his way along the river southeastward, camping on July 17 near present-day Minco. Fourteen miles east of there, on July 18, Lieutenant Johnston and his company departed for Fort Washita. On July 21 Boone's unit reached the hilltop where Fort Mason had once stood. The men visited the ruins of Chouteau's trading post four miles away. From there the regiment followed the old military road laid out by Lieutenant Seaton in 1835 along the north bank of the Canadian, finding it in extremely bad condition.

The dragoons had lived on buffalo meat for the past two months; but being out of the buffalo range now, their food supply was running very low. To their good fortune, they came upon a Creek village in what is now southern Seminole County. The Creeks there had good farms and an abundance of stock. The Indians supplied food to the famished soldiers during a respite in a beautiful grove of oaks near a spring.

After resting there for a day, the dragoons pushed on for Edwards's store. En route a soldier named Seiter was killed when a loaded rifle was accidentally knocked down and discharged, striking the man in the back. Seiter was buried on the north bank of Little River just north of the old Seminole town of Sasakwa.

Edwards's place was reached the following day. Here, Boone's diarist noted, was a large tree carved with a finger pointing to where the soldiers of the Leavenworth expedition had died in a sick camp and were buried. The dragoons learned at Edwards's that Johnston's detachment had become lost in the hill country of the Blue River and had run out of provisions. Leaving Johnston and five men with their wagon, Anderson had come to Edwards's store for food and help.

Boone and his men marched for Fort Gibson, anxious to arrive now as they neared their home base. They reached the post on July 31 and formed on the parade grounds after seventy-nine days in the saddle. It had been a grueling ride, the main product of which was the descriptive journal produced by Lieutenant Buford.[22]

Even as Boone was ending his reconnaissance, a small Texas party made its way into the southwestern region of Indian Territory. Joseph C. Eldredge, superintendent of Indians affairs for the Republic of Texas, had been sent by Republic president Sam Houston to work out treaty arrangements with the tribes that frequented north Texas. Of particular concern were the then-powerful and hostile Comanches. Eldredge was accompanied by Thomas Torrey of Torrey's Brazos

River trading house and guided by several Delaware frontiersmen.²³

Eldredge crossed the Red River on July 9, passed by Warren's trading post at the conflux of the Red River and Cache Creek. Established by trader/merchant Abel Warren around 1840, the remote palisaded fort served as a convenient meeting place for frontier traders and the prairie tribes of western Indian Territory and northern Texas until it was closed in 1846.²⁴ A visitor to the post, Colonel William J. Weaver of Fort Smith, described a frontier scene there:

> We were aroused one morning by whoops and yells and the trampling of horses around the enclosure. Several hundred Comanches had arrived and many were setting up their buffalo skin lodges close by the fort. Young men dashed around on horseback, old women were shrieking and children were chattering and playing. Little columns of "slow rising smoke" were seen above the gypsy kettles suspended from tripod sticks. Young women were "toting" water in water skins on their backs, while other girls led ponies laden with calf-skin water bags. Women were stretching and pegging buffalo skins on the ground and scraping them. Others were unloading buffalo meat from the ponies and cutting it in slices for frying. Many of the young men were staking out their horses and rubbing them. Old dignitaries stood around, smoking and waiting for the kettle to stew. Our stock of horses and cattle were driven into the enclosure, where they were secured in the sheds inside, and the gates were carefully closed and securely fastened.²⁵

Eldredge moved on to a Wichita village further up the creek, where he conferred with a Wichita chief before moving on to a nearby Keechi village. There he found a portion of the command of Colonel Jacob Snively that had gone north from Texas across Indian Territory to pillage Mexican trade along the Santa Fe

Trail in Kansas. A command of U.S. Dragoons had forced the command to surrender and retreat back to Texas.

Eldredge eventually located a Comanche village on the west side of the Wichita Mountains. He and his party were well treated by the head chief, Pah-hah-yuco, despite the wish of many of the Comanche tribesmen to kill the Texans as revenge for the 1840 massacre of Comanche chiefs at San Antonio. The Comanches' deep, abiding distrust of the Texans prevented the tribe from attending the ensuing treaty council held at Bird's Fort north of present-day Fort Worth, Texas.

On November 20, 1843, Cherokee agent Pierce M. Butler, who was serving as a U.S. commissioner, set out from Fort Gibson to conduct a council with the Comanches and other tribes along the Red River. Butler's party, which included artist John Mix Stanley, rode south to newly established Fort Washita, where they were joined by Lieutenant Anderson and a company of dragoons. Heavy rains held them at the post for a time before they pushed on up the Red River to Warren's trading post. On December 3 Butler set up camp opposite the mouth of Cache Creek and sent out messengers to persuade the Indians to come in.[26]

The Comanches arrived the next evening under Chief Buffalo Hump. Pah-hah-yuco, they said, could not come. He was in mourning over the death of his son, who had been killed in a fight with Mexicans. Pah-hah-yuco had burned five of his six magnificent lodges, killed nearly all of his horses and mules, and thrown aside all of his ornaments and wearing apparel, keeping only his robe. "I must cry and mourn till the green grass grows," the chief had said. "I have scattered ashes on my head. I can do nothing during the season of my grief."[27]

In addition to the Comanches, the Wacos, Kichais, Caddos, Anadarkos, Ionies, and Tawakonis arrived—

only the Wichitas and Kiowas were absent. Butler made no peace agreements with the Indians, but laid a foundation with the Plains tribes for future efforts by the United States. Possibly the greatest contribution of the journey was the paintings made by artist Stanley, who painted several Comanche men and women in addition to prairie and camp scenes.[28] "This gallery, as a work of art, deserves patronage, and, as laying the foundation for a gallery to show forth the truthfulness, the resources of our great West," insisted a man who had viewed Stanley's work on exhibit in Washington, D.C. "It is worth a hundred statistical reports as a means of useful information."[29] Tragically, many of Stanley's paintings were destroyed in a Smithsonian Institution fire in 1865, though a few remain to provide scenes of early Oklahoma and its native life.

Abert's March

In the fall of 1845 Captain John C. Fremont arrived at Bent's Fort on the Arkansas River of present-day Colorado on his third exploring expedition across the continent. While there, he assigned West Point graduate Lieutenant James W. Abert, son of John J. Abert, chief of the U.S. Topographical Corps, to lead a party from Bent's Fort to Fort Gibson via the Canadian River. Abert was also to branch off from the Canadian and explore the headwaters of the Washita River.

Abert afterward believed that he had done so. But, in fact, it was not the Washita that Abert followed into what is now Oklahoma. Just as Long had mistaken the Canadian for the Red River, so Abert and his men mistook the North Fork of the Red River for the Washita. The party was guided by the famous mountain man Thomas "Broken Hand" Fitzpatrick, but this region of the West was entirely new to him.

Abert's march was nonetheless an interesting and revealing journey across the Texas Panhandle and the

James W. Abert led a difficult march from Bent's Fort in Colorado eastward along the Canadian River to Fort Gibson in 1845. (*National Cyclopaedia of American Biography*)

buffalo range of western Oklahoma, all of which was still dominated by the Plains tribes. Unbeknown to Abert and others at the time, his expedition was actually the first U.S. exploration of the northernmost headwaters of the Red River, a feat that Captain Randolph B. Marcy set out to accomplish seven years later.

Abert's party consisted of twenty-eight soldiers, two black servants, and three guides, with Lieutenant William G. Peck, also a West Pointer, as second in command. Fitzpatrick would be appointed the first agent for the Cheyennes and Arapahos of the upper

Arkansas the following year. Two other guides were Bent traders John Hatcher and Caleb Greenwood. The group was equipped with four ox-drawn wagons, the first wagons to travel the entirety of the Canadian route; fifty-six mules; seven horses; and four tents. Their scientific apparatus were very limited. Abert had managed to obtain only a sextant and a chronometer for determining latitude and longitude. Eight head of cattle were driven along to serve as food.[1]

Fremont, who wished to eliminate any competition for the publication of his own exploration records, had issued orders against the keeping of any private journals. Nevertheless, a young Missourian named Isaac Cooper maintained a day-by-day record of the expedition. In publishing it, he used the nom de plume François Des Montaignes. Cooper's account adds colorful details to Abert's official transcript of the journey.[2]

Before departing Bent's place, Abert had the opportunity to attend a peacemaking council among the Cheyennes, Arapahos, and a visiting delegation of Delawares, who had recently killed fifteen Cheyenne warriors in a fight. During the council—which was interpreted by Bill Guerrier (Gary), father of Edmund Guerrier, for whom Geary, Oklahoma, is named—the Delawares invited the Cheyennes to attend a grand council at the Salt Plains of Indian Territory, where they could work out a peace agreement. Although the Cheyennes and Arapahos had made peace with the Comanches and Kiowas at Bent's Fort in 1840, they were still concerned about venturing below the Arkansas.[3]

On August 18, 1845, Abert and his exploring party moved down the Arkansas to Purgatory River and then southward down that stream. Most of the men were mounted on mules and rode with their rifles ready across their pommels. The wagons set a slow but steady pace as they moved through Raton Pass. There they met an Apache mule-and-dog train and visited an encampment of Cheyennes. On one occasion Lieutenant Peck's mule became frightened and galloped away with a sketchbook containing notes of the march. The mule was recaptured only after a six-mile chase.

The company had experienced a small hailstorm in coming through the pass; then as the men approached the plains of eastern New Mexico on August 28, a sudden drenching rainstorm turned into a barrage of hail "as large as musketballs."[4] The storm drove the men to find shelter beneath the wagons.

Now the travelers began to see herds of wild horses, and there was a strong awareness among them of entering the land of the Comanches, though actually Kiowas were dominant in the Texas Panhandle at this time. Abert and his men knew that the Comanches were still infuriated over the killing of their chiefs in San Antonio, and white men were at great risk in their country. Frontier-wise Fitzpatrick directed the building of a log corral interlaced with branches for protection at night. The men all slept with their loaded guns at hand, muzzles to their feet, prepared to be awakened at any moment by the war cry of Comanche attackers.

On September 3 the explorers followed an "ancient trail" along the north bank of the Canadian.[5] The trail had probably been made by New Mexican Comanchéros who came with their two-wheel carts to trade with the Indians. Abert's pace was slowed by the rough country, which greatly hampered wagon travel. Increasingly the men could see distant figures of Indian scouts sitting their horses atop the bluffs rimming the river valley and watching their movements. One group of Indians finally responded to the display of a white flag and came riding down to meet the party. They proved to be Kiowas, who were accompanied by some Crows, their old allies on the headwaters of the Missouri River. The joint party had just returned from a raid as far south as Chihuahua, Mexico.

Hatcher, who had been at Bent's Fort Adobe post on the Canadian until recently when it was abandoned, was well liked by the Kiowas. Using some wrapping paper in which to roll some tobacco, he constructed the Indians some "segaritos" to smoke. Abert, who found the Kiowas brave, energetic, and honest, was amazed at the way they chatted, laughed, and joked— much in contradiction to his preconceived notions about Indians.[6]

Like other tribes of the Plains, the Kiowas wore buckskins, supplemented by blankets and robes. The ornamentation of the men was particularly noticeable. Their hair was braided into long queues, sometimes lengthened by the addition of horsehair until they reached the ground. The queues were usually decorated with convex silver discs. On the heel of their moccasins, the men wore a fringed appendage some eight to ten inches in length. The Kiowa women followed the dress of northern tribes—leather cape, tunic, leggings, and beaded moccasins.[7]

The expedition was due west of present-day Borger, Texas, on September 13, when they met a party of conical-hatted Comanchéros who were on a trading excursion to the Indians. Two days later, three miles above the site of Adobe Walls and near the sand hills where Oñate may have made his departure from the Canadian, Abert decided it was time to cut away southward to the headwaters of the Washita as Fremont had ordered. At this point Hatcher and Greenwood began their return to Bent's Fort. The Kiowas also departed.

Abert did not indicate that he visited Fort Adobe. But Isaac Cooper must have, for he described the abandoned trading post as "a series of rude log or block houses" to which the Comanches and Kiowas came annually to traffic their hunting spoils.[8] The fort was burned by the traders, Cooper said, to prevent other traders from using it.

Now bearing south along Spring Creek (Abert called it Arrow Creek) to Red Deer Creek (Abert's Elk Creek), the travelers were forced to search downstream for a couple of miles to find water. A happy-natured young Kiowa named Tiah-na-zi, who had come along as a temporary guide, instructed them on how to reach the Washita (to him, Buffalo Creek). He also warned them to beware of the Comanches. He said that they sometimes spotted stragglers and lanced them in sight of friends whose mules were too slow to provide help. He also warned that the Comanches might mistake them for Texans. Moreover, Comanche chief Red Jacket, who held an especially great hatred for the Texans, was camped nearby at Antelope Hills.[9]

Abert's march took him through the area of present-day Pampa, Texas, and on southward to the North Fork of the Red River, having unknowingly bypassed the headwaters of the Washita, which were to the east of his march. It was a hot, dry, grueling trek that was lengthened by growing doubts about the directions the young Kiowa had given them.

The heat simmered off the Llano Estacado, and mirages formed before the travelers' eyes, magnifying rabbits into deer, buffalo skulls into Indian warriors on white steeds, dry land into glimmering pools of water. An Indian rider hovering along the distant horizon had the appearance of a giant. Finally the ground began to fall away, and before dusk a long line of bluffs presented the hopes of a river. With parched mouths and throats, the men pushed across the badly cut terrain to discover only scorching, dry sand. Downstream some two miles, however, they located a pool of precious water.[10]

As they moved down the stream, the travelers saw more and more Indians on the surrounding bluffs. The foreboding of a Comanche attack hung over the small band. On the night of September 17 a sentry sounded the call of "Turn out! Turn out!" He had seen figures moving about in the dark shadows beyond the camp. The men posted themselves for an attack, but none came. Finally the long ears of their mules ceased to stand forward rigidly in alarm, and the men relaxed. Nevertheless, they had lost most of their night's rest.[11]

The next morning the ground seemed to sprout Indians all around. Abert quickly displayed a white flag. The Indians proved to be another band of Kiowas under Chief To-ha-sun, or Little Mountain. The Kiowas were hungry and cold from having spent the night around the camp trying to discern if the strangers were Americans or Texans. The explorers gave the tribesmen tobacco and food.

Little Mountain proved to be very intelligent and helpful. He pointed out the smoothest route for their wagons, though he and his elders were confused by the map that had been made for Abert's party by an Indian at Bent's Fort. The Kiowas were undecided whether the stream they were then on ran into the Red River or the Goo-al-la (Canadian). The old men, women, and children, some wearing Navajo blankets, flocked to the expedition's camp bringing robes to trade. Among them was a captive Spanish woman of great beauty. The Kiowas were sorely disappointed to find that the Tabbyboos had no trade goods.[12]

A number of the Kiowa women had their hair cut short and their faces slashed in mourning for deceased relatives. Little Mountain's very elderly and wrinkled father wore a strange costume combining a sealskin cap from far to the north and a tattered uniform of a Mexican soldier from far to the south. The uniform, as well as the old man's attractive Mexican wife, had been presented to him by Little Mountain. The woman said that she had been a prisoner for four years.[13]

Abert and his men continued on down the North Fork of the Red until it bent sharply toward present-day Shamrock. They left the river there in a course that ran mostly east by north and forded the Sweetwater (known to Abert as Lone Tree or Big Tree Creek) close to its intersection with the 100th meridian. The men feasted on the abundant wild grapes along the river before moving on. Crossing the divide between the Sweetwater and the Washita, on the night of September 23 the expedition camped just east of present-day Cheyenne, Oklahoma, where the Washita makes a horseshoe bend to the north.[14]

They had now entered the heart of the buffalo range, and the size of the herds increased as the travelers advanced toward the Canadian. A large panther was aroused and "made a most picturesque appearance, as he made his retreat over the neighbouring hills."[15] A fawn killed by the party and left near the camp that night was devoured noisily by a bear. Packs of large gray wolves trailed the party along the bed of the river.

The explorers moved northeastward to approach the Canadian at the foot of its northward bend just west of present-day Leedey. Now they were able to see Antelope Hills rising above the horizon some sixteen miles to the west. Abert sketched the hills from there. Buffalo herds provided the group with an ample supple of fresh meat as the men followed the windings of the Canadian eastward along its north bank. They discovered an abandoned Comanche camp northeast of Leedey and near it a spring-fed creek that offered much improved water over that of the Canadian.[16]

Buffalo in great numbers, bear, deer, wild turkey, playful herds of mustangs, and a variety of bird life entertained the explorers as they continued southeast. On one occasion a large, handsome roan stallion dashed up close to the head of their column and pranced slowly alongside in curious observation for a time. Finally he flicked his long tail and galloped off, his mane flowing in the breeze as he joined his drove in the happy luxury of their wild freedom.

The party went into camp on the north bank of the Canadian southwest of present-day Geary on October 1. From there the travelers could see a range of buttes several miles beyond the river that they took, correctly, to be the dividing ridge of the Washita and Canadian.

Abert sketched these also. The next night the explorers experienced their first frost of the season. Despite this, Abert took a bath in the cold channel of the Canadian and returned to camp to enjoy a feast of buffalo brisket, ribs, and marrow bones that had been roasted, broiled, and fried over the "merry campfires" of the four messes.[17]

A drizzling rain set in as the group passed south of the site of today's Oklahoma City and then past those of Moore and Norman to reach the tangled bottom of Chouteau Creek. There on October 9 the party visited the ruins of Fort Holmes and Chouteau's trading post, which Cooper indicated had been erected in 1836 and abandoned in 1839. All that now remained of the fort were three or four upright posts that presided over the two stone chimneys still standing in blackened ruins and the rotting remains of some abandoned wagons.[18]

Cooper and a friend named Rivan, who had lived there as a boy, climbed the chimney to unfurl a handkerchief flag in commemoration. A road overgrown with weeds and bushes was visible leading away from this place where once Indians had camped, dragoons had marched, and frontier traders had unloaded their wagons of barter mercantile. Desolate though the fort was, it was a welcome reminder of civilization to all.

Now the party moved on through the forests of the Cross Timbers, still following the north bank of the Canadian. The men killed what they first thought was a wild hog, but then found that it carried a brand. Later they would learn that Creek trader James Edwards had once sent a white man and two slaves up the river to establish a trading post. A cabin had been built, but the black men deserted it in fear of the Indians. Later the white man's scalped corpse was found amid the charred ruins of the cabin. His hogs, which the Indians would not eat, were left to run wild.[19]

The sunburned, unshaven, and travel-worn party reached Edwards's place at the mouth of Little River on

The Abert party marches along the Canadian River of the Texas Panhandle. (James W. Abert, "Report of an Expedition Led by Lieutenant J. W. Abert")

October 15. The rude collection of huts housed the trading posts of Edwards and Thomas Aird. The latter maintained fields of corn and sweet potatoes. Present also were industrious Creek Indians dressed in colorful shirts of red flannel, sashes, and turbans. Bead-worked pouches hung at their sides. The travelers willingly traded their burdensome powder, lead, and tobacco for foodstuff. Resisting Edwards's invitation to rest and let their mules graze for a few days, Abert took up his march again the following day.

At the mouth of the North Canadian, Abert directed Fitzpatrick to lead the main party on to Fort Gibson. He, Peck, and one soldier then headed east to the conflux of the Canadian and Arkansas rivers to make astronomical observations. After visiting among Cherokees at Webber's Falls for a brief time, the three continued on up the west bank of the Arkansas to Fort Gibson. On the road between Fort Gibson and St. Louis, Abert encountered a steady stream of white-topped wagons headed southwest for Texas.[20]

William Gilpin. (*National Cyclopaedia of American Biography*)

Another incursion by a U.S. military unit occurred during the spring of 1848. Concerned over depredations committed on the Santa Fe Trail in Kansas, Lieutenant Colonel William Gilpin, commanding the newly established post of Fort Mann, conducted what was intended to be a punitive expedition into northwest Indian Territory. He led a force of mule-mounted infantry down the Santa Fe Trail to El Moro, New Mexico, then scoured the country back eastward along the Canadian River, crossing the Texas Panhandle to Antelope Hills. From there he turned northward across Wolf Creek, Beaver Creek, and the Cimarron River, returning to Fort Mann on May 30. This attempt to intimidate the Indians was a wasted effort. Much of the country had been burned off ahead of him, and Gilpin found no Indians and very little game.[21]

These initial military intrusions were prefatory to the opening of two important new wagon roads across Indian Territory. The Texas Trail across eastern Oklahoma would carry a flood of white homesteaders by way of Missouri to the foundling state of Texas. It would also create new white-occupied settlements along its route within the territory. Still another great westward migration would flood the region in 1849 following the discovery of gold in California. The California Road along the Canadian River would serve as a route for many of the gold seekers and enhance the advancement of settlement up that stream within the territory.

The Gold Rush Trails

In the spring of 1849 Captain Randolph B. Marcy and a command of dragoons were providing military escort to a California gold rush caravan along the Canadian River trail. At an encampment one evening the officer overheard a conversation between his two guides, one a Comanche and the other Marcy's highly regarded Delaware scout Black Beaver. Beaver, who had considerably more acquaintance with the world of white people than the other, was instructing the untutored Comanche concerning the roundness of the earth. The Comanche's response was to gaze at the Delaware with intense scrutiny and demand to know if Beaver took him for a child or an idiot.

Black Beaver calmly replied that neither was the case. The white people had found not only that the earth was round but also that it circled the sun. The Comanche remained incredulous. Anyone could look out across the prairie, he argued, and see quite easily that the land was flat. Moreover, his grandfather had

Randolph B. Marcy.
(*Appleton's Cyclo-
paedia of Ameri-
can Biography*)

once ridden to the west end of the earth and had seen
the sun set behind a vertical wall.

Beaver persisted, adding information about steam
engines that powered boats and locomotives and other
amazing things he had seen among white people. The
response of the Comanche to each was an exclamation
that translated roughly into "Hush, you fool!" It was
then that Marcy decided to enter the conversation. He
instructed Black Beaver to tell the Comanche about the
magnetic telegraph. The instrument, he said, could
send a message as far as one thousand miles and obtain
an answer within ten minutes. Beaver listened with
interest but failed to relay the information to the
Comanche. Marcy urged him to do so, but Beaver shook
his head. "I don't think I tell him that, Captain," he
said. "The truth is, I don't believe it myself."[1]

The incident is revealing of the cultural differences
existing between the white person and the Plains
Indian of that day. It also reflects the great changes that
were soon to come following the California gold rush.

Nothing like this covered-wagon invasion had ever crossed the great Central Plains of the Indian and the buffalo before. No longer would the Plains be separate and apart from the rest of the nation; now they would become a connecting link between East and West. Indian Territory was no exception; as Gregg had shown, it offered routes that could be traveled earlier in the spring than those to the north.

Fort Smith and the nearby community of Van Buren, Arkansas, were the jumping off points for most of those who crossed Indian Territory on their way to the gold fields. These two border villages quickly became outfitting Meccas for many who were rushing pell-mell to California. People flocked there from all parts of the thirty states with wagons, horses, oxen, mules, and cattle. The streets were thronged with newcomers to the West. Many dressed in eastern garb or in recently purchased high boots and large "California" hats. All looked out of place here on the frontier's edge. They mingled with the rifle-toting, bearded frontiersmen in soiled buckskins and blanketed Indians whose head feathers stood above the busy mob that swirled in and out of the stores.[2]

Merchants did a large trade in guns and ammunition, yokes and harnesses, canned goods and condensed foods, smoked meats, soap, clothing, water casks, shovels, picks, butcher knives—whatever was needed to survive the long and hazardous trip across the prairie. Horse and mule traders from Indian country drove their herds across the Arkansas River at Fort Smith and sold them at good prices. There were not enough wagons to satisfy the demand, and local residents often found there was no food left in town for themselves.

Men gathered in small conclaves to hear the stories of adventure and hardship related by frontiersmen. They learned how to organize overland companies, talked over their concerns regarding Indians, and shared their excitement over the forthcoming adventure and the great wealth they hoped to find in California. Few of them fully realized the extent of the difficulty they were undertaking—the bad roads made worse in inclement weather, the problems in finding food and forage on the prairie, and the obstacles presented by the mountains they would ultimately have to cross.

Gold had been discovered in California in January 1848, and by September the news had reached the general public in the East. It happened that during this interim period, a military reconnaissance was made of a possible wagon route from Fort Gibson to Santa Fe. The survey was conducted by a company of First Dragoons under Captain Abraham Buford, who had been with Boone's exploring party of 1843.

In July 1848 Buford and his men followed the course of the Arkansas River from Gibson to the Cimarron. They traced that stream to Rock Saline, much the same as the first James-McKnight expedition of 1822. From Rock Saline, Buford cut southwest to the Beaver Creek fork of the North Canadian. He continued along it the length of the Oklahoma Panhandle to the Cimarron Springs of the Santa Fe Trail. En route the dragoons hewed down banks of ravines and constructed bridges for wagon crossings. Arriving in Santa Fe on September 9, he reported back that he had found good camping grounds with an abundance of wood, water, and grass, plus innumerable buffalo.[3]

But it was Gregg's route, which had been publicized by his book *Commerce of the Prairies*, that promoters at Fort Smith and Van Buren hawked. Their advertisements brought a flood of gold rushers pouring into the two villages during the spring of 1849. Some came overland and others via the steamboats that plied the Arkansas River. The resulting surge of business had its profits even for the prairie Indians: "The traders here get their stock from the Creeks and Choctaws who get

Abraham Buford. (U.S. Military Academy)

them from the Comanches who steal them from the Mexicans," observed the *Arkansas State Democrat* of April 27, 1849.

The first gold rush group to depart Arkansas was a band of young Arkansas farmers with a train of pack mules. They left in March 1849 and were soon followed by a St. Louis company, also with pack mules.[4] Hard on their heels was a sixty-five-man party from New York. Well equipped with good wagons, the New Yorkers left Fort Smith on March 26. Thus began what would at times be virtually a continuous line of covered wagons lumbering slowly along the Canadian River. Each night campfires dotted the trail westward along the townless prairie.

In 1849 there were only three embryonic settlements touched by the Canadian road west of Arkansas. The Choctaw agency near present-day Spiro offered several stores for purchasing food and some good camp sites. North Fork Town, located at the mouth of the North Canadian, contained three trading houses amid the Creek settlement there. At the mouth of Little River were the trading houses of Aird and Vore and that of Edwards. These places offered horses, beef, grain, and blacksmithing to travelers. They were the last chance for these invaluable services before travelers reached far, faraway Santa Fe or Albuquerque.[5]

Although now vacant, Chouteau's old trading post at the far side of the Cross Timbers was considered a final gathering point before gold rushers shoved off across the prairie. It was a place to fix axles, tighten the iron rims of wagon wheels, mend harnesses, and shoe horses. Sometimes supplies could be obtained from merchants whose wagons traveled this far with a caravan, such as Aird and Vore of Little River were known to do. Here, too, before venturing off into Indian country, a traveler could post letters to home with a company mail carrier, a trader, or a military person returning to Fort Gibson or Arkansas.

Some who followed Gregg's route along the north bank from Edwards's place found the road extremely difficult. The wagons fought rugged passes, miry ravines, and steep ascents. As a result, a route along the south bank of the river soon became the choice. But when the spring rains came, as they did profusely in 1849, there were no good roads. The heavily laden wagons sank bottom deep into the mud, and the entire line often halted for exasperating delays. Men waded into the mire to heave and pry with poles as drivers cracked their whips and embellished the air with profanity at their straining teams. From Chouteau's westward, the standard route was along the south bank of the Canadian.

Responding to public demands that a military escort be provided for the gold seekers, General Arbuckle appointed Marcy to the task. Marcy was also instructed to survey a railway route as he went. Marcy's command consisted of twenty-six First Dragoons under Lieutenants John Buford and fifty Fifth Infantry troops under Lieutenant Joseph Updegraff and Montgomery P. Harrison—whose brother Benjamin Harrison, president of the United States in 1889, would issue the order opening Oklahoma to settlement. Lieutenant James H. Simpson of the Topographical Corps, who went along as an observer, kept a log of the journey, as did Marcy himself.[6]

The command crossed the Poteau River near Fort Smith on April 4, 1849, with eighteen wagons, a sixteen-pound howitzer, and wheel-mounted traveling forge, each drawn by six mules. Moving to Edwards's, the unit went into camp on the south side of the Canadian, where several days were spent repairing wagons and purchasing cattle and feed. It was there that Marcy hired noted Delaware guide Black Beaver.

Emigrant trains were already ahead and behind when Marcy left Edwards's on May 1 and made his way past the Delaware Mountains and up the Canadian's south bank. Reaching Chouteau's on May 9, the group went into camp to await the arrival of the consolidated 479-member Fort Smith and California Emigrating Company.[7] This large convoy had departed Fort Smith on April 11 with seventy-five ox-drawn wagons and a large stock of riding and packhorses and mules. The slow-moving caravan took the north bank route and suffered much delay because of the poor trail.[8]

Traveling with this party was Dr. John R. Conway of Little Rock, who was taking his wife and family of ten children to California. His oldest child was seventeen-year-old Mary, a vivacious girl who rode a handsome black horse most of the way.[9] Both Buford and Harrison became enamored of the girl and courted her. It was Lieutenant Simpson, however, who suggested that an unusual rock butte west of present-day Hinton, Oklahoma, be named Rock Mary in honor of the girl.

Harrison won the contest for Mary's affection, but her parents rejected an en route wedding. Plans were laid for their marriage in California, but tragedy awaited the young couple before this march was done.

Lieutenant Simpson climbed atop the formation and unfurled a flag as Marcy requested. He was followed by several others who wished to survey the surrounding countryside from the rock's summit. "The rock is situated solitarily in a prairie plain," Simpson wrote, "its height some sixty feet; its base some two hundred feet in diameter. In form it is like a pound-cake well puffed up and partially broken at its centre. Two turret-like projections are seen protruding from its top."[10] (Twenty years later in 1869 General Phil Sheridan and journalist DeB. Randolph Keim would stop to ascend Rock Mary themselves while traveling from newly founded Fort Sill to Fort Supply. The view, Keim would write, was "sublime beyond comparison."[11])

There was great concern among the California gold rushers regarding the Comanches. The tribe had committed numerous depredations in Texas during the preceding winter. However, few of the gold seekers knew that Jesse Chisholm, who traded among the Comanches, had acted as a peacemaker on their behalf. Earlier he had told the Comanches of the invasion of white people that was to take place and secured their promise not to interfere.[12]

Furthermore, Chisholm had invited a band to come to the settlements at Little River and discuss the situation with Seminole agent Marcellus Du Vall and with the Creeks.[13] With the Comanches now convinced that the gold rush invasion of their land meant a profitable trade, both Indian and white traders safely entered the Comanchería to deal for horses and mules to sell to the California immigrants. A group of immigrants following the Gregg route across western Indian Territory in May 1848 was surprised by a friendly visit from a large band of Comanches. The Indians had with them some five thousand mules, which they offered to barter for "anything of value but money."[14]

While traveling just west of Antelope Hills, Marcy was met by four Kiowas on their way to Mexico to steal horses and mules. As he neared Tucumcari, New Mexico, he encountered a large village of Comanches under Chief Is-a-ki-ep, or Wolf Shoulder. The chief expressed a strong friendship for the Americans.

The Comanches were all mounted on strong-looking horses or mules. They wore leggings and moccasins with a buffalo robe or a woven blanket about their waists. Their ears and arms were decorated with large brass rings, while some of the fancier young men had enhanced their attire with bright red cloths, beads, and buffalo-hair queues.[15]

Black Beaver engaged Is-a-ki-ep in a sign-language conversation, and a large crowd gathered around in curiosity. Marcy asked Black Beaver what the chief had to say. Much to his embarrassment, the Delaware explained that the chief had brought two "wives" for the escort commander. Marcy hastily replied that he already had a wife and wished no more. Is-a-ki-ep thought that Marcy was "the strangest man he ever see[n]."[16]

Despite accounts heard in Fort Smith that the Comanches had attacked a gold rush company and killed forty people, the Comanches remained friendly to Marcy's group and to succeeding travelers.[17] Nevertheless, the rule of safety in numbers was a good one for those venturing onto the prairie, as four Germans who left Gibson in July learned. Heading up the Arkansas River route laid out by Buford the summer before, the Germans were just past the site of present-day Tulsa when they met a band of twenty Comanches who were driving a herd of mules. The Indians appeared to be friendly, and the Germans joined them in traveling west for two or three days. On the way half of the Indians departed with the mules, and the rest remained with the Germans until evening. Then they, too, left.[18]

During the night the German who was posted as a sentry was shot through the back with an arrow and killed. An attack by unknown assailants left one of the other three badly wounded. The men fled into the night, leaving behind all of their possessions. For eight days they wandered about the countryside without horses or guns. Their only food was a stray dog that followed them. Finally the three made it to Thomas Aird's store at Little River. There they were fed and their wounds tended.

Later that summer while visiting at Fort Washita, Comanche chief Pa-ha-u-ca insisted that it was the Quapaws who committed the act. The Fort Washita commander thought, as Aird did, that the Comanches were really the guilty ones.[19] Nevertheless, there is no disputing that all in all the California gold rush migration suffered little harassment from the Comanches and other tribes of the region.

Lieutenant Harrison of Marcy's command was not as fortunate. The wagon train escort left the California-bound party at Albuquerque and explored a new route on its return to Fort Smith, blazing a trail across southern New Mexico and central Texas. Near Big Spring in far west Texas, Harrison rode out to investigate a ravine that had caught his curiosity. When he failed to return, a search party was sent out. They found his mangled, nude corpse; he had been scalped and stripped of his clothing.

Black Beaver read the signs that told his expert eye that Harrison had met two Indians, thought to be Kiowas. The officer had dismounted and smoked with them, only to have his gun captured and to be taken prisoner. Tying the young officer on his horse, the Indians led him to some timber, where one of them shot him in the back of the head with his own rifle. Harrison's body was packed with charcoal inside a wagon bed and carried back to Fort Smith for interment.[20]

Upon reaching a branch of the Clear Fork of the Brazos, Marcy's command came across a Comanche village headed by Se-na-co, a "dignified, fine-looking old man."[21] The chief carried letters from Texas Indian agent Robert Neighbors and others testifying to his good will for whites. The Comanches were interrogated concerning Harrison's murder. They insisted that they knew nothing about it and thought that the Kiowas were probably guilty.

Marcy and his detachment arrived at Preston on the Texas bank of the Red River on November 6, crossed the river there on a flat boat, and reached Fort Washita on November 10. While at the fort, Marcy encountered another exploring party under Lieutenant Nathaniel Michler. Having marched north from San Antonio with fourteen civilians and wagons, Michler was searching out a route for an intracontinental railroad under orders from Secretary of War Jefferson Davis.

After failing to recruit the trail-weary Black Beaver for a guide, Michler moved westward along the north bank of the Red River to Beaver Grove in Jefferson County, Oklahoma. Crossing the Red River near present-day Terral, Michler moved on down the ridge separating the Big and Little Wichita rivers of north Texas. Following the general course of Marcy's return route, Michler and his men reached El Paso.[22]

The Gregg route up the Canadian and Buford's Cimarron River road were not the only routes across Oklahoma to California. Another important passage was established by Cherokee gold rushers up the Arkansas River to its juncture with the Santa Fe Trail in Kansas. It was not surprising that the Cherokees, who had been familiar with gold mining in their Georgia past, would be interested in the California rush. As early as February 1849 meetings were held at the Cherokee courthouse in Tahlequah to make plans to go to California.

Considerable interest was expressed at the meetings, and some 130 people, both Indian and white, accumulated at the Grand River saline on April 23 to organize. The Cherokees attending did not like the Canadian route, and some consideration was given to Buford's road. But in the end the largely Indian group headed its forty wagons and four hundred oxen, horses, and mules up the Arkansas River.

Passing the mouth of the Little Arkansas, the site of present Wichita, Kansas, the party struck north to the Santa Fe Trail and followed it west. In Colorado one party continued on the trail toward New Mexico, but one group cut off toward the juncture of Cherry Creek and the South Platte. On June 22, 1849, the Cherokees found traces of gold in the bed of Ralston Creek. Two more days of search, however, failed to reveal more of the precious metal, and the party moved on through Salt Lake City to California. Ten years later, in 1858, another party of Cherokees would return to the Colorado site and ignite the Colorado gold rush.[23]

Still another road to California developed out of the Texas routes of Marcy and Michler. It ran from Fort Smith across the southeastern corner of Indian Territory to Preston, Texas. From there it crossed vast acres of central Texas to El Paso, thence on westward across southern New Mexico and Arizona. This would eventually become the overland mail route serviced by the Butterfield stage line.

The California gold rush trail had pierced the Comanche barrier and laced the prairies with the ominous arteries of white civilization. This was only the beginning.

Military Explorations

Captain Randolph Marcy stood in awe before the gushing spring that issued forth from a chasm at the bottom of Palo Duro Canyon. He and his small group were, he felt certain, the first white men ever to view this natural spa deep in the bowels of the Texas Panhandle. The remoteness of the site, along with the towering rock escarpments of Palo Duro, effectively guarded the spring from happenstance discovery. Marcy's search for the headwaters of the Red River had drawn him irresistibly over the uncharted plains to this place. Discovery of this idyllic spot in the far wilderness filled him with great emotion.[1]

Marcy's 1852 exploration of the Red River was one of several explorations of Oklahoma conducted by the U.S. military at midcentury. The land that only a few years before had been promised as the inviolable domain of the Indian had now caught the interest and curiosity of the U.S. government. These explorations were initiated, in part, to locate sites for frontier forts from which the U.S. military could provide for the removal tribes against the marauding of the tribes of the prairie. These were difficult tasks for the thinly manned and poorly subsidized army.

But in large part the forts served the cause of national expansion. The California gold rush had given impetus to the westward movement. Military escort was needed for the ever-increasing migration and transportation across the Indian-dominated Central Plains. Also making an appearance were surveying crews sent to better define the tribal areas. These usually followed no established trail but cut directly across the land with their wagons, chains, tripods, and notebooks.

The task of surveying the north boundary of the Creek lands in Oklahoma was assigned in 1849 to Lieutenant Lorenzo Sitgreaves, who was assisted by Lieutenant Israel C. Woodruff, both of the U.S. Topographical Corps. Other members included Dr. Samuel W. Woodhouse, a surgeon and naturalist; assistant surveyor and civil engineer Isaac W. Smith; a wagonmaster; and thirty crewmen. Woodhouse would provide the first comprehensive report of the topography, geology, flora, and wildlife of the region and add new species of plants and animals to the knowledge of the day. Under Sitgreaves's direction, the surveying party worked a line eighty miles north from Fort Gibson to the northeast corner of Creek country. There on the banks of the Grand the surveyors found the old Union Mission, established in 1820, now deserted and in ruins, although inhabited by a Cherokee woman whose husband had followed the gold rush to California.[2]

Turning due west, the surveyors camped on September 6 at the site of ten Indian houses that made up the Creek town of Tallassee—today's Tulsa. They paused long enough to witness a Creek stick-ball game before moving on westward to a point known as Bald Eagle Mound, west of present-day Stillwater. Having endured a long streak of rainy weather, Sitgreaves halted the survey for the season on October 20. The party returned via Tallassee and from there followed a course paralleling the Arkansas River back to Fort Gibson.[3]

Completion of the line to the 100th meridian was thus delayed until the next season. During the interim, however, Sitgreaves was assigned elsewhere, and it was left up to Woodruff, an 1836 graduate of West Point, to finish the work.[4]

As preparations were being made to continue the effort in May 1850, the Osages issued a dire threat. If the surveyors came onto their hunting grounds, the Indians said, they would be killed. The threat was not made without cause. The Osages had seen surveyors in Kansas and knew them to be the vanguard of white encroachment. Nor was the warning taken lightly. The surveyors understood well how vulnerable they were on the prairie, as an officer noted: "The men are unavoidably separated a considerable distance from each other or in parties of two or three, and are unable, most of them, to carry arms . . . and are at the mercy of any evil disposed band of Indians they may encounter."[5]

Nonetheless, the survey continued. Two new members were assistants William C. Meyhew and Joseph R. Smith. Meyhew, a pioneer daguerreotypist, would make some of the first photographic impressions in Oklahoma. Joseph Smith, a nineteen-year-old New Yorker who would later become a colonel surgeon in the U.S. Army, maintained a detailed and exuberant diary of the day-to-day events of the survey.[6]

Additionally, there were a wagon master and thirty men, plus some Indian scouts and couriers. The crew included ax men, instrument carriers, flag bearers, chain men, and target men. Thirteen wagons carried

———————————————————————➤

Explorations of the 1850s *(opposite page)*

1. Woodruff—1850   4. Whipple—1853
2. Marcy—1851   5. Johnston—1857
3. Marcy (Red River)—1852   6. Beale—1858

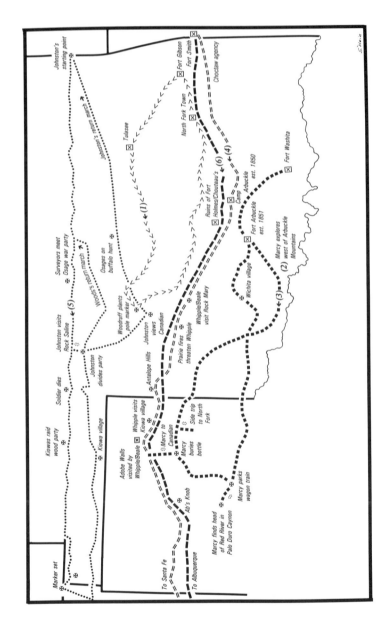

Johnston's starting point

Marker set

To Santa Fe

To Albuquerque

Kiowas raid wood party

Soldier dies

Johnston visits Rock Saline (5)

Surveyors meet Osage war party

Woods's return march

Johnston's return march

Tulasee

(1)

Osages on buffalo hunt

Woodruff plants pole marker

Johnston views Canadian

Johnston divides party

Kiowa village

Adobe Walls visited by Whipple/Beale

Ab's Knob

Marcy finds head of Red River in Palo Duro Canyon

Whipple visits Kiowa village

Marcy to Canadian

Marcy buries bottle

Antelope Hills

Prairie fires threaten Whipple

Whipple/Beale visit Rock Mary

Side trip to North Fork

Marcy parks wagon train

Wichita village

Marcy explores west of Arbuckle Mountains

(2)

(3)

(4)

(6)

Ruins of Fort Holmes/Chouteau's

Camp Arbuckle

Fort Arbuckle est. 1851

North Fork Town

Fort Gibson

Fort Smith

Choctaw agency

Fort Arbuckle est. 1850

Fort Washita

camp equipage and supplies. The wagons were ox drawn, the oxen being chosen because of the Indian preference for horses, which could be stampeded more easily. There were also a traveling forge with blacksmith tools procured from Fort Gibson and a spring wagon containing the surveying instruments.

The party departed Fort Gibson on July 1 and moved up the Arkansas River to Tallassee. Picking up the survey line, Woodruff and his crew worked their way west to the ending point of Sitgreaves's survey and continued on. When smoke was spotted rising skyward ahead of them, it brought a warning from the Indian scouts that other Indians were in the vicinity. Everyone should be on the lookout, they said. Fording the Arkansas River, the party went into camp near the mouth of the Cimarron. The surveyors remained there from July 13 through 26, adjusting their transit and taking astronomical observations. They also mowed and stacked hay to be used on their return trip, though it so happened that they came back by another route. Young Joseph Smith described the camp as looking like a large farm, with haystacks, horses, oxen, wagons, and washed clothes drying on lines.

The men fished, tended their stock, read, hunted, wrote letters home, and waited anxiously for Indian express riders to arrive from Fort Gibson with the mail. Temperatures rose, eventually exceeding 100 degrees and lending to the discomfort caused by flies and ticks. But Smith was having a good time riding his pony Kickapoo and investigating the mysteries of the still-wild West. Meyhew worked at getting his daguerreotype apparatus in operation. His first attempts were unsuccessful, but eventually he was able to take images of the men with their horses as well as a group picture.

The Indian hunters daily brought in venison and wild turkey for the crew. Four Delaware Indians arrived at the camp one day, but they posed no threat. Isaac Smith had already led a thirteen-man detachment on a survey ahead up the Cimarron when on July 27 Woodruff put the remainder of the party in motion on a due west line along that river. He found the traveling and surveying difficult because of the steep-banked gullies and creeks that even horses could not cross. The men saw their first buffalo north of what is now Yale.

It was probably in the vicinity of present-day Marshall that they met a party of Delaware hunters on August 13. The Indians' horses were loaded with dried buffalo meat and venison. The one woman with them was completely unclothed except for a pair of buckskin leggings. She rode her horse astride a saddle like the men. The Delaware spoke a smattering of English, and they assured the surveyors that there were no Comanches in the area.

Joseph Smith was with the detachment that had separated from the main party, taking along blankets, food, two barrels of water, and a keg of whiskey in one of the wagons. The soldiers soon came onto a large herd of buffalo, which Smith described as "the most terrific looking monsters."[7] They encountered them again at two o'clock one morning when a herd strayed into camp and woke everyone with "their incessant bellowing."[8]

The presence of buffalo, as was often said on the frontier, meant that Indians were not far away. The next evening four Comanches appeared in camp. They were peaceful and remained only a short time, but on the following day a group of fifteen or more appeared. These Indians were more demanding. Smith gave up his neck and pocket handkerchiefs and a comb as proof of friendship. The Comanches broke the comb and divided it among themselves. They also helped themselves to the group's provisions. Still unsatisfied, they forced the surveyors to take them back to the main camp. They eventually departed without causing any trouble. Later, however, a Frenchman with the group was butchering a buffalo he had killed when four

Comanches rode up and ordered him away. He returned to camp thankful to still have his scalp with him.

The intense heat continued, and water became increasingly scarce. The situation was made even bleaker when the surveyors discovered that Indians had burned off the prairie beyond the Cimarron. For as far as the eye could see, there was only charred, black prairie. Smith led an all-day search for water. The bone-wearying effort was fruitless, but that night a severe windstorm struck the camp. Behind it came rain, providing the badly needed moisture.

With spirits revived, the surveyors moved on westward through low scrub-oak country. Pools of water found in a range of gypsum hills proved to be heavy with Glauber's salt content, and the water gave both the men and their animals diarrhea. An "elegant spring" was discovered near present-day Okeene, Oklahoma, on August 24. Four men sent ahead to look for water along the survey line found none east of the North Canadian. The river itself was dry except for pools where the buffalo had stomped the sands. The four did see a large number of buffalo along with deer, turkey, and a few bears.

A hard rain set in, holding the surveyors in camp during August 26 and 27. The men caught water in every available vessel until the rain ceased on August 28. That evening they built several campfires from wood of the native cedars and lay about singing to the merry tune of a fiddle.

With the surveying season nearing an end, Woodruff decided that it was unnecessarily costly to continue on to the 100th meridian. Planting a large post to mark the conclusion of the work (possibly in the vicinity of present-day Seiling), the surveyors began their return by way of the North Canadian. This route provided better grass and water than their previous route.

Even as the Woodruff surveyors were "chaining" their way back up the North Canadian in late August 1850,

Marcy was leading another detachment of troops from Fort Smith. His orders were to establish a westerly military post on the Canadian. With him were thirty-one ox-drawn wagons carrying building materials, supplies, and equipment for the planned fort. He also had two artillery field pieces, a portable forge, and a herd of cattle.[9]

Marcy's journey to New Mexico via the Canadian River and back across the sea of raw country of West Texas had been only the first of several important explorations that the infantry officer would make. The Massachusetts native had graduated from West Point in 1832. He had seen battle service with the Fifth Infantry during the Mexican War at Palo Alto and Resaca de la Pluma. After the war he was stationed at Fort Towson.[10] Marcy's descriptive report of the New Mexico journey had proved him to be an alert observer with exceptional ability at reporting his discoveries in a lucid and interesting manner. As a result, he was soon placed at the lead of other explorations.

The August heat was so fierce when he left Fort Smith that Marcy was forced to travel at night. Even so, his oxen began dying off. Guide Black Beaver recommended that instead of continuing on west to Mustang Creek as Marcy had planned, they halt near the site of present-day Byars, Oklahoma. Marcy agreed, there establishing a cantonment, which he named Camp Arbuckle. Troops were quartered at the Canadian River post through the winter of 1850–1851. One of the officers was Lieutenant Rodney Glisan, assistant surgeon, whose book *Journal of Army Life* tells of frontier hunting adventures in the game-rich country along the Canadian River.[11]

The War Department decided that the post should be located farther west, closer to the Plains tribes. Accordingly, Marcy was ordered to make a thorough reconnaissance of the region between the Canadian and the Red River. With a few Creek Indian guides and a small detachment of troops, he departed Camp Arbuckle on January 9, 1851. Moving southwest, he skirted the Arbuckle Mountains and marched up the Red River as far as the mouth of Cache Creek. The site that he selected for the new post, however, was on Wild Horse Creek four miles south of the Washita and some seven miles west of present-day Davis.[12] Lieutenant Glisan described the construction of Fort Arbuckle in a letter of May 12, 1851:

> We are living, and are expecting to live for some months, in tents. The carpenters and extra-duty men are engaged in erecting the men's barracks; which will be built from hewn logs, with the chinks stopped with small pieces of wood and clay loam. The floors will be of puncheons, and the roofs of clapboards. The chimneys will be constructed of stone and clay. The buildings will be arranged into an oblong rectangular parallelogram, with a line of barracks on each side for the men—the commissary and quartermasters buildings at one end, and the officers' quarters at the other. The hospital, which will be erected so soon as the private soldiers are under cover, will be a long one-story log building divided into four compartments—one of which will be used as a dispensary, with the steward's room adjoining— the next as wards for the sick—and the fourth as a kitchen. This building will be erected a short distance outside of the garrison.
>
> The sutler's store is about a hundred yards north of the commissary buildings. Just under the hill is a limpid spring of icy water, gushing forth in a stream powerful enough for a first-class water power.[13]

Later that same year Marcy was selected to escort General William G. Belknap into Texas, where another military post was to be established on the trace Marcy had cut across Texas in returning from New Mexico in 1849. The purpose of this new fort was to protect the settlers who were pushing farther and farther north

Trap Mountain on Cache Creek as depicted by artist James
A. Suydam. (Randolph B. Marcy, *Exploration of Red River*)

into upper Texas. Departing from Fort Smith again,
Marcy marched to Fort Arbuckle and from there across
the Red River to the headwaters of the Brazos.

After several days of exploration, General Belknap
selected a site near some Tawakoni, Caddo, and Waco
villages. The fort would carry his name, Fort Belknap.
During the return trip to Fort Washita, the general
became ill and was placed in an army ambulance.
Upon arrival, it was discovered that en route he had
died in the wagon.[14]

Marcy was especially intrigued with the unknown
and virtually unexamined upper reaches of the Red
River. Pedro Vial had traversed the area in 1786–1787.
The maps he had produced reflected the courses of the
North and South Forks of the Red River fairly accur-
ately. But all previous attempts by American exploring
parties had failed: Pike in 1806, Freeman-Custis that
same year, and Long, who had mistakenly coursed the
Canadian instead of the Red, in 1820. Abert had visited
the head of the North Fork, but he did not know which

river it was.[15] Even the Indians, Marcy noted, avoided the region because of the bitter and unpalatable water there.

While in Washington, D.C., Marcy called the region to the attention of the army adjutant general. Marcy suggested that he be permitted to lead an expedition up the Red beyond the mouth of Cache Creek. He felt that his being on friendly terms with the Comanches would provide him access that others could not obtain. His request was granted, and orders were issued in March 1852.[16]

Proceeding to Fort Smith and then to Preston, Texas, where his transportation was stored, Marcy requisitioned supplies, subsistence, and baggage to support his command in the field for five months. Once his 120-man expedition was organized, Marcy marched to the mouth to Cache Creek. He was met there by his wagons from Preston, along with a herd of beef cattle that would provide subsistence during the march. To avoid the worst of the afternoon heat and to give the stock time to graze, the expedition began its day's march at three o'clock in the morning and went into camp around eight hours later, at eleven.

In setting off on this exploration, Marcy was accompanied by Corps of Engineers Captain George B. McClellan, a good friend and later to be son-in-law. Others included Lieutenant Joseph Updegraff; Dr. George G. Shumard of Fort Smith; Captain J. H. Strain, a Fort Arbuckle trader; and James R. Suydam of New York City. Suydam drew the sketches that later accompanied Marcy's official report of the journey.[17] Also along were a Mexican boy named John; Marcy's servant, Uncle Andrew; several civilian teamsters; and five Delaware and Shawnee scouts headed by John Bushman, a Delaware who was highly regarded as a guide and interpreter. Bushman spoke Comanche fluently and was, as Marcy described him "a man of eminently determinate and resolute character, with great powers of endurance and sound judgment."[18]

This was to be far more than mere exploration, however. A thorough examination and record would be made of the geology, minerals, mammals, reptiles, fish, insects, and plant life. The party would be kept busy collecting and storing samples, making meteorological observations, and investigating the mysteries of this heretofore unstudied part of the West.

The expedition marched westward along the south side of the Wichita Mountains and then turned north. They were near the future site of Camp Radziminski on May 27 when they met a small hunting party of Wichita Indians under elderly chief Canje-Hexie. The Indians had a large number of horses and mules, all heavily loaded with jerked buffalo meat, plus ten wild horses they had captured on the prairie. The Wichitas instructed the travelers on the land ahead, warning them of the scarcity of water—falsely, Marcy thought.[19]

On the North Fork the expedition passed the high-cliff area where Dodge and Catlin had found the Wichita village in 1834. Following a route that took the explorers west past present-day Mangum and then north, they went into camp on June 6 near the site of present-day Sayre. Here Suydam, for whom Marcy named the creek on which they were located, sketched the circle of wagons and tents, depicting the activity of the camp.[20]

Moving west, the expedition found a clear stream fringed with cottonwood and surrounded by a valley of wild rye grass that the horses found very tasty. Marcy named the water course Sweetwater Creek.[21] Following up its north bank, the expedition crossed the 100th meridian into Texas. They now encountered numerous Indian trails and deserted campsites, which Black Beaver identified as being of Kiowa and Comanche origin. Seventeen years later, in 1869, George Armstrong Custer and a force of Seventh Cavalry and Nineteenth Kansas Volunteers would meet the Cheyennes here and rescue two white women captives.

On June 13 the command was encamped near the future site of Fort Elliott, Texas. From this place Marcy made a side exploration to the southwest, reaching the North Fork of the Red. Returning to the main party, Marcy set his caravan of ox-drawn wagons into motion again, traveling eleven miles to reach "a very beautiful stream of good spring water."[22] He named the watercourse Kioway Creek; today it is known as Red Deer Creek.

Evidently mistaking it for a tributary of the Sweetwater and considering it to be the apex of the Red River's northern extension, Marcy had a bottle buried at the foot of a large cottonwood tree near the head of the stream. In it was placed a note reading: "On the 16th day of June, 1852, an exploring expedition, composed of Captain R. B. Marcy, Captain G. B. McClellan, Lieutenant J. Updegraff, and Doctor G. C. Shumard, with fifty-five men of company D fifth infantry, encamped here, having this day traced the north branch of Red River to its source. Accompanying the expedition were Captain J. H. Strain of Fort Washita, and Mr. J. R. Suydam, of New York City."[23]

Also, the tree was blazed with the message "Exploring Expedition. June 16, 1852." Most likely the bottle still lies buried somewhere in the vicinity of present-day Hoover northeast of Pampa. From this location Marcy made a side trip of "about twenty-five miles" to the mouth of Sandy Creek on the Canadian River just north of present-day Borger, Texas. Traveling with eleven members of his expedition, Marcy was gratified to reach the Canadian, which he had traveled on his way to Santa Fe in 1849. He made note of the wagon road, much traveled by the California gold rushers, migrants, and traders, that passed along the river's bank. He also recorded the existence of a giant cottonwood tree that stood on a tributary of the Canadian. It measured nineteen and a half feet in circumference at five feet above the ground. On the north bank stood four other cottonwoods, their trunks blazed by travelers. Suydam sketched the rugged terrain, and Marcy ordered a cottonwood tree on the north bank blazed with the date of their visit.

Marcy now set forth to explore the southern branch of the Red River. Proceeding southwest across the North Fork, the explorers reached another pleasant stream with pure water that ran over a bed of gravel. Marcy named it for McClellan, whom he believed was the first white man ever to set eyes on it. The southwesterly movement was continued across meadows of short buffalo grass. On June 27 the party arrived at the main South Fork of the Red. The stream was known as "Prairie-dog-town River" by the Comanches because of the abundance of prairie dog villages along its banks.

Marcy was determined to locate and explore the ultimate reaches of this main channel of the Red River. The terrain had now become so badly cut and rough that it was impossible to continue with the wagons. On June 29 Marcy left the main body of his command in camp under the charge of Lieutenant Updegraff while he proceeded ahead on horseback with McClellan, Suydam, and a ten-man escort.

The course of the river led into even rougher terrain, with deep gorges and towering rock cliffs that rose precipitously from the riverbed. The explorers were now in the great Palo Duro Canyon southeast of present-day Amarillo, rediscovering the enormous chasm that had originally been stumbled onto by Coronado. Following the branch of Palo Duro known as Tule Canyon, Marcy ultimately reached what he believed to be the apex of the stream, where its cool, sparkling waters spouted forth from the base of a rock cliff. Suydam sketched the scene. Climbing to the rim of the canyon, the men found the treeless reaches of the Llano Estacado stretching endlessly away to the distant horizon.[24]

Marcy was satisfied that he had accomplished his goal. He had explored each of the principal headwater

Randolph Marcy stood in awe of a spring at the head of the Red River deep in Palo Duro Canyon in the Texas Panhandle. (Marcy, *Exploration of Red River*)

branches of the Red River. Rejoining the main camp of the expedition, he ordered the return march on July 4. The expedition followed the higher ground of the South Fork's north bank, which was less cut by dry ravine washes. As the expeditioners again passed south of the Wichita Mountains, they discovered a Wichita

The Wichitas and Taovayas resided in neatly fenced, cultivated, thatched-hut settlements. (Randolph B. Marcy,
Exploration of Red River)

village. Thus far they had seen many Indian signs but
few Indians. But east of the Wichita Mountains on
Rush Creek, they came onto active villages of Wichitas
and Caddos.[25]

The Wichitas, they found, still resided in the rounded,
thatched huts first described by Coronado at Quivira.
The towns were surrounded by cornfields with rail
fences. Crops, which were ready for harvesting, included corn, pumpkins, beans, peas, and melons. The
Caddos lived in much the same manner, both tribes
depending on the buffalo for their main subsistence.
Also, both possessed large herds of horses and mules.
Many of the animals carried Mexican and American
brands.

From Wichita chief To-sa-quash, or White Tail, Marcy
learned some surprising news. It had been reported at
Fort Arbuckle that Marcy's entire expedition had been
massacred by the Comanches on the head of the Red
River. The story had been accepted as fact by everyone.
It was known that the Comanches were very angry over

the new forts being built in their country, some of their people having been killed near them.[26]

After ransoming a fifteen-year-old Mexican captive from the Wichitas, Marcy pushed on to Fort Arbuckle. The expedition arrived there on July 28 after more than two months in the field. There he learned that the rumor of his expedition's massacre had created sensational headlines around the country. The story had been initiated by some Wichitas and Waco Indians visiting Fort Arbuckle in early July. They said they had heard the story from a band of Comanches who had visited their camps.[27]

In the face of this hearsay evidence, the story had been accepted as fact by the Fort Arbuckle commander. The officer had even requested funds from the War Department to conduct a war of revenge against the Comanches. Newspapers around the country had picked up on the story, fostering strong public antagonism toward the Indians and martyrdom for Marcy. The Fort Worth Herald had run a banner headline: "MASSACRE! MELANCHOLY AND DISTRESSING NEWS! MURDER OF CAPTAIN MARCY'S COMMAND BY THE COMANCHES!"[28] There had even been a funeral service for him at Greenwich, Massachusetts, with many of his relatives, including his cousin Governor William L. Marcy of New York, in attendance.[29]

Upon Marcy's arrival at Fort Arbuckle, a courier was sent galloping to Fort Smith with the news, which was then relayed by mail to Memphis and from there to Washington City by telegram. A few days later a search party of fifty dragoons from Fort Worth and Fort Graham in Texas arrived at Fort Arbuckle having hit Marcy's trail and followed it there.[30]

Meanwhile, the War Department had come under criticism for not sending out a stronger, better-armed force on this exploration. As a result, the government announced plans to bolster its frontier army, adding unexpected benefit to this supposed "Custer Massacre" of 1852. Even without that benefit, Marcy and his men had explored an unknown part of the West and brought back a large amount of scientific information about the area. Now the forty-year-old Marcy would become acclaimed as one of America's foremost explorers, his reputation rivaling that of John C. Fremont.

➤ 17 ─────────────────────────

Whipple's Railroad Route

The Cherokee Nation, whose main body had been reunited in eastern Indian Territory in 1838, played a major role in governmental attempts to pacify and work out peaceful relations with the prairie tribes to the west. In June 1853 the Cherokees sent a delegation of their leading men to attend a grand council of thirteen different tribes at a "high point on the North Canadian."[1] These tribes included the Comanches, Kiowas, Kichais, Creeks, Delawares, Cherokees, Shawnees, Chickasaws, and Choctaws.

It was an all-Indian meeting; the United States was not invited or represented. The Cherokees attempted to persuade the Comanches and Kiowas that with Texas having become part of the United States in 1845, they would now have to give up their practice of holding white captives. Jesse Chisholm, the noted prairie trader, served as interpreter-general for the council. Such ventures into the raw environment of the prairie Indians provided a wealth of experience and knowledge of the region to men such as Chisholm and

Black Beaver, who as guides conveyed this information to men who came to explore the Plains.

The issue of captives held by the prairie tribes was raised again the following month when Indian agent Thomas Fitzpatrick met with the Kiowas and Comanches at the now-abandoned Fort Atkinson on the Santa Fe Trail.[2] The chiefs strongly rejected Fitzpatrick's exhortation regarding release of Mexican captives. The captives, they said, were now wives, mothers, or some other part of their tribal family.

The chiefs also complained that they did not want military forts in their country. They said that the soldiers destroyed their timber and ran off their game, creating hostility and causing trouble. The council and debate lasted for several days. Eventually the prairie tribes signed a treaty with the United States on July 27, 1853, stipulating that they would cease their practice of taking prisoners. However, it is doubtful that they fully understood the clause or took it seriously, as U.S. surveyor Lieutenant Amiel Weeks Whipple would soon discover.[3]

When Whipple arrived at old Camp Arbuckle in August 1853 with a railroad surveying expedition, he was in dire need of a quality guide. He greatly hoped to recruit either Jesse Chisholm, Black Beaver, or John Bushman to take him across the prairie to New Mexico. But Chisholm, who had been away from his home for some time, had his own affairs to attend to. Besides, he insisted, the prairie Indians were angry over white intrusions onto and across their lands. He said that they would very likely burn the prairie in front of the expedition.

Whipple also had little luck with the other two guides. Black Beaver, who lived in a small log hut at the abandoned Camp Arbuckle, then known as Beaversville, was too ill to go. John Bushman said that he feared the return trip back across the prairie from New Mexico alone. And he expressed grave concern about

Amiel Weeks Whipple. (*National Cyclopaedia of American Biography*)

the serious drought that the country was experiencing: "Maybe you find no water," he warned; "maybe you all die."[4]

The Whipple survey was one of several approved by Congress and implemented by Secretary of War Jefferson Davis. The purpose of the surveys was to ascertain the best railroad route from the Mississippi River across the Plains and the Rocky Mountains to the Pacific Ocean. The central route survey along the thirty-eighth and thirty-ninth parallels, crossing Indian Territory, was assigned to the command of Lieutenant Whipple of the Topographical Corps. Whipple, a native of Massachusetts and graduate of the U.S. Military Academy, had previously conducted surveys of the United States–Mexico border.

It was mid-July 1853 when Whipple's party of professional men—botanists, physicians, naturalists, topographers, artists, astronomers, surveyors, and others—departed Fort Smith. They had with them a dozen wagons and a two-wheeled scientific "carretela."[5] Using Marcy's 1849 map as a guide and stopping at Marcy's camping spots, Whipple's caravan moved to the Choctaw Agency at Skullyville. Here three more wagons and teams were hired from Able Warren, the former Red River trader who was now engaged in freighting to frontier army posts. Whipple would make an extensive record of this expedition across the prairies; so would Lieutenant David S. Stanley and German artist H. B. Möllhausen, who had been commissioned as a naturalist for the expedition by the Smithsonian Institution.

From Skullyville the surveyors struck the Canadian River and followed its south bank past the Delaware Mountains to old Camp Arbuckle. Warren guided them that far before turning back. A scattering of Delawares headed by Black Beaver still resided there. The Delawares grazed cattle on the surrounding tall-grassed pastures, planted fields of rice, and enjoyed the harvest of their peach orchards. But, Whipple reported, the band was living in degraded slothfulness and diseased conditions. At the time of his arrival, the inhabitants of the former post were engaged in drunken revelry, with whiskey brought to them by Creek traders.[6]

The travelers were impressed with Black Beaver. Expedition artist Baldwin Möllhausen described him as a meager-looking man of middle size, with long, black hair that framed a clever but melancholy face. The frontier-famous guide entertained the party with stories of his travels and adventures in the far West. He had seen the Pacific coast on seven occasions, he said. He had helped the Americans in war and had taken many scalps among the Blackfeet and other tribes.

Black Beaver spoke English, French, Spanish, and some eight different Indian languages.[7]

Whipple offered Black Beaver as much as $5 a day to serve as a guide, but the frontiersman was too ill. His wife had convinced him that if he went with Whipple, he would never return to his family again. The expedition remained at Camp Arbuckle for four days, repairing wagons and shoeing mules. Whipple was still endeavoring to locate a frontier-experienced guide who would be able not only to lead the way but also to find water on the prairie. None of the other Delaware scouts would take the job.

Whipple sent for Jesse Chisholm. The frontiersman came, but he rejected Whipple's offer of more money and provisions than guides had ever made before. Finally, in exasperation, Whipple declared angrily that he was annoyed and offended. Anyone as intelligent as Chisholm, he insisted, would see the value of a transcontinental railroad and would not refuse to help in the exploration for one.

Chisholm relented, though he still would not go himself. He offered instead the services of a Mexican boy named Vincente, in later life known as George Chisholm. Chisholm had purchased Vincente from the Comanches six years before at the price of $200 in goods. He had promised the boy his freedom when he came of age.[8]

Vincente, one of seven children so rescued by Chisholm, had a sister still with the Comanches. He was a small, black-eyed youngster of fourteen who had been held by the tribe for over eight years. The boy spoke English and Comanche fluently in addition to being adept at sign language. He was a bright and agreeable youngster but, as Whipple would learn, possessed of the independence and love for hunting of a Comanche. Whipple agreed to pay the boy $25 a month plus his passage home.[9]

With a guide thus procured and driving cattle purchased from Chisholm, Whipple and his entourage set
forth on Marcy's trail once more. It did not take long for
Chisholm's prediction regarding prairie fires to come
true. On Walnut Creek southwest of present-day Purcell, two Indians were spied setting fire to the dry
prairie grass. The flames roared toward the caravan,
forcing the surveyors to set backfires and burn an area
of safety about their camp. The smoke was thick
enough to obscure the sun as they moved on.[10]

The California gold rush wagon road had now become
so overgrown that Whipple's party lost it in the vicinity
of Walnut Creek. Drifting to the south, they met two
Waco Indians, who first claimed to be Kichais. They
wore blue cotton blankets about their waists, head-
dresses of eagle feathers, moccasins, and brass wire
bracelets. Their bodies were painted with vermilion,
and their earlobes were pierced with short sticks. The
Indians had no guns, but they carried twenty-six-inch
bows made of the tough bois d'arc (Osage orange) wood,
and their leather quivers were filled with red-shafted,
steel-tipped arrows that were said to be poisoned.[11]

The Wacos spoke no English, Spanish, or Comanche.
Nonetheless, after they had eaten and smoked, Vincente
conducted a rapid-fire conversation with them in sign
language. His graceful hands conveyed ideas faster than
could have been done with words. One of the Wacos
offered to show Whipple the wagon road, but the Indians
deserted them before it had been located. However, the
party soon met a Kichai from a band that was then
residing at the former Fort Holmes–Chouteau post
site. The Indian found the trail for the surveying party.
Möllhausen made sketches of the Wacos and Kichais,
and Whipple recorded as much of their vocabulary as
possible. The Kichai was rewarded for his help with a
shirt, a string of beads, a pipe, tobacco, and a silver
dollar.

On August 25 a courier from Fort Smith arrived with the last mail the company would receive before pushing onto the prairie. With the Cross Timbers behind the surveyors, they moved westward on Marcy's trail. While crossing present-day Caddo County, they were struck by a wind- and rainstorm. Despite this, the burning of the prairie continued as they made their way across Custer County. On one occasion a raging grass fire driven by high winds forced them to countermarch and take refuge in a ravine. A temporary opening was beat out in the wall of flame, and the expedition pushed through. For mile after mile from there the men moved across a fire-blackened prairie. Even at night the glow of distant prairie fires could be seen. Whipple speculated that the Indians were burning away the dead grass for the return of the buffalo in the spring.[12]

Even with the dryness of the season, the surveyors found ample springs and ponds of water in the creeks. The area of Rock Mary, where curious-shaped mounds rose forth from a field of sand, impressed Whipple as "the evil genie of an evil place."[13] As they approached Antelope Hills on September 3, Whipple and the others sighted their first buffalo. This single animal was enough to send Vincente galloping off on his white pony, pistol in hand. He was unsuccessful in his hunt, but more straggler buffalo were found in the region, and some were killed.

Crossing the Texas-Oklahoma border on September 6, the expedition moved through prairie dog towns and across sandy arroyos to Dry Creek (Red Deer Creek at Canadian, Texas). Game was now plentiful. Vincente killed a fat doe, and several wild turkeys were bagged from a flock in a thicket near the river. Five buffalo managed to elude the pursuing hunters, however, and a cougar spotted near camp also escaped.

A party of hunters led by Lieutenant Stanley spied some Indians stealing down a draw toward the expedition's camp. A parley with them revealed that they

Members of the Whipple survey halt for a rest on the trail. (Amiel W. Whipple, "Report of Exploration for a Railroad")

were Comanches from a large village north of the Canadian. The Comanches were taken to the camp—as prisoners, Whipple stated—and interrogated. With Vincente off indulging his passion for hunting, little could be learned from them. Whipple made them a gift of a pipe and some tobacco and permitted them to leave.[14]

A little farther along, the Americans encountered the huge cottonwood tree that Marcy had visited and measured the year before. Möllhausen described the tree as being twelve feet in diameter, with mighty, far-reaching arms. Its bark was engraved with Indian-cut figures of rattlesnakes and long-necked horses. The artist enjoyed a recess from the heat as well as from the back of his mule by relaxing in the shade of the giant tree. He ruminated on the centuries of history that the tree had witnessed.[15] In later years an Indian reported that the tree had burned, likely from having been struck by lightning.

Signs of mounted Indians had increased, and at mid-afternoon on September 9 the expedition came upon an Indian encampment located on the opposite bank of a small stream. The village, which consisted of twenty or more lodges, was caught by surprise. An instant alarm went up among the Indians when the surveying caravan was spotted. The women and children began a mass exodus from the encampment, while a small force of warriors assembled on the creek bank facing the visitors. The warriors, mounted on prancing ponies, were ready with bows in hand and arrows between their fingers. Their silver trappings glistened in the sun as they milled about like disturbed hornets.[16]

Vincente saved the day by tying a white handkerchief to the ramrod of his rifle and waving it. The relieved Indians immediately responded with shouts and signs of friendship. An old medicine man, virtually naked and afoot, came across the stream to hug Whipple and Stanley and voice his liking for Americans. The expedition doctor, whom Stanley pointed out as the party's medicine man, also received a special hugging from the old man.

The Indians, who were Kiowas, insisted that, as friends, the Americans were obligated to visit their camp and hold a council. Whipple consented and forded the creek to the village. He accommodated the old man's fervent desire and let him ride across atop the carretela. The Americans were met by two Mexicans who had come to trade flour, biscuits, and sugar for buffalo robes and horses. They complained that the Indians had taken most of their goods, and they wished to accompany the expedition to New Mexico.[17]

In the village was a Mexican woman, José Maria, who had been captured seven years before at the age of twenty. She was now the third and favorite wife of an elder Kiowa chief, Ku-tat-su, or the Sorrel Horse. By him she had borne a very pretty blue-eyed son, then three years of age. She was watched closely and was given little chance to speak. However, José Maria managed to convey to Vincente in Spanish her soulful wish that the Americans save her from captivity and send her and the child to her home in Rio de Nacos. A Mexican boy captive was also in the village.[18]

To greet the visitors, the Kiowa warriors had painted their faces bright yellow and the part in their long, black hair with a streak of bright red vermilion. They carried excellent hardwood bows ornamented with brass nails, silver disks, and wampum beads. Their arrows, measured at twenty-eight inches, were steel-tipped with multicolored feather fins. Their wolf-skin quivers, buckskin leggings, and moccasins were decorated with beadwork and silver plates. Long silver-decked horsehair queues trailed almost to the ground behind them, while brass rings with bones and shell trimmings hung from their ears. All wore brass bracelets. One of the chiefs wore a large silver cross, which Whipple thought had likely been taken from a Mexican church.[19]

In the center of the village was a scalp-draped pole guarded by an old woman who would let no one near it. Another pole held a beautiful headdress with a scarlet feather train some eight feet long. Whipple attempted to trade for it, but he could produce nothing that would persuade the Indians to barter. The Kiowas said that their great chief Little Mountain was on a buffalo hunt to the north. Two other large camps of Kiowas were nearby.

The matter of the Mexican captives was broached by Whipple during his council with the chiefs. After the pipe had been passed about the circle of Kiowas and whites, the old chief talked of the strong friendship his people felt for the Americans, who only recently had given them presents (at Fort Atkinson), including blue blankets for each tribal member. The Americans had promised there would be more presents, he said, if they would remain friendly to travelers on the prairie.

Whipple then presented each of the five chiefs with a red blanket, some beads, and tobacco. But the Kiowas were disdainful of the presents, saying that they expected at least a blanket for each member of the band, plus calico for the women and children.

Angrily Whipple replied that if the gifts were not satisfactory, they could be returned, that the Americans could try powder and lead in preserving the peace with the Kiowas. It was in this climate of ill feelings that Whipple brought up the matter of the Mexican captives. He insisted that he wished to restore them to their families and friends.

The American officer was not prepared for the reaction of Chief Ku-tat-su, who became convulsed with anger, his face contorting with fury. It was not the act of a friend, he stormed, to come among his band and try to separate wives and children from husbands and fathers. The Kiowa was eventually calmed somewhat when Whipple agreed that no one would be taken who did not wish to go. To soothe the chief further, Whipple presented him with a cow for food. The Kiowas were pleased and proceeded to entertain their guests by goading the animal into flight and then pursuing it on horseback as they would a buffalo.

Vincente, meanwhile, had become greatly agitated. According to his Comanche upbringing, he believed that when the Kiowas directed their first puffs from their pipe to the sun, they were being sorcerers. He felt they were trying to cast an evil spell on the Americans. Whipple questioned the other Mexican prisoner— Andres Nuñares of Chihuahua, who had been taken prisoner five years before—about this. The captive said that it was simply the method used by the Kiowas in invoking their blessing.

When Whipple offered to take the captive boy with him, Andres declined. He said that he was the owner of twelve mules, all broken to the saddle, as well as a number of wild mares and colts. He did not wish to give them up, and he had no particular complaint against the Indians. He said that if José Maria was provided a bridle bit for her horse, she would be able to join them at the next camp. Whipple produced the bit for Andres to give her. After assisting the visitors with a vocabulary of Kiowa words and being given some presents in return, the happy captive went leaping and whooping back to his lodge.

The old chief came to the Americans' camp early the following morning with his son in tow, requesting a present for the boy. José Maria came up behind, riding a sorry-looking pony with only a thong for a bridle and no bridle bit. She looked very sad, and her expression pleaded for rescue. But her husband scolded her sharply, and she returned dejectedly to the Kiowa village. When Whipple demanded the return of some camp items that had been taken by the Kiowas, the chief left as if to comply. But as soon as he reached his camp, the conical lodges began disappearing from the landscape. With travois packed and ready to move, the Kiowas sat mounted on their fleet ponies and watched as the Americans departed.

A party of Comanchéros and Pueblo Indians from New Mexico who were in the camp had had a disagreement with the tribesmen. Fearing for their lives, they now took the opportunity to depart with the expedition as it moved on up the Canadian. Mounted on mules and wearing conical sombreros and serapes, they had come with flour and bread to barter for Kiowa and Comanche horses and buffalo robes. They had not had much success, they said, as most of the prairie tribes were still to the north on their fall hunting tour. Nothing more was seen of the Kiowas or of José Maria and Andres.

On the second day beyond the Kiowa camp, Whipple rode across the Canadian to visit the site of Adobe Walls. He described it as being "finely situated in a grove of trees, and containing a spring of water within the court. An acequia from the river insured the garden in front from the ill effects of the season."[20] He noted that the site was now desolate, its only use being to designate a ford.

The Canadian River now led the expedition southwest past the site of present-day Borger, Texas. The expedition did not encounter any more Indians on the Llano Estacado; but as the route turned back westward, the expeditioners again found signs of a huge encampment in the river valley. The Pueblo Indians said the camp of an estimated three hundred lodges, six hundred warriors, and one thousand horses had probably been Comanche.[21]

It was now mid-September as the surveyors pushed on westward. Initially Stanley found that "the scenery of this extensive plain is indeed beautiful,"[22] but he soon became acquainted with the phenomena of dreary mirages when columns of smoke appeared to be rising from a burning prairie and the false images of cliffs and trees appeared ahead. When the expedition finally departed from the river's valley, Stanley noted in his journal, "I felt a feeling of regret at parting with our old friend the Canadian, in whose turbid, but wholesome water I had so often quenched my burning thirst."[23] Locating a campsite beside a spring and a vineyard of wild grapes, Whipple paused on the Texas–New Mexico border to permit a much-needed rest. With the New Mexico mountains rising on the horizon, the expedition crossed the border on September 19 and left behind the "ocean prairie."[24]

The ensuing Civil War and postwar railroad construction across Kansas would preclude construction of a transcontinental railway route along Whipple's Canadian River route from St. Louis to the Pacific.[25] Nevertheless, the Whipple expedition, with excellent chronicles by Whipple, Stanley, and Möllhausen, would provide extensive lore concerning Indian country and its inhabitants.

Surveys and Swords

The years 1857 through 1860 were an active time in Indian Territory in terms of peaceful exploration as well as hostile military action. Even as the U.S. government continued its surveys of Indian lands, the forces of conflict between the Native tribes and intruding whites were coming to issue. The Plains tribes did not like the invasion of their hunting grounds by eastern migrants and government parties. But generally the whites went on their way; the Indians' most hated and dreaded enemy was Texas.

White settlements, including those of immigrant Germans, were pushing deeper and deeper into the Comanchería of Texas, driving the Native tribes north. The Comanches and their allies, in particular the Kiowas, conducted persistent and bloody raids against the settlements. The Texas Rangers fought back with search-and-destroy forays against Indian encampments. It was only a matter of time before the determined Texans would cross the Red River and invade the Indian Territory sanctuary from which the Indians struck.

Both U.S. military forces and the removal Indians from eastern Indian Territory would join in.

Meanwhile, government surveys continued to explore the Territory. John McCoy, son of Reverend Isaac McCoy, had chained the Cherokee Outlet in 1837. It was resurveyed again during 1851–1852. In 1857 Congress approved two new explorations that included the area of present-day Oklahoma. These were the Johnston survey of the southern border of Kansas—thus the northern border of Indian Territory and what is now the Oklahoma Panhandle—along with a potential railroad route across northern Indian Territory, and the Beale survey for a government wagon route along the Canadian River.

Lieutenant Colonel Joseph E. Johnston, a First Cavalry West Pointer from Virginia, was placed in charge of the Kansas border survey. The weather was extremely cold in May 1857 when Johnston departed Fort Leavenworth, Kansas, with four companies of First Cavalry and two of Sixth Infantry. John E. Weyss was the head surveyor, while John H. Clark and Hugh Campbell were assigned as astronomers. John Connor and two Delaware Indians served as guides.

The survey would take the expedition westward along the Kansas–Indian Territory line to New Mexico and back again. On the return, a belated order came for Johnston to also examine the country for the most practicable railroad route to the Rio Grande. This forced the officer to split his command into two divisions in order to examine more of Indian Territory than had been originally planned.[1]

Johnston kept a day-by-day account of the journey. By July 4 the expedition was camped five miles east of the eventual site of the Chilocco Indian School in Indian Territory. In recognition of the national holiday, Johnston ordered his troops into military formation, while a salute was fired by the field battery. None of the officers knew at the time that four years later they

Officers of Joseph E. Johnston's survey of the northern boundary of Indian Territory in 1857 were soon forced to choose between Union and Confederacy. (*Appleton's Cyclopaedia of American Biography*)

would be fighting on opposing sides in a bloody civil war. Johnston himself would resign his rank of brigadier general to enter Confederate service.

As the party surveyed west along the border on July 8, they met Chief Black Dog with thirty to forty Osage warriors. The Osages said that they were searching for Comanches, evidence that intertribal warring was still the rule of the land. The surveyors worked their way on west, reaching the area just north of present-day Gate, Oklahoma. A soldier died and was buried there. North of present-day Beaver, two Kiowas were spotted on July 30. The Indians came up and shook hands all around with the men.

After riding for a time with the party, the Kiowas went their own way. When the Indians came back later, the surveyors decided that they were sizing up the infantry guard. The Kiowas bided their time until an opportunity presented itself. They waited until a wagon was out of sight of the guard beyond a low ridge. Then the Indians shot the driver and drove the team off as fast as it could go. The unmounted infantrymen ran after the wagon and fired a few shots in vain. When a cavalry unit was sent in pursuit, the troops found the wagon, but with the horses missing. They also discovered the body of the driver where he had been thrown from the wagon after being shot. In falling he had grabbed onto the wagon's singletree. It was still in his grasp in death.

On August 16, at the Cimarron crossing of Aubrey's Cutoff of the Santa Fe Trail, a trade was conducted with New Mexican traders coming up the Cimarron River. Final astronomical calculations were made by the surveyors on September 10, and a marker was set at the head of Willow Creek.

On September 16 the expedition camped on McNees Creek near where a trader named McNees and a comrade had been killed on their way home from Santa Fe in 1828. The expedition surveyed to the New Mexico border at the northwestern tip of the Oklahoma Panhandle and beyond. The party then moved south to Rabbit Ear Creek. On September 20 the surveyors began their return on a course that was a bit more southerly. Near present-day Hardesty, they encountered a small Kiowa encampment. The chief promised to surrender the pair that had murdered the soldier as soon as both were found. A brisk trade was conducted by Johnston's men for buffalo robes, moccasins, lariats, and other items.

Upon arriving again at the Buffalo Creek–Cimarron River juncture west of present-day Buffalo, Oklahoma, Johnston divided the command. The wagon train was sent back to the starting point at the Kansas-Missouri border under Captain Thomas J. Wood. This segment of the expedition moved on east along the Cimarron and turned north to rejoin the old line of march and follow it eastward to the Missouri line.

Johnston, acting in line with his new orders to seek out a railroad route to the Rio Grande, led his division southward to within sight of the Canadian River south of Seiling. From there he followed a fairly direct northeast line back to the original starting point at the southeast corner of Kansas. Johnston's expedition finished its survey on October 29, 1857, after four and a half months in the field.

Even as other government surveys were being planned, the first hostile invasion of western Indian Territory took place. In April 1858 a force of Texas Rangers supported by Indians from the Brazos reservation near Fort Belknap invaded Indian Territory. Commanded by Captain John S. "Old Rip" Ford, the rangers were looking for stolen horses and Indians to attack. Marching north along the east side of the 100th meridian, they came onto Indian buffalo hunters near Antelope Hills.[2]

Following the hunters, the rangers crossed the Canadian River and on May 12 attacked a Comanche village encamped along Little Robe Creek. An undetermined number of Indians were killed, twenty-three woman and children were taken prisoner, and the village was burned. One Comanche chief killed during the fight was later discovered to be wearing a Spanish coat of mail beneath his buffalo robe. The coat was cut into pieces and divided among the rangers as souvenirs.

Still another attempt to punish the Comanches was made the following month. This foray was led by Chickasaw Indian agent Douglas Cooper at the head of a combined force of Chickasaws, Choctaws, and Cherokees. Early in 1858 the Seventh Infantry stationed at Forts Washita and Arbuckle had been ordered to Utah to help put down the Mormon rebellion there. Left behind was only a small and illness-stricken force under Captain Enoch Steen at Fort Washita. Cooper decided that this left the immigrant Indians along the Red River virtually unprotected. Accordingly, the militant-minded agent organized an expedition of "woods Indians" to raid the troublesome prairie tribes.[3]

Accompanied by Lieutenant James E. Powell, First Infantry, and guided by Black Beaver, Cooper and his Indian command departed Fort Arbuckle on June 30. Moving down the old Marcy–Black Beaver trace toward the Red River, they arrived at the mouth of Beaver Creek near present-day Ryan, Oklahoma, on July 4. There the unit crossed an Indian trail, which Cooper believed had been made by the Comanches that Ford had attacked. Warriors of the band had told the Wichitas that they were ashamed to go back to their people until they had gone to Texas to commit reprisals.

Cooper also found a stake with a note attached to it. The note stated that a party of U.S. surveyors had passed that way on July 3. This party, headed by A. H. Jones and H. M. C. Brown, was tracing the 98th meridian to mark the eastern border of the new Leased District. The district, lying between the 98th and 100th meridians, had been established by an 1855 treaty with the Choctaws and Chickasaws as a reserve for many of the Plains tribes of Texas and Indian Territory.

Driving northwest toward the Wichita Mountains, Cooper's force crossed still another trail. This was a well-worn wagon trace that ran north and south between Fort Belknap and Fort Laramie. It was said to have been the route of a Mormon emigrant train that in 1846 had settled temporarily in the Cross Timbers country of southern Indian Territory. Cooper and others had accused the Mormons of attempting to incite the Comanches, Kiowas, and Wichitas to attack U.S. supply trains on their way to Utah.

On July 8 Cooper arrived at the old Wichita village on Cache Creek visited by Marcy in 1852. It now stood deserted. Black Beaver explained that the tribe lived in constant dread of the Texans on the one side and the

———————————————————————➤

Pre–Civil War Intrusions and Boundary Surveys *(opposite page)*

1. Ford—1858
2. Cooper—1858
3. Van Dorn—1858
4. Van Dorn—1859
5. Jones/Brown—1860
6. Clark/Weyss—1860
7. Sedgwick/Stuart—1860

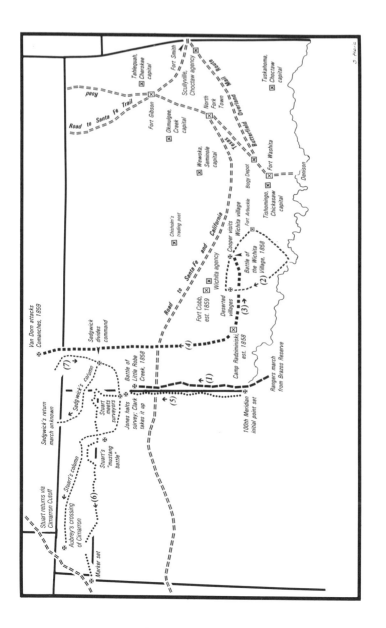

Comanches on the other. However, the Wichitas still conducted trade with both the Comanches and Kiowas. Five miles up Cache Creek, the expedition came onto an old Waco town and, above that, an "ancient Wichita village."[4]

Here, it appeared, buffalo and Indian trails converged from all directions. Cooper felt that this beautiful, spring-fed site surrounded by high bluffs would make an excellent Wichita agency location. He also thought it would be a choice spot for a military post. He was, of course, presaging the location of Fort Sill, which would be established there eleven years later by Generals Sheridan and Custer.

Picking up a trail, which Black Beaver pronounced to be that of the Wichitas, Cooper followed it to that tribe's village on Rush Creek. Some 150 huts stood surrounded by over one hundred acres under cultivation with corn. The chief assured Cooper that there were no Comanches presently south of the Canadian, the main body being at the Salt Plains. Seven Comanche bands had leagued together, the Wichita leader said, in order to conduct a war of vengeance against the Texans in retaliation for the Ford attack.

Black Beaver was sent to contact the surveying party. Having discovered McClellan's error, the surveyors were preparing to move farther west. Cooper, with his horses now badly jaded and his followers weary, turned back to Fort Arbuckle. Although he had found no Comanches, he felt that he had at least proved that the woods Indians were not afraid to go out onto the Plains and fight the Comanches.

At the same time that these events were occurring in western Indian Territory, a party of Cherokees was making its way up the Arkansas River to the Rocky Mountains. They were led by Georgian Green Russell, who was married to a Cherokee woman. He had heard stories of the gold particles that the Cherokees had discovered in Colorado ten years before. The Russell party finds on Cherry Creek during the summer of 1858 would trigger the Pike's Peak gold rush.

Even as reports from the Colorado gold region were reaching the United States in the fall of 1858, a new government expedition was preparing to cross Indian Territory. This venture was to survey a wagon road along the Canadian River from Arkansas to New Mexico. In charge was Lieutenant Edward F. Beale. He had already made two trips to the West Coast, where he took part in the struggle for California alongside Kit Carson and later served as an Indian agent.[5]

The increasing immigration to California had created the need for better transportation routes across the Plains. In September 1858 John Butterfield's Overland Mail Company began its operation from Fort Smith to El Paso and on west. Another stage line had been established across the territory along the Canadian to Santa Fe, but Comanche trouble made the route a dangerous one without military escort.

Beale, however, plunged eagerly into his assignment. After organizing his expedition at Fort Smith, he set out on his journey on October 28, planning to meet his military escort somewhere along the trail. He carried with him a copy of Gregg's *Commerce of the Prairies*, "the best book ever written on prairie life, and particularly valuable to me."[6]

Beale sent his brother, George Beale, ahead to Fort Arbuckle to secure the services of either Black Beaver or Jesse Chisholm as a guide. But George discovered that, as it had been with Whipple, neither of the two men would agree to serve. Both insisted that because of the recent hostilities, the Comanches would burn off the grass, and the animals of the expedition would perish.

Still hopeful of persuading one of the two frontiersmen to help, Edward Beale pushed ahead. He followed the south bank of the Arkansas and then that of the Canadian to the North Fork. In his report he recommended that a bridge be built across the San Bois River. An iron bridge was later erected a few miles east of Stigler. Instead of following Marcy's California trail along the south bank of the Canadian, Beale crossed the river at North Fork Town, "an insignificant village [with] nothing inviting in its appearance."

From there he used the old Fort Holmes military road to Little River, where he was welcomed by Thomas Aird "with kindness and hospitality." Beale recommended another bridge for Little River. After waiting five days for his military escort, which did not arrive, Beale pushed on up the north bank of the Canadian. En route he passed the home of Jesse Chisholm, which was located near the road in southern Pottawatomie County two miles east of present-day Asher, on November 12. Chisholm's place, Beale noted later, was the most forward settlement on the Canadian River at that time.

Somewhere along the way—Beale does not give the circumstances—Chisholm was persuaded to join the expedition, which now moved at a leisurely pace to allow the military escort to catch up. On the trail near present-day Purcell, Beale found stagecoaches of the new Canadian River mail line waiting for the expeditioners. The owner, R. Frank Green, was unwilling to send the stages across Comanche country without an escort.

On November 14 the surveying party reached Chouteau Creek and the site of old Fort Holmes. Beale and Green rode up the river some three miles from their camp and located the abandoned post. Beale found a human skull, which he tied on the back of his saddle and took to camp. After cutting down the banks of Chouteau Creek for passage of his wagons, Beale recrossed the Canadian at this point and continued his march along Walnut Creek.

On November 19 a storm struck, leaving six inches of snow on the road. The expedition, still waiting for escort troops to arrive, moved even more slowly as it passed the site of present Oklahoma City. Finally on November 26 Lieutenant Steen arrived with his company and two pieces of artillery. This addition brought the unit's count to 130 men. Now moving on in better spirits, the expedition passed Rock Mary on November 29.

While in camp at the head of what the Indians knew as Sugar Tree Valley (Sugar River), Beale and a companion took their rifles and explored the chasm that is presently known as Red Rock Canyon near present-day Hinton, Oklahoma. Although it was too late in the year to witness the maple trees in their fall orangy red, Beale was impressed with its deep banks and wide, level floor filled with "sugar trees" and fine springs. "Here," he noted in his journal, "would be a charming place for California travelers to come and winter with their stock and start on in the spring."[7] Beale dubbed a nearby group of the unique formations Steen Buttes in honor of his escort commander.[8] Beale thought that this point on the east edge of Comanche country would make an excellent location for a military post from which to protect the immigration and mail.

Expert hunters Delaware Dick and Little Axe, a Shawnee, kept the expedition supplied daily with fresh meat. "We dined today on buffalo, fat raccoon, venison, and marrow bones," Beale noted in his journal on December 3. "On our wagon was wild turkey, and opossum, and side of bear, and Mr. Baker this evening killed a good bunch of rice birds, or, as we call them at home, reed birds. The President himself could not sit down to such a table."[9]

East of Antelope Hills a north-south wagon trail was discovered. Beale said it was the trail of a man named Prole who, a year before, had led a large gold rush party onto the Plains. The group had become lost and by twisting and turning every direction had finally hit the Washita and made it back home.

Chisholm now insisted that this was as far along the river as he knew the country. Having great respect for the frontiersman's good judgment, Beale persuaded him to continue on for a way. He named a stream that they passed on December 8—Whipple's Dry River west of Antelope Hills—for Chisholm. Beale stayed with Whipple's route along the bank well into the Texas Panhandle. Although he fails to mention the giant cottonwood told of by both Marcy and Whipple, he does make note of the sand hills northeast of present-day Borger, Texas. On December 16 he paid a visit to the ruins of Adobe Walls, observing that the Indians had recently camped there. "It was pleasantly situated, having a spring and good stream of water, and up the valley, at the mouth of which it is built, timber sufficient."[10] North of present-day Borger, Beale named an isolated butte for his black servant, who had accompanied him on two previous trips from ocean to ocean. He dubbed it Ab's Knob.[11]

Now breaking from the Whipple route and cutting south away from the river, Beale laid out a road more directly toward Albuquerque. He rested over a month at Hatch's Ranch on the Gallinas River in New Mexico, visiting there with his old friend Kit Carson. Beale then journeyed on to Albuquerque.

Despite the peaceful passage of the Beale expedition, the war fever had not subsided on the prairie. During the summer of 1858 Major Earl Van Dorn was sent from Texas to pursue the Comanches north of the Red River. Leading four troops of Second Cavalry, Van Dorn established a military post on Otter Creek north of the Red River. He named it Camp Radziminski in honor of Polish-born Lieutenant Charles Radziminski, a Second Cavalry officer who had died a few weeks earlier.[12]

Upon learning from friendly Indian spies that a large entourage of Comanches was visiting the Wichitas on Rush Creek, Van Dorn made an overnight, thirty-six-hour march to reach the village. In a surprise attack at

Earl Van Dorn. (*Frank Leslie's Illustrated Newspaper,* June 6, 1863)

dawn, the U.S. troops killed fifty-six Comanches and destroyed 120 of their lodges.[13] Van Dorn struck the Comanches again during the spring of 1859 when he led his troops north into Kansas. Finally locating a Comanche encampment in Clark County, Van Dorn fell on it, killing forty-nine tribespeople and taking thirty-six prisoners.[14] These attacks, and others by troops from Fort Arbuckle, kept the western prairie in a state of turmoil and hostility. The Comanches now turned their anger toward the Santa Fe Trail of Kansas, where they began to wreak their vengeance on wagon trains.

Having discovered in 1858 that McClellan had established the initial point for the 100th meridian some forty miles too far east, Brown and Jones had halted their survey for that season. They returned the following summer to determine a new initial point and began running their line north. During 1859 they reached a point nineteen miles beyond the Canadian River, due west of present-day Arnett, Oklahoma, and only a few miles from where Ford had attacked the Comanche camp.

Their line of survey was taken up in 1860 by John Clark and John Weyss, who were surveying the Texas

Panhandle. Having recently traced the western line of the Panhandle, Clark and Weyss arrived at the Canadian River and the 100th meridian where Jones and Brown had left off in 1859. On June 8 Clark and Weyss worked their way to the northeast corner of the Texas Panhandle, then continued west surveying and erecting monuments along the border separating the present-day Texas and Oklahoma panhandles. A severe drought gripped the country, and water was so scarce as to force the surveyors to desert their line and go north to Beaver Creek.[15]

By a quirk of fate during this operation, the surveyors were met June 12 on Wolf Creek in the Texas Panhandle wilderness just east of present-day Lipscomb, Texas, by a company of U.S. troops under Lieutenant James E.B. Stuart. Stuart's detachment was part of a command of Major John Sedgwick that had marched from Fort Riley, Kansas. Sedgwick's mission was to chastise and punish the Indians by striking their home camps.[16] Lieutenant Stuart was assigned to keep a daily record of the trek. With four companies of First Cavalry and two of Second Dragoons, Sedgwick made a steady march to the Pawnee Fork in western Kansas where a military depot had been established. There he found the Santa Fe Trail flooded with covered wagons streaming to the gold fields in Colorado.

After establishing Camp Alert (soon to be renamed Fort Larned) at the Pawnee Fork, Sedgwick marched south, guided by the famous scout Fall Leaf and five other Delawares. At the Cimarron the outgoing trail of the Johnston survey, the map of which was available to the command, was still evident; signs of the survey's return march were discovered at Buffalo Creek.

On June 1 the command went into camp on Wolf Creek, or Middle River as it was then known, just above its juncture with Beaver Creek. Several of the officers wished to go on south to Antelope Hills. Sedgwick chose instead to split his command and send

James E. B. Stuart. (*Apple-* *ton's Cyclopaedia of Ameri-* *can Biography*)

John Sedgwick. (*Appleton's* *Cyclopaedia of American* *Biography*

Stuart with one segment up Wolf Creek, while he took the remainder up the Beaver.

Stuart headed up Wolf Creek on June 11. Interestingly, in part the route was precisely the one that Stuart's Civil War foe, George Armstrong Custer, would take eight years later on his way to attack the Cheyennes on the Washita River. Stuart found several deserted Indian camps, but no Indians. He went into camp that night on the south bank of the river near present-day Fargo, Oklahoma, with good water, timber, and grass. He also recorded an abundance of deer, turkey, and black bear. On June 12 the detachment passed by the site of present-day Gage, crossing and recrossing Wolf Creek several times. Just beyond the 100th meridian, the soldiers met the Clark-Weyss surveyors.

Stuart continued on up Wolf Creek into the Texas Panhandle, then turned north to Beaver Creek, failing to find the Indians he sought. On June 15 the detachment sighted what looked to be a party of Kiowas. Leaving packmules behind, the troops charged forward eager for battle, only to find that their prey was a herd of wild horses. Stuart later referred to it wryly as his "mustang battle."

Without making contact with Sedgwick, who had explored the Beaver ahead of Stuart and returned to Larned, Stuart continued up the river's north bank to the Santa Fe Trail at Aubrey's Crossing of the Cimarron.[17] There Stuart posted a letter to his wife with an express rider who was being sent for provisions. The dragoons made their way back to the Pawnee Fork base via Aubrey's Cutoff.

This would be the final military action within Indian Territory preceding the outbreak of the Civil War the following spring. The war would bring an end to the Indian Territory's period of initial exploration by white people and for a time set it even farther apart from the national whole.

Into the Grasp of War

When the Civil War erupted in 1861, Indian Territory stood greatly changed from the pristine wilderness it had been in 1820. No longer was it a tribal haven untouched by the outside world. Although the region would remain a part of the American frontier for a time, its natural state had been altered by the advent of white intrusion and the arrival of sophisticated tribal groups. Now there were Native farms and villages scattered among the eastern forests with roads between. Steamboats plied the Arkansas River, exchanging trade goods with eastern ports and connecting people in the territory to relatives and friends in the United States.

The immigrant tribes, particularly the Five Civilized Tribes, had reframed their tribal societies. Adapting themselves to many ways of white society, they had organized governments, built towns, created schools, and developed agricultural and trade economies. Wealthier tribal members sent their children off to eastern seaboard schools such as Princeton to be educated. The common tribespeople, however, were often extremely poor and dependent upon the treaty-owed assistance of the United States.

These woodland tribes had already been forced to give up their hunters' existence. Much of the animal life along the Canadian that had been reported by Long in 1820, and even by Abert in 1845, was gone. The elk, deer, black bear, wolves, wild horses, and buffalo present then had largely been killed off or driven away. While passing down the river in 1858, Beale had noted: "We find an abundance of small game, such as partridges and prairie chickens; but [hunter] Delaware Dick finds little for his rifle, as the Indians here have hunted out the larger game."[1]

Outside influence on the territory was ever increasing. The explorations and surveys had been adventurous and revealing, but they were nonetheless harbingers of change. The day of intrusion by the railroad and white settlement would come after the war. But even now the march of American empire was pushing other Indian tribes into the territory. This meant more guardian military forts, more Indian agencies, and increasing white influence.

Although under attack, the Plains tribes remained in control of the western prairies between the Arkansas and the Red rivers. They still moved their lodges from stream to stream, hunted the buffalo, and held fiercely to the way of life they knew and loved. The principal component of their existence was that the great buffalo herds still grazed the prairie. As long as there were buffalo, the Plains tribes could feed their families.

Citizen pressure in Texas had forced the closing of the two Brazos River reservations (Upper Brazos and Lower Brazos) and the removal of those tribes to Indian Territory. Late in 1858 a group of Texans who called themselves the Erath County Rangers went on an Indian-hunting foray. They located a friendly camp of reservation Indians under Choctaw Tom and fell upon it during the night. Seven Indians, including three women, were murdered while asleep in their beds. The agents restrained the Indians from retaliating, but fear and near-panic swept the north Texas settlements. Texas governor Hardin R. Runnels attempted to have the Erath Rangers arrested, but a white grand jury refused to indict the men.[2]

At Gainesville, Texas, a company of rangers was enlisted for three months' service to combat the Comanches. Another group called the Regulators was organized with the idea of chastising the Indians for thefts of stock and other depredations. The hysteria increased when false rumors circulated to the effect that the Caddos had killed nine people, among them a young girl whose throat had been cut from ear to ear. Also contributing to the situation was a campaign of Indian hatred spewed forth by fanatical John R. Baylor.[3]

Baylor, agent for the Upper Brazos Reserve, had been forced to flee the Fort Gibson area earlier because of his involvement in a murder there. His dislike for Indians resulted in a feud with Indian superintendent Robert Neighbors, who was sympathetic to the tribes. Neighbors dismissed Baylor as Comanche agent and appointed Matthew Leeper to replace him. Following this dismissal, Baylor began publication of an intensely racist newspaper called *The White Man*. With it he began stirring up dissension among whites. To this point there had been little trouble between the Indians of the Lower Brazos Reserve and the white settlers of the region. But with the murder of Choctaw Tom's people and the agitation by Baylor, the Texas frontier flamed with hatred and conflict.

Depredations committed in north Texas were inevitably blamed on the reserve Indians even though investigations showed that they were entirely innocent. In February 1859 Neighbors recommended that the tribes be moved north of the Red River for safety. Baylor and his followers were by no means satisfied with a solution that did not involve blood vindication. He began organizing an armed force for the purpose of exterminating the reserve bands.[4]

Gathering together some 280 men of a self-styled "Front Army of Defense," on May 23 Baylor advanced onto the Lower Reserve. Once there, he let himself be faced down by Captain Joseph B. Plummer, who headed a force of First Infantry assigned to protect the Indians. As Baylor's army retreated, a member murdered an eighty-year-old Indian man. The warriors of the reservation responded by attacking the invaders, killing three of them and wounding several more. Baylor retreated to the village of Fort Belknap, where he sent out a call for one thousand volunteers to wipe out the reservation Indians.[5]

Major Earl Van Dorn meanwhile brought up three companies of troops from Camp Radziminski under orders to disarm the so-called rangers. This move, along with the army forces already on hand, stymied Baylor's offensive. After a time the aggregation of Texans wearied of Baylor's oratory, which produced no action, and began departing for home.

Now came approval from Washington, D.C., for Neighbors to remove his Indians from the Brazos reserves to a district leased from the Choctaws and Chickasaws in Indian Territory. On June 30 Neighbors and a party of headmen from the reserve tribes arrived at Fort Arbuckle and met with Indian superintendent Elias Rector from Fort Smith. Under escort of Major William H. Emory, commanding officer at Arbuckle, the party toured the new Leased District.

The party visited the Medicine Bluff Creek site that Cooper had once recommended as a choice place for an agency. Rector did not like the location, citing creeks that overflowed and left stagnant ponds. This situation, he said, had in past times spread disease among the Wichitas and decimated them badly. He stated a preference, instead, for a site near the Washita River.[6] In a council with the chiefs on July 1, Neighbors and Rector

Along with Fort Cobb, Fort Arbuckle constituted U.S. military presence in Western Indian Territory at the start of the Civil War. (*Harper's Pictorial History of the Civil War*)

assured the chiefs that they would be residing on land owned by the United States and, as such, would receive the full protection of the government from all harm there. The chiefs expressed satisfaction with the country and agreed to make the move from Texas.[7]

On August 1 agent Robert Neighbors led 1,051 Indians from the Upper Brazos Reserve toward the Red River. These included the Caddos, Anadarkos, Kichais, Wacos, Tawakonis, Tonkawas, Absentee Shawnees, Delawares, and Penateka Comanches. The entourage included wagons, Mexican carts, army ambulances, cattle, horses, and dogs. They were escorted by two companies of Second Cavalry under Lieutenant George H. Thomas. At Steen's crossing of the Red River just east of the mouth of the Big Wichita River, the group was joined by 370 Comanches of the Lower Brazos Reserve under agent Matthew Leeper. The combined party then continued on to the new Leased District.[8]

On October 1, 1859, Major Emory arrived with troops from Fort Arbuckle to establish a new post three miles from the agency. Backdropped by a caprock bluff, it

William H. Emory. (*Harper's Pictorial History of the Civil War*)

consisted of a rectangle of picket-style quarters that were daubed with clay and featured dirt roofs and floors. A sandstone and adobe shed served as a commissary. The post was named Fort Cobb in honor of Howell Cobb, a Georgia politician.

Although the Sedgwick-Stuart expedition was the last major U.S. exploration into Indian Territory prior to the Civil War, one more military march was made across Oklahoma at the outbreak of the war. The Union quickly saw that its meager forces in the territory had little chance of holding out against the Texas Confederates, whose troops threatened the region. Accordingly, orders were issued to Emory, now at Fort Smith. He was to go into the territory, dismantle the

Fort Smith, Arkansas, was the starting point for many pre–Civil War intrusions into Indian country. (Amiel W. Whipple, "Report of Exploration for a Railroad")

Union bases there, and salvage as many fighting men and as much military equipment as possible. Leading the Fort Smith garrison, Emory marched first to southernmost Fort Washita. Gathering men and families, private belongings, military armament, and supplies from that post, he continued on to Fort Arbuckle. The Texans occupied Fort Washita behind him and then set out in hot pursuit.[9]

En route to Arbuckle, Emory was overtaken by Lieutenant William W. Averell. He carried orders for Emory to repair to Fort Leavenworth in Kansas. After gathering in the Fort Arbuckle garrison and equipment, the growing convoy of wagons and horses hurried on west to Fort Cobb. With Cobb's contingent added to his charge, Emory set out for Kansas.

Personnel of the march included 759 military men and 150 family members, clerks, blacksmiths, teamsters, and others who did not wish to be left behind under Confederate control. There were 600 horses, 500 mules, and 90 vehicles. The caravan was a mile in length. Baggage was piled into wagons and buggies, and wives and children snuggled into places of comfort atop for the long ride ahead. Drivers lashed their teams, and the Union retreat from Indian Territory was under way.

Black Beaver served as a guide for the exodus. The Delaware had been reluctant to leave behind the 400 head of cattle he had accumulated on the new reserve. When he asked for time to gather them so they could be driven north, the Fort Cobb commander advised him, "Let the cattle go and save your scalp."[10]

Black Beaver decided that this was good advice. He led the Union retreat on a course through the area of present-day Minco, Oklahoma, northward up a route that would one day become the Chisholm Cattle Trail, past the site of Blackwell, and on to Kansas. As the refugees passed through Lawrence, Kansas, the editor of the *Lawrence Republican* reported that he had met Black Beaver on the street. The Delaware laconically explained why he left Indian Territory, "Bad white and fool red man talk about seceding and raise Texas flag and swear he scalp Yankee Indian."[11]

With the retreat of Union forces, an era of exploration of Indian Territory came to an end. Now would follow four years of warfare and deadly hatreds as many of the tribes split internally between North and South. During this time the social and economic progress of the immigrant tribes would be wiped out. Houses, barns, and fences were burned. Crops would be destroyed and not replanted. Horses, cattle, and other livestock would be either confiscated or stolen. Tribespeople would live in bitter enmity with one another. After the war would come the harsh period of Reconstruction, when the federal government would exact retribution from the dissident tribes that had fought with the South.

In western Indian Territory the tribes were freed for a time from military chastisement for their raiding in Texas and along the Santa Fe Trail. Not until the war

The outbreak of the Civil War, which ended the period of white exploration of Indian country, was followed by military attacks, slaughter of the great buffalo herds, intrusion of Texas cattle being driven to Kansas railroads, and eventual opening of Indian Territory to non-Indian settlement. (R. I. Dodge, *The Plains of the Great Southwest*)

was done could an effective force be mounted for any new invasion of their prairie stronghold. But after 1865 whites arrived in increasing numbers, some as soldiers who waged war against the home camps of the Native Indian and some as hunters who mercilessly slaughtered the buffalo until the Plains were empty of them. Behind these whites came the Texas cattle drovers and cattlemen, pushing their herds northward to Kansas and eventually binding the prairies with barbed wire.

In 1886 the Santa Fe built its line across the midsection of the territory, directly through an area that had come to be known as the Unassigned Lands. Known popularly as the Oklahoma Lands, the region became the target for a series of intrusions—the Oklahoma Boomer Movement—led by Kansan David L. Payne.

This section at the heart of Indian Territory was eventually opened to non-Indian settlement by presidential proclamation in 1889. Other areas soon followed, and by the end of the century the bountiful country that had been so solemnly promised as a permanent home to Native peoples had been conquered.

➤ ─────────────────────────────────────

Appendix
Profiles of Oklahoma Explorers

James William Abert
James W. Abert was born in Mount Holly, New Jersey, November 18, 1820, the son of Colonel John James Abert, chief of the Topographical Engineers. The younger Abert graduated from West Point in 1842 and took part in a survey of the Great Lakes in 1843–1844. Following his Canadian River reconnaissance of 1845, he served in the Mexican War. In 1848 he became an instructor in drawing and painting at West Point. He served in the Seminole War and in the Civil War, when he was wounded. He attained the rank of major of U.S. Engineers before resigning from the army in 1864. He was later honored with a brevet rank of lieutenant colonel. After leaving the service, he became a professor of mathematics and drawing at the University of Missouri at Rolla. He died in 1871.

Richard H. Anderson
Richard H. Anderson, a member of Boone's 1843 exploration, was born October 7, 1821, near Slatesburg, South Carolina. He graduated from West Point in 1842 and was commissioned as a second lieutenant in the First Dragoons. In 1846

he won acclaim during the Mexican War for his brilliant cavalry maneuvers in assistance of the capture of Mexico City. He resigned his captain's rank at the outbreak of the Civil War to join the Confederacy. He fought in numerous Civil War battles. At Gettysburg the three brigades under his command penetrated the center of the Union line, but lack of support forced them to fall back. Anderson held important commands in the Shenandoah Valley and Wilderness campaigns, rising to the rank of lieutenant general before the war ended. He died at Beaufort, South Carolina, June 26, 1879.

Matthew Arbuckle

Matthew Arbuckle, longtime commander of Fort Gibson and namesake of Oklahoma's Arbuckle Mountains, was born in Greenbrier County, Virginia, in 1776, entering the army in 1799 as an ensign. He was made captain in 1806, major in 1812, lieutenant colonel in 1814, and colonel of the Seventh Infantry in 1820. He served in the Indian wars and in 1830 became a brevet brigadier general. Arbuckle held commands at New Orleans, Fort Smith, and Fort Gibson. At Gibson he was actively engaged in Indian affairs and in the extension of U.S. influence to the frontier. He served in the Mexican War and died June 11, 1851, at Fort Smith.

Edward Fitzgerald Beale

Edward F. Beale, who surveyed a wagon road along the Canadian River in 1858, was born at Washington, D.C., February 4, 1822. He was the son of George Beale, a navy paymaster who held the Congressional Medal of Honor for gallantry on Lake Champlain in 1814. Edward's mother, Emily Trustum, was the daughter of a famous naval commodore. While attending Georgetown University, he was appointed by President Jackson to the Naval Academy, graduating there in 1842. In 1845 he sailed to California and from there was sent overland across the continent to carry vital dispatches to Washington, D.C. He returned to California and fought in the Battle of San Pasqual, joining Kit Carson in a heroic effort to penetrate Mexican lines to secure reinforcements. He was appointed superintendent of Indian affairs for California in 1852, and in 1853 he conducted a railroad survey through Colorado and southern Utah. After his survey of 1858–1859, he was appointed surveyor general of California and Nevada. In 1876 President Grant appointed him minister to Austria-Hungary. He died in Washington, D.C., April 22, 1893. Bayard Taylor described him as a pioneer in the path of empire.

Jesse Bean

Jesse Bean, leader of the Ranger unit that toured central Oklahoma in 1832 with Washington Irving, was born in Tennessee. He became a captain of mounted rangers on June 16, 1832. In August 1833 he was appointed captain in the first dragoon regiment that was formed. He resigned from the service May 31, 1835, and died May 31, 1855.

Pierre Beatte

Not much is known of Beatte except that he was a highly esteemed and dependable guide for travelers of early Oklahoma. He has been referred to by various spellings of both his first and last names. Ellsworth claimed that he was a Quapaw Indian; Irving, that he was a mixture of French and Osage; Latrobe, that he was of mixed Quawpaw and French Creole blood. Thompson B. Wheelock said that Beatte was a Frenchman who had lived most his life among the Indians. It appears that he was the namesake of Beattie's Prairie near Maysville, Oklahoma.

Black Beaver

Black Beaver, one of the premier Indian explorers of Oklahoma and the West, was a noted chief of the Delaware tribe, who were notorious as wanderers. Beaver guided many trips to the West Coast with Oregon- and California-bound wagon trains and was often a guide for Marcy, who spoke of him almost reverently. Black Beaver served in the Mexican War at the lead of a company of mounted volunteer Shawnee and Delaware Indians. During the post–Civil War years, he was a model figure as an Indian agriculturist and stockman and often served as a mediator with the warring Plains tribes. Black Beaver died at Anadarko, Oklahoma, May 8, 1880.

John R. Bell

John R. Bell, a native of New York and leader of one division of the Long expedition of 1820, was admitted to West Point in 1808 and graduated January 3, 1812, being commissioned as a second lieutenant of light artillery. He was promoted to first lieutenant the following August; to captain October 10, 1814; and to brevet major October 10, 1824, for ten years' faithful service in one grade. He died April 11, 1825.

Louis Bingier

Louis Bingier was born in France in 1773 prior to his family's migration to New Orleans, where his father became a wealthy exporter and a prominent member of Louisiana's aristocracy. Bingier was raised in luxury at the family's White Hall plantation. He was probably educated in France. Described as a big, fearless man who could whip two or three men of ordinary size, he proved to be the black sheep of his family. He became heavily indebted through gambling, left New Orleans, and spent two years roaming through Missouri, Arkansas, and Oklahoma. At Arkansas Post he was involved in slave trading with John D. Chisholm, grandfather of Jesse Chisholm. In later years Bingier became a surveyor in Louisiana, where at the age of over fifty he married a girl barely out of her teens. He died in 1860 at the age of eighty-seven.

Benjamin Louis Eulalie de Bonneville

B. L. E. de Bonneville, who explored southeast Oklahoma in 1830, was born near Paris, France, on April 14, 1796. His father was a radical intellectual and close friend to General Lafayette and John Howard Paine, author of "Home Sweet Home." At the age of seventeen Bonneville came to America with his mother and in 1815 graduated from West Point. He saw service in New England until 1820, when he was assigned to road building in Mississippi. Bonneville was sent to Fort Smith in 1821 and served there and at Fort Gibson until 1832. Taking a leave of duty, he led a 110-man party to the Green River to engage in the fur trade. Upon his return, he found he had been dropped from the army. Over the protest of his fellow officers, President Jackson reinstated him to rank. He returned to Gibson, but social pressures caused him to be reassigned. Bonneville won a lieutenant colonel's rank for his gallantry during the Mexican War. He was brevetted brigadier general after retiring in 1865. He lived his final years at Fort Smith, dying there June 12, 1878. He was given lasting fame by Washington Irving's book *The Adventures of Captain Bonneville, U.S.A.*

Nathan Boone

In addition to being a historical military figure of early Oklahoma, Nathan Boone was also involved in much of its exploration. The youngest child of Daniel Boone, he was born March 2, 1780 or 1781 in Kentucky. In 1799 his family moved to Missouri, where Nathan gained high reputation as a leader of militia and as an Indian fighter. He arrived in Indian Territory in 1832 as captain of a company of mounted rangers. He helped survey the Cherokee-Creek boundary and was the commander of Fort Wayne in 1838. In addition to the one in this book, he led numerous military excursions into unknown areas of present-day Oklahoma. He served in the army until 1853, retiring with the rank of lieutenant colonel. He is believed to have died in 1856 and is buried at Ash Grove, Missouri.

William Bradford

William Bradford, the first commanding officer of Fort Smith, Arkansas, was a native of Virginia and Kentucky. He was appointed as a captain in the Twenty-first Infantry in 1812. He won the rank of brevet major in 1814 and the regular rank of major in 1818. Transferring to the Fourth Infantry in 1822, he resigned in May 1824 and died October 20, 1826.

Abraham Buford

Abraham Buford, who was involved in several Oklahoma explorations, was born January 18, 1820, in Woodford County, Kentucky, of a family well known as breeders of blooded horses. He graduated from West Point in 1841 and was assigned to frontier service with the First Dragoons. He won a brevet captaincy for action at Buena Vista during the Mexican War. He resigned from the U.S. Army in 1854 to become a stock breeder. When the Civil War began, he was appointed a brigadier general in the Confederate Army. He was severely wounded at Lindville in December 1864. After the war he returned to his stock farm and was very successful for a time. His only son died in 1872 and his wife a short time later. Financial reverses resulted in the loss of his home. Buford took his own life on June 8, 1884.

Pierce Mason Butler

Pierce Mason Butler, Cherokee agent who led a peacemaking expedition to Cache Creek, was born April 11, 1798, in South Carolina, where he attended a military academy. He entered military service in 1819. As an officer in the First Infantry Regiment, he was involved in the founding of Fort Gibson in 1824. In 1829 he resigned from the army to become president of a bank in Columbia, South Carolina. In 1836 he was appointed as a lieutenant colonel in a volunteer regiment to fight in the Seminole War in Florida. On his return, he was elected governor of South Carolina in 1838. He was appointed Cherokee agent in 1841 and immediately reported to his post at Fort Gibson. He organized a volunteer unit and became its colonel during the Mexican War. He was wounded in the Battle of Churubusco but would not retire from the field. He continued to lead the advance until shot in the head and killed August 20, 1847.

George Catlin

George Catlin, famous Indian artist who accompanied the Leavenworth expedition of 1834 to the Wichita Mountains, was born at Wilkes-Barre, Pennsylvania, July 26, 1796. He was trained as a lawyer, but his talent as a portrait painter won out. He developed his skills as a self-taught portrait artist before turning to Indian subjects. His younger brother Julius, a graduate of West Point, had been with the First U.S. Infantry when it established Cantonment Gibson in 1824. Julius resigned from the army in 1826, in part to return home and encourage George in his painting of western life. In 1829 Catlin traveled to St. Louis and from there to the upper Missouri River, where he spent five years becoming familiar with the Indian tribes and painting portraits of Indian figures. He made more than five hundred paintings and sketches, which he exhibited on tour in New York City, Baltimore, and Washington, D.C., and, from 1839 to 1845,

Europe. In 1853 he began traveling the jungles of Central and South America in a canoe to paint Indian life there. He died December 23, 1872, in Jersey City, New Jersey.

George Chisholm (Vincente)

George Chisholm, whose real name was Vincente de Huersus, was rescued from Comanche captivity and adopted by trader Jesse Chisholm. The younger Chisholm served as a government scout and interpreter at Fort Sill, Oklahoma, until 1874, when he resigned in a disagreement with General Ranald S. Mackenzie. De Huersus then took up residence among the Creek Nation, his wife being a member of that tribe. Vincente died at Yeager, Oklahoma, November 1, 1917.

Jesse Chisholm

Jesse Chisholm served the United States, Texas, and the immigrant tribes as a mediator with the Plains tribes. Chisholm, born between 1804 and 1806 in Tennessee, was half Scotch and half Cherokee. He came west to Arkansas with the first Cherokee migration in 1810. He went up the Arkansas River from Fort Gibson with a gold-search party in 1826 and made a trip to California via the Texas route in 1839. As an Indian trader and Indian mediator, he traveled between his home on the Canadian River into southwestern Oklahoma and deep into Texas and took trade goods north to Fort Leavenworth. Having established a road between his post at Council Grove in present-day west Oklahoma City and Wichita, Kansas, he became the namesake for the Chisholm Cattle Trail that followed the same path. Chisholm died during an Indian trade session on the Salt Creek tributary of the Cimarron River, April 4, 1868.

Auguste Pierre Chouteau

Colonel Auguste Pierre Chouteau, eldest son of Pierre Chouteau, was born May 9, 1786, at St. Louis and entered West Point in 1804. He graduated in June 1806 and served as an aide to General James Wilkinson on the southwestern frontier. Chouteau resigned from the army in 1807 and that same year accompanied Ensign Nathaniel Pryor in his attempt to return Mandan Shehaka to his people. Chouteau became one of the ten partners of the Missouri Fur Company.

In 1815 he accompanied Jules de Mun to the upper Arkansas River, being captured and imprisoned by the Spanish in 1817. In 1823 Chouteau bought the trading house of Brand and Barbour at Three Forks, where he became good friends with Sam Houston. Chouteau married an Osage woman and resided in a plantation-style home on the Grand River but remained active on the Indian frontier. He died December 25, 1838, near Fort Gibson.

It was his father, Jean Pierre Chouteau, who persuaded an Osage band to move to the Verdigris River and who established the first trading post in present Oklahoma. Colonel Chouteau's brother Paul was also active in early Oklahoma, as was his nephew (Paul's son) Edward Chouteau.

Douglas Cooper

Douglas Cooper, a native of Mississippi who as Choctaw agent led a military sweep of southeastern Oklahoma in 1858, had served under Jefferson Davis during the Mexican War. At the outbreak of the Civil War, Cooper was commissioned a colonel and later as brigadier general in the Confederate Army as commander of the First Choctaw and Chickasaw Regiment, which saw Civil War action in Indian Territory. He remained among the Choctaws and Chickasaws after the war, dying at Fort Washita on April 30, 1879.

Francisco Vásquez de Coronado

Francisco Vásquez de Coronado, born around 1510, was made governor of Nueva Galicia, Mexico, in 1538. Hearing tales of the dazzling wealth of the Seven Cities of Cíbola, he led a great expedition north into southeast Arizona. Although he discovered the Grand Canyon, he found no wealth. Led by stories of the Turk, he marched northeast across the Oklahoma Panhandle in search of Quivira. Returning to Nueva Galicia, he became involved in a fruitless war. He was dismissed as governor in 1544 and spent the remainder of his life in obscurity in Mexico City, dying in 1554.

Jefferson Davis

Jefferson Davis, an officer with the Leavenworth expedition of 1834, was best known as president of the Confederate States. He was born June 3, 1808, in Todd County, Kentucky, his father being a Georgia revolutionary soldier. At an early age the family moved to Mississippi. Davis attended Transylvania College in Kentucky and graduated from West Point in 1824. After serving in Indian Territory, Davis resigned from the army, married the daughter of Zachary Taylor, and settled on a plantation in Mississippi. He was elected to Congress in 1845. The following year he organized a regiment of Mississippi volunteers and led them in the Mexican War. After the war, in which he saw considerable action, Davis rejected a presidential appointment of brigadier general and returned to Congress. Upon election of his friend Franklin Pierce as president, Davis was appointed secretary of war, serving as such until 1857. He was again in the Senate when the Civil War began but quickly resigned and returned home to become commander in chief of Mississippi troops. On February 18, 1861, he was inaugurated as provisional president of the Confederacy. After the war he was incarcerated at Fortress Monroe. Released in May 1867, he visited Canada and England until he could legally return to Mississippi. There he became president of a life insurance company and wrote a history of the Confederacy. He died December 6, 1889, in New Orleans while on a trip.

James Henry Dawson

James H. Dawson, who conducted several Oklahoma explorations and first surveyed roads in the state, was born in Baltimore, Maryland, September 3, 1799. His schooling is unclear, but he was commissioned as a second lieutenant in the U.S. Army, August 13, 1819. He was at Fort Smith in 1825 and moved to Fort Gibson, where he married the daughter of Assistant Surgeon John W. Baylor. In addition to several explorations, Dawson joined Pierce M. Butler in surveying a road between Fort Gibson and Fort Smith. Dawson resigned from the army in 1835 and became a planter and slave dealer near Pine Bluff, Arkansas. He returned to Three Forks as Creek agent in 1842. In 1844 he shot and killed a man in an argument and fled the country to avoid arrest on the charge of murder. He was captured in Texas by an Arkansas group in 1845 and taken to Little Rock. However, his arrest was declared to have been illegal, and he was released. He died at Westminister, Maryland, January 13, 1879.

Appendix

Henry Dodge

Henry Dodge, who conducted peace talks with the Plains tribes on the North Fork of the Red River in 1834, was born in Vincennes, Indiana, on October 12, 1782, but he grew up in Ste. Genevieve, Missouri. Having been a district sheriff and territorial marshal, Dodge commanded a company of mounted riflemen in the War of 1812. He quickly rose to the rank of major general. Moving to Wisconsin, he fought in the Black Hawk war. In 1832 the mounted rangers became a part of the First Dragoon Regiment, in which he was named a colonel. Following his Indian Territory service, Dodge led an expedition to the Rocky Mountains in 1835. The following year he was appointed governor of newly organized Wisconsin Territory. He served two terms as a territorial delegate to Congress and was reappointed to his governor's post in 1845. When Wisconsin became a state, he was elected to the Senate. Dodge died at Burlington, Iowa, June 19, 1867.

Claude Charles Du Tisné

A native of Paris, France, Claude Charles Du Tisné came to Canada sometime prior to 1708. In 1714 he arrived at Mobile on the Gulf of Mexico in charge of a detachment of soldiers. From there he conducted an exploration to the Ohio River. In 1716 he was sent with twenty men to bring the chief of the Natchez Indians to a conference and in doing so successfully was appointed second in command of Fort Rosalie at Natchez, Mississippi. In 1717 Du Tisné led forty men on an overland journey from Mobile to Canada, returning the following year with his family. Commissioned to explore Missouri River country, he visited the Osages and Wichitas. In 1722 he took part in an expedition against the Fox Indians of Illinois and afterward served as French commandant in Illinois until his death in 1730.

Henry Leavitt Ellsworth

Henry L. Ellsworth, who toured Oklahoma with Washington Irving in 1832, was born in Windsor, Connecticut, November 10, 1791. He was the son of Chief Justice of the U.S. Supreme Court Oliver Ellsworth and twin brother of William Wolcott Ellsworth, governor of Connecticut. After graduating from Yale and Litchfield Law School, he practiced law and engaged in agriculture. He was president of Aetna Insurance Company. In 1832 President Jackson appointed him as a commissioner to attend the removed tribes. Ellsworth wrote a descriptive account of his trip to Indian Territory. Returning to the East, he was elected mayor of Hartford in 1835 but soon resigned to accept an appointment as U.S. commissioner of patents. In that office he assisted his friend Samuel B. Morse in obtaining a $30,000 grant to test his telegraph invention. After resigning in 1845, Ellsworth moved to Indiana, where he continued his work in advancing agriculture and agricultural machinery. Poor health made him return to Fair Haven, Connecticut, where he died on December 27, 1858.

William Helmsly Emory

William H. Emory, former commander of Fort Arbuckle who led the Union retreat from Indian Territory in 1861, was born of colonial descent in Maryland. Emory graduated from West Point in 1831. In 1838 he was assigned to the Topographical Corps and helped survey the U.S.-Canada border. During the Mexican War he was appointed chief engineer of the army and won two brevets for meritorious service in battles at San Pasqual, San Gabriel, and Plains of the Mesa. After the war he helped survey the California-Mexico border. He won more honors for his Civil War service and was commissioned as a major general of volunteers in 1865. Emory's wife was a granddaughter of Benjamin Franklin. He retired from the army in 1876 and died December 31, 1887.

Thomas Fitzpatrick

Thomas Fitzpatrick, born around 1799, was a member of Abert's expedition across Oklahoma in 1845. One of the most famous of the mountain men—ranking with Carson and Bridger—he was involved in much of the history of the early West: a member of Ashley's trapper company in 1823, participant in battles with the Arikaras, second in command with Jedediah Smith's penetration of Wyoming in 1824, a noted fur trader, leader of emigrant trains to Montana and Oregon, guide to Fremont in 1843–1844, and first agent, in 1846, for the Cheyenne and Arapaho Indians. Known among the Indians as "Bad Hand"—a rifle burst had blown off two fingers— Fitzpatrick died at Washington, D.C., February 7, 1854.

John S. Ford

John S. Ford, who led a Texas Ranger invasion of Indian Territory in 1858, was born in South Carolina, May 26, 1815. Later he moved to Tennessee, where he studied to become a doctor. In 1836 he went west to Texas, joining in the fight for Texas independence. In 1844 he was a member of the Republic of Texas congress, and for a time he published a newspaper at Austin. During the Mexican War he fought with John C. Hays's regiment of Texas Rangers and rose to captain of rangers in 1849. He continued his political and newspaper activity until called to his Indian campaign in 1858. Later he led the Texas Rangers against Mexican bandits. When Texas seceded, Ford became a Confederate colonel and saw action along the Rio Grande until the war's end. For several years he was superintendent of the Deaf and Dumb Asylum at Austin. He died at San Antonio in 1897.

Jacob Fowler

Jacob Fowler, who kept a rough but descriptive diary of an 1821 trapper expedition from Oklahoma to Colorado, was born in New York in 1765. At an early age he moved to Kentucky, where he worked as a surveyor as well as for the U,S. government in the West. He later became a partner with Hugh Glenn at Cincinnati in supplying various army posts. One of these was Fort Smith, the location of which led him to his coadventure with the Glenn party to Oklahoma and the Rocky Mountains. Fowler died at his home in Covington, Kentucky, in 1850.

Hugh Glenn

Hugh Glenn, leader of an 1821 trapping party up the Arkansas River, was born in Berkeley County, West Virginia, January 7, 1788. His father was a native of Scotland. By 1803 Glen had moved to Kentucky, and he became a major in the militia there. He moved on to Cincinnati, Ohio, where he was captain of a company that was recruited at the start of the War of 1812. In 1814 he became a partner with Jacob Fowler in furnishing supplies to the Army of the Northwest. In 1817 the men entered into a contract to furnish provisions and supplies to garrison troops at eight frontier outposts and to Indians who came in to those posts. One of these was Belle

Point, or Fort Smith. He later operated one of the first trading houses at Three Forks. His trading expedition to the mountains and then to Santa Fe and back to Missouri was the first by that route. Although Thomas James did not like or trust him, Glenn was said to be a gentleman in both manner and practice. He died at Cincinnati, May 28, 1833.

Rodney Glisan

A native of Linganore, Maryland, Rodney Glisan graduated from the medical department of the University of Maryland in 1849. After practicing medicine for a year, he was appointed as an assistant surgeon in the U.S. Army. He served on the Plains for five years and in Oregon during the Indian wars from 1850 to 1861, when he resigned his commission. After a year's practice in San Franciso, he settled in Portland, Oregon, where he led a notable medical career. He traveled widely throughout the United States, Central America, and Europe. Glisan authored numerous articles on medical science as well as books on his army experiences, travels abroad, and a *Text-Book of Modern Midwifery.*

Josiah Gregg

Josiah Gregg's book *Commerce of the Prairies* was an invaluable guide to early-day travelers across Indian Territory. Gregg was born July 19, 1806, the son of an Illinois farmer. Smallish and often sickly, Gregg tried his hand at both medicine and law but did not fit well in either. His poor health led him to join a merchant caravan to New Mexico, and he found the trail much to his liking. After his return from his 1839 journey across Oklahoma, he made another tour from Fort Smith to Cache Creek and back via Chouteau's post on the Canadian. After trying a variety of vocations, Gregg returned to the trail in 1846. During the Mexican War he joined General John Ellis Wool's army as a doctor and correspondent. His interest in collecting and identifying plants of the West and Mexico brought him recognition as a naturalist, with several plants being designated as *greggi.* Gregg followed the gold rush to California, eventually losing his life while exploring the unknown country north of San Francisco. He died on February 25, 1850. Buried on the trail, his gravesite has been lost to record. He had never married.

Montgomery Pike Harrison

Montgomery P. Harrison, an officer with Marcy's expedition up the Canadian River in 1849 and brother of President Benjamin Harrison, was born in Indiana and became a cadet at West Point in July 1842. He was commissioned as a second lieutenant in the Seventh Infantry in July 1847, transferring to the Fifth Infantry the following September. He was killed by hostile Indians near the Colorado River in Texas on October 7, 1849.

Ethan Allen Hitchcock

Ethan A. Hitchcock, who investigated tribal conditions in eastern Oklahoma in 1841–1842, was a grandson of the famous Ethan Allen. Hitchcock was born at Vergennes, Vermont, May 18, 1798, and graduated from West Point in 1817. After graduation he became an instructor and commandant of the Corps of Cadets at the military academy. Hitchcock was credited with ending the bloody Seminole War in Florida through diplomacy. A man of literary ability and unimpeachable honesty and courage, he saw action in several battles of the Mexican War, where he won the brevet of colonel. He commanded the U.S. Army's Pacific Division from 1851 to 1855 and rose to major general of volunteers during the Civil War. He died August 5, 1870, at St. Louis.

Theophilus Hunter Holmes

Theophilus H. Holmes, who constructed Fort Holmes at the mouth of Little River in 1834, was born November 13, 1804, the son of North Carolina governor Gabriel Holmes. The younger Holmes graduated from West Point in 1829 and served in Florida, Texas, and Indian Territory. Holmes was a close friend of classmate and fellow officer at Fort Gibson Jefferson Davis. Holmes was brevetted a major for Mexican War service and was in command of recruiting at Governor's Island, New York, when the Civil War began. He resigned from the U.S. Army and was appointed brigadier general, and later major general, by Confederate president Davis. Holmes was given important war assignments but proved to be inadequate as a commander. He died June 21, 1880.

Washington Irving

Washington Irving, whose classic *A Tour of the Prairies* is an important document of early Oklahoma history, was born in New York City, April 3, 1783, the youngest of eleven children. Educated for the bar, his love and skills as a writer soon emerged. He had already won great literary success with such stories as "The Legend of Sleepy Hollow" when he went to Germany in 1826 to attend to his health and to study German folklore. He had just returned from Europe after seventeen years there when he made his trip to the West. Afterward, among his other works were *Astoria* in 1836 and *The Adventures of Captain Bonneville* in 1837. He died at his home on the Hudson River of New York on November 28, 1859.

Edwin James

Edwin James was born at Weybridge, Addison County, Vermont, on August 27, 1797. After graduating from Middlebury College in 1816, he studied botany and geology at Albany, New York, for three years, as well as medicine under his doctor brother. James wrote the official account of the Long expedition of 1820, which was published in Philadelphia and London. In 1823 he became an assistant surgeon in the U.S. Army and was stationed at Fort Crawford (Prairie du Chien) and Mackinac, Michigan, where he compiled several Indian spelling books. He also translated the New Testament in the Ojibway language. In 1837–1838 he was subagent for the Pottawatomie Indians at Council Bluffs, Nebraska. He spent his last years on a farm near Burlington, Iowa, where he ran a station for escaping slaves on the underground railroad. He died October 28, 1861, at the age of sixty-four.

Thomas James

The worth of Thomas James's account of his visits to western Oklahoma in 1821 and 1823 has generally been underappreciated. James was born in Maryland in 1782 but moved west with his family to Kentucky, to Illinois, and then to Florissant, Missouri, in 1807. At the age of twenty-seven he enlisted with a fur company and spent several years on the upper Missouri. Following his two expeditions into present-day Oklahoma, he turned to milling for a time in Monroe County, Illinois. In 1825 he was elected a general in the Illinois militia and served in the Illinois state legislature during 1826–1828. He fought in the Black Hawk war as an officer commanding a "spy battalion." He died at Monroe, Illinois, in December 1847.

Abraham R. Johnston

Abraham R. Johnston, a dragoon officer involved in Oklahoma exploration during the early 1840s, was a native of Ohio who graduated from West Point in 1830. He was commissioned as a second lieutenant in the Second Dragoons and was made a captain in 1846. Soon after, in December 1846, he was killed in the Mexican War battle of San Pasqual.

Joseph Eggleston Johnston

Joseph E. Johnston, who led a survey of the Oklahoma-Kansas border in 1857, was born near Farmville, Virginia, February 3, 1807. An 1829 graduate of West Point, he was named quartermaster general of the U.S. Army with the rank of brigadier general in June 1860. He resigned April 22, 1861, when Virginia seceded from the Union. Involved in many key battles for the South, he rose to the rank of full general in the Confederate Army and was appointed by General Robert E. Lee as commander of the Army of Tennessee. Johnston died March 21, 1891, at Washington, D.C., where he had served one term in the House of Representatives from Richmond, Virginia.

Other officers with him on the 1857 survey were Richard Brooks Garnett, who became a Confederate brigadier general and was killed at the Battle of Gettysburg on July 3, 1863; Benjamin Franklin Smith, who became a brigadier general of volunteers in the Union Army; and Owen Kenan McLemore, who entered Confederate service as a lieutenant colonel, dying of wounds from a Civil War battle, September 14, 1862.

Stephen Watts Kearny

Stephen W. Kearny was born in Newark, New Jersey, August 30, 1794. He was a lieutenant in the Thirteenth Infantry when the War of 1812 began, and he distinguished himself in the assault on Queenstown Heights. In 1813 he became a captain and as a lieutenant colonel of the First Dragoons was third in command during the 1834 Leavenworth expedition. By June 1846 Kearny had risen to brigadier general and commanded the Army of the West, which marched from Bent's Fort to capture Santa Fe. After establishing a provisional government there, he marched on to California, where he was twice wounded in the Battle of San Pasqual. For this and other action, he was promoted to major general. He was made military governor of California in 1846. In 1847 he joined the army in Mexico, where he served as military and civil governor of both Vera Cruz and Mexico City. He contracted a disease in Mexico and died there in October 1848.

Bernard de La Harpe

Bernard de La Harpe, a French soldier and explorer, had been given a grant on the Red River prior to 1817. The French Council of Louisiana made him commandant over the Nassonite, Cadodauinou, Nadaco, and Natchitoches Indians. He was assigned to explore both the Arkansas and Red rivers for France and do all he could to establish trade with the Spanish of Texas and New Mexico. He left New Orleans in December 1718 to explore and contact the tribes concerning trade. He became commander of the trading center and Jesuit mission at Arkansas Post and in 1722 ascended the Arkansas River beyond the site of Little Rock.

Charles Joseph Latrobe

Charles J. Latrobe, who visited Oklahoma with Irving in 1832 and penned his own account of the trip, was born March 20, 1801, in London, England. A nephew of architect Benjamin Henry Latrobe, who helped design and build the U.S. Capitol, Charles Latrobe was well educated and well traveled in the United States, Mexico, Africa, and Europe. He accompanied Pourtalès on the western tour as a tutor to the prince. Latrobe was the author of a number of books, including *Crayon Miscellany, A Visit to South Africa,* and *The Rambler in North America.* He died in London, December 2, 1875.

Henry Leavenworth

Henry Leavenworth, who died while exploring Oklahoma, was born in New Haven, Connecticut, on December 10, 1783.

His father was a revolutionary soldier. When the parents separated, Henry went with his father to Delhi, New York. There he studied law and was admitted to the bar in 1804. He began his military career during the War of 1812 and rose to the rank of colonel by 1815, when he took a leave to serve in the New York legislature. He commanded a unit that built Fort Snelling, Minnesota, in 1819. In 1823 he led U.S. forces against the Arikara Indians and was afterward brevetted as a brigadier general. In 1827 he built the post that bears his name, Fort Leavenworth, Kansas. Early in 1834 he was put in command of the entire southwestern frontier, with instructions to negotiate peace among the warring Plains tribes. He died July 21, 1834, at Camp Smith on the Washita and is buried at Fort Leavenworth.

Stephen Harriman Long

Stephen H. Long, who led an exploring expedition through Oklahoma in 1820, was born in Hopkinton, New Hampshire, December 30, 1784. After graduating from Dartmouth College in 1809, he joined the army engineers. Long was an instructor at West Point for two years before being promoted to the rank of major in the Topographical Corps. His first explorations were on the upper Mississippi. After his trip to the Rocky Mountains, Long explored the upper Minnesota River and the U.S.-Canada border region. He helped survey several Baltimore and Ohio Railroad routes and from 1837 to 1840 was chief engineer for the Atlantic and Great Western Railroad. He was appointed as chief of the Corps of Topographical Engineers with the rank of colonel in 1861. He died in Alto, Illinois, September 4, 1864.

James B. Many

James B. Many, onetime Fort Gibson commander who led a military reconnaissance from Gibson to the Washita River in 1833, was born in Delaware on June 4, 1798. He became an officer in the U.S. Army in 1798. In 1804 he was in command of troops that took over from the Spanish at Arkansas Post. Many served on the frontier for nine years before being transferred to New York and then to New Orleans. He was ordered to Fort Gibson when it was constructed in 1824, and he served as commandant at both Gibson and Fort Smith. In

1836 he was in charge at Fort Jesup, Louisiana, and marched to Shreveport to expel Republic of Texas forces that had crossed the border to disarm the Caddo Indians. After retirement from the military, Many spent the rest of his life in Louisiana, dying February 23, 1852.

Randolph Barnes Marcy

Randolph B. Marcy, the most active explorer of Oklahoma and north Texas, was born in Greenwich, Massachusetts, April 9, 1812. His father was secretary of war under Polk. After graduating from West Point in 1832, Marcy saw service in Michigan and Wisconsin Territories and Texas. During the Mexican War he was involved in the battles of Palo Alto and Resaca de la Palma. After his Indian Territory tour, he played a brief role in the Seminole War in Florida in 1857. That same year he served in Colonel Albert S. Johnson's Mormon expedition. During the Civil War Marcy served as chief of staff to son-in-law General George B. McClellan. Marcy retired in 1881 after serving as inspector general of the army. He died in New Jersey on November 22, 1887.

Richard Barnes Mason

Richard B. Mason, member of the Leavenworth expedition and builder of Camp Holmes in 1835, was born in Fairfax County, Virginia, January 16, 1797. At age twenty he was appointed a second lieutenant in the Eighth U.S. Infantry. Mason fought in the Black Hawk war at the Battle of Bad Axe, and in 1833 he was made a major in the First Dragoons at Fort Des Moines. He was appointed lieutenant colonel in 1836 and was assigned to Fort Gibson, which he came to command. In 1847 he was transferred to California, where he became the first military governor. In 1848 he was brevetted as a brigadier general and soon returned to the East. His report on the discovery of gold in California was the most authentic ever published and was distributed around the world. He died of Asiatic cholera at Jefferson Barracks, Missouri, July 25, 1850.

George Brinton McClellan

George B. McClellan, member of Marcy's 1852 search for the headwaters of the Red River and namesake of Oklahoma's

McClellan Creek, was born in Philadelphia, Pennsylvania, December 3, 1826. His grandfather had fought at Bunker Hill, and his father was a doctor. McClellan was educated by private tutors before attending the University of Pennsylvania for two years. Upon graduation from West Point, along with Stonewall Jackson and Ambrose Burnside, in 1842 he was assigned to the Army Corps of Engineers. He served in the Mexican War, taking part in several battles and having his horse shot from under him in one contest. Afterward he saw service in Indian Territory, Texas, Oregon, and Washington. In 1857 he resigned to become chief engineer of the Illinois Central Railroad, later becoming president of the St. Louis, Missouri, and Cincinnati Railroad. When the Civil War began, he was made major general in command of the Department of the Ohio. In May 1862 he was appointed major general in the U.S. Army and replaced General Winfield Scott as commander of all the armies of the United States. Unhappy with McClellan's inaction in moving against the South, President Lincoln removed him from command on November 7, 1863. McClellan ran against Lincoln for the presidency in 1864, losing badly in the electoral vote. After the war McClellan worked at various engineering assignments until he was elected governor of New Jersey in 1877. In his later years he wrote articles for magazines as well as his autobiography. He died October 29, 1885, at Orange, New Jersey.

Isaac McCoy

Isaac McCoy was born near Uniontown, Pennsylvania, on June 13, 1784. In 1790 he moved with his parents to Kentucky, where he received some public school education. In 1804 he and his new wife took up residence in Indiana, where he was ordained to preach in the Baptist church. In the ensuing years he conducted missionary work among the western Indians and took part in the removal of the Ottawa and Miami tribes to the West. In 1827 he published *Remarks on the Practicability of Indian Reform* and was soon after invited to meet with John C. Calhoun, secretary of war. Accepting a government position as surveyor and Indian agent, McCoy was active in surveying lands involved in Indian removal. McCoy wrote a *History of the Baptist Indian Missions* and published numerous pamphlets on tribal affairs. His proposal for an Indian state was not accepted by the U.S. government, even though he surveyed a tract of land near Ottawa, Kansas, for an Indian capital. He died at Louisville, Kentucky, June 21, 1846.

Leonard McPhail

Leonard McPhail, who kept a journal of the 1835 Camp Mason peace council near present-day Lexington, Oklahoma, was a native of Maryland. He entered the U.S. Army in November 1834 and was sent to Fort Jackson at New Orleans for a short time before being assigned to the Second Dragoons at Fort Gibson. He was attached to the Seventh Infantry during the Mexican War, seeing duty at Matamoras, Palo Alto, and Resaca de la Palma. After the war he remained at Matamoras and was promoted to surgeon. He and his younger brother both resigned from the service on April 30, 1849, but for what reason is not known. He died in 1867.

Athanase de Mézierès

Athanase de Mézierès, who visited the Spanish forts on the Red River in 1778, was a native of Paris, France. He came to America about 1733. He was a brother-in-law of the duke of Orleans and had been a longtime French soldier in Louisiana when he was appointed lieutenant governor of the Natchitoches district in 1769. He was instructed to appoint licensed traders for the friendly Red River tribes and to stop the trade in stolen horses and Indian captives at the Taovaya villages. In 1770 he summoned the chiefs of the Taovaya, Tawakoni, Yscani, and Kichai Indians to a meeting near present-day Texarkana, Texas, and made treaties with them. In 1772 he toured their country, going as far west as the Brazos River and on to San Antonio. His account of this notable expedition provides our first views of the Indian tribes there. In May 1779, while making a tour of the north Texas tribes, de Mézierès suffered an injury. Upon arriving at San Antonio, he learned that he had been appointed governor of Texas. Before taking office, however, he died on November 2, 1779.

Nathaniel Michler

Born in Eastern, Pennsylvania, in 1827, Nathaniel Michler graduated from the U.S. Military Academy in 1848. As a member of the Topographical Engineer Corps, he helped survey the Mexican boundary during 1851–1857. During 1857–1860 he was chief engineer of the survey to build a ship canal from the Gulf of Darien to the Pacific. In the Civil War Michler served with the Union Armies of the Ohio and Cumberland and was involved in several important battles, creating defensive works. He rose to the rank of brevet brigadier general. Following the war, he was involved in various engineering projects along the East Coast. He held the regular rank of lieutenant colonel when he died in New York in 1881.

Heinrich B. Möllhausen

Heinrich B. Möllhausen, a member of Whipple's railroad survey across Oklahoma in 1853, was born January 27, 1825, near Bonn, Germany. The artist arrived in America in 1849. In 1851 he was a member of an expedition led by the duke of Württemburg on an expedition to the West. Möllhausen returned to Germany, then came back to America in 1853 to join the Whipple expedition as topographer and artist. An active writer and scholar, he served as librarian for King Frederick William IV, dying in Berlin, May 28, 1905.

Lucius B. Northrop

Lucius B. Northrop, who led a detachment to Wolf Creek in northwestern Oklahoma in 1838, was a native of South Carolina. He graduated from West Point in July 1827. In August 1833 he was transferred to the dragoons as a brevet second lieutenant. Northrop was a member of the Leavenworth-Dodge expedition of 1834. He was made first lieutenant on July 4, 1836. At the outbreak of the Civil War, he resigned his commission to become a colonel in the Confederate Army. He died February 9, 1894.

Thomas Nuttall

Thomas Nuttall, the botanist who kept a detailed journal of his scientific explorations of eastern and central Oklahoma in 1819, was born January 5, 1786, in Yorkshire, England. He served seven years as an apprentice printer before emigrating to the United States. Through the encouragement of botanist Dr. Benjamin S. Barton of the University of Pennsylvania,

Nuttall became a student and eventual expert on North American flora. He identified many new genera and species of plants. In addition to his Arkansas River trip, Nuttall made expeditions to the Columbia River and to Hawaii. He eventually became a lecturer on natural history at Harvard and was curator of the botanical gardens there. He was much published, one of his books being *A Manual of the Ornithology of the United States and Canada*. He returned to England in 1842 and died at Lancashire on September, 10, 1859.

Juan de Oñate

Juan de Oñate, Spanish conquistador who crossed Oklahoma in 1602, may have been born in New Spain (Mexico). Per a 1595 contract with the viceroy of New Spain, Oñate led an army north to conquer and settle New Mexico in 1598. He established a Spanish settlement there and harshly put down a Pueblo Indian revolt. After his trip to Oklahoma and Kansas, he led an expedition west to the Colorado River, following it to lower California. He resigned as governor in 1609. Because he had found no gold, he was convicted on charges of misconduct in 1614 but was eventually pardoned before his death in 1624.

William Guy Peck

William G. Peck, a member of Abert's 1845 march down the Canadian, was born October 6, 1820, in Greenwich, Connecticut. A graduate of West Point, he was with the Army of the West under General Kearny in its march on Santa Fe. Afterward Peck was an assistant professor at West Point until resigning in 1855. He taught physics, engineering, mathematics, mechanics, and astronomy at the University of Michigan and Columbia, himself earning a Ph.D. from Columbia and LL.D. from Trinity. Additionally, he authored several significant scholarly works in his professional areas. He died at Greenwich, Connecticut, February 7, 1892.

Albert Pike

Born in Boston December 29, 1809, Albert Pike attended Harvard briefly, then became a grammar school principal. He wrote a descriptive account of his trip across Oklahoma and the Staked Plains in 1831. Settling in Arkansas, he became a lawyer, newspaper editor, and contributor of poetry to *Blackwood's Magazine*. He commanded a regiment during the Mexican War. At the outbreak of the Civil War, he became a Confederate Indian commissioner and negotiated treaties with both the immigrant and Plains tribes. He later became a Confederate brigadier general. After the war Pike returned to the law profession, retiring in 1880. He was an active Mason, and today the Masonic Temple in Washington, D.C., is dedicated largely to his memory.

Zebulon Montgomery Pike

Zebulon M. Pike, whose expedition of 1806 led to Oklahoma exploration, was born in Lamberton, New Jersey, January 5, 1779, but was raised and educated in Pennsylvania. His father, a captain in the Revolutionary Army, was brevetted a lieutenant colonel in the Regular Army. Zebulon was appointed ensign in his father's regiment in 1809 and rose to captain's rank in 1806. On his exploration of the Southwest, he was captured by Spanish forces and held in 1807. In 1813 he commanded an expedition against Toronto. During the engagement he was killed when a magazine exploded and buried him under a mass of stone. Pike died April 27, 1813. He is the namesake of Pike's Peak in Colorado.

Albert-Alexandre de Pourtalès

Albert-Alexandre de Pourtalès, who accompanied the Ellsworth-Irving tour of central Oklahoma in 1832, was born in Switzerland on October 10, 1812. A member of a royal family, he held the title of comte de Pourtalès and was known to Americans as a count or prince. His family estates were in Switzerland and Bohemia. Irving described him as being talented but youthfully spirited and prone to wild adventures. Pourtalès died in Paris on December 18, 1861.

James E. Powell

English-born James E. Powell enlisted in the U.S. Army in 1847 from Maine. He was appointed second lieutenant in the First Infantry in 1855 and was upgraded to first lieutenant in 1856. Serving with the Union during the Civil War, he was made a brevet major in 1862 when he was commended for his gallantry and meritorious service. He was killed in the Battle of Shiloh on April 6, 1862.

Nathaniel Pryor

Nathaniel Pryor, who was involved in several explorations of early Oklahoma, was born in Virginia. He is most famous as a sergeant with the Lewis and Clark expedition of 1804–1806. Afterward Pryor was in charge of a military detachment that returned Mandan chief Shehaka to his people. He was appointed infantry ensign in 1807 and second lieutenant in 1807 and rose to captain before being honorably discharged in 1815. He engaged in the fur trade at Arkansas Post for a time before securing a license to trade at Six Bulls, where he married an Osage woman. Pryor was highly regarded as an Osage subagent and as a frontiersman. He died in June 1831.

Thomas Say

Thomas Say, a naturalist and member of the Long expedition who accompanied Bell down the Arkansas River in 1819, was born in Philadelphia, July 27, 1787. He was the founder of the Academy of Natural Sciences in 1812 and took part in scientific visits to islands along the southern coast of the United States. He was widely known for his collection of insects. Among his principal published works were *American Entomology* and *American Conchology*. In 1821 he was made curator of the American Philosophical Society and became professor of natural history at the University of Pennsylvania in 1822. Say, who was often in poor health, died at New Harmony, Indiana, October 10, 1834.

Augustine Fortunatus Seaton

Augustine F. Seaton attended the U.S. Military Academy in 1828 and following graduation was assigned to the Seventh Infantry as a second lieutenant in 1833. After building the military road from Fort Gibson to Camp Holmes near present-day Lexington, Oklahoma, and attending the treaty there, he returned to Fort Gibson, where he died soon after on November 18, 1835.

Washington Seawell

Washington Seawell, journalist of the 1835 Camp Holmes council, was born in Virginia in 1802. Upon graduation from West Point in 1825, he was assigned to the Seventh Infantry as a disbursing agent of Indian affairs, then as adjutant general and aide-de-camp to General Matthew Arbuckle. After frontier service, Seawell served with the Second Infantry at Monterey, California, in 1849. He saw action in the Mexican War, eventually rising to colonel of the Sixth Infantry. He was removed from active duty in 1862 because of exposure-caused disability. He was transferred to California in 1863 and remained there to become a brevet brigadier general in 1865. After retirement Seawell remained in California and owned one of the largest ranches in Sonoma County. He died in San Francisco, January 9, 1888.

John Sedgwick

John Sedgwick, 1859 explorer of the Oklahoma Panhandle, was born in Cornwall, Connecticut, September 13, 1837. He graduated from West Point in 1837 and was assigned to the First U.S. Cavalry as a major in 1855, seeing action both in the Seminole War in Florida and in the Mexican War. Sedgwick was active on the early western frontier in Kansas and Colorado Territory prior to the Civil War. He served with the Union Army during the war, fighting at Chancellorsville, and won a brilliant victory at Rappahannock Station with a surprise night attack. Sedgwick attained the rank of major general before being killed at Spotsylvania, Virginia, on May 9, 1864.

George Champlin Sibley

George C. Sibley, whose curiosity led him to the Salt Plains of northwestern Oklahoma in 1811, was born at Great Barrington, Massachusetts, April 1, 1782, the son of John Sibley. Educated at Fayetteville, North Carolina, the younger Sibley was appointed a clerk in the Indian Bureau at St. Louis in 1808. He accompanied a military detachment to a point near Sibley, Missouri, and helped construct Fort Osage. He later was stationed there as factor and then as Indian agent, serving as a major during the War of 1812. In 1825 he was one of three commissioners assigned to mark the Santa Fe Trail across Kansas. He and his wife established a school for girls at St. Charles, Missouri, where he died January 1, 1863.

James Hervey Simpson

James H. Simpson, an officer diarist with Marcy's Canadian River survey of 1849, was born in New Jersey on March 9, 1813. After graduating from West Point in 1832, he was assigned to artillery and served in the Seminole War. He joined the Topographical Corps as a first lieutenant in 1838 and saw duty in surveying the Great Lakes region and the western plains. In 1859 he explored a new route from Salt Lake City to the Pacific coast. Simpson served with the New Jersey volunteers during the Civil War and was captured at Gaines's Mills. He was brevetted brigadier general in 1865 and became chief engineer of the Interior Department. After the war he was active in improving harbors and river navigation and in building bridges, including one at Little Rock. He retired in 1880 and died March 2, 1883, at St. Paul, Minnesota.

Josiah Simpson

Josiah Simpson, a dragoon officer with Boone's 1843 exploration of western Oklahoma, was born in New Brunswick, New Jersey, February 27, 1815. He graduated from Princeton in 1833 and the University of Pennsylvania in medicine in 1836. He served in the Florida war as a U.S. Army assistant surgeon, receiving commendation from General Zachary Taylor. Simpson received further commendations during the Mexican War. He was attending surgeon at Bellow's Island, New York, from 1848 to 1855. He was then promoted to surgeon and held the medical director's post at various army departments. He died in Baltimore on March 3, 1874.

Lorenzo Sitgreaves

Lorenzo Sitgreaves, 1849 surveyor of Creek lands in Oklahoma, graduated from West Point in 1827. After serving in the artillery, he was reappointed to the Topographical Engineers in 1838. He was awarded a brevet captaincy for his gallant and meritorious service at the battle of Buena Vista during the Mexican War. He died May 14, 1888.

David Sloane Stanley

David S. Stanley, who chronicled Whipple's railroad survey across Oklahoma in 1853, was born June 1, 1828. A native of Ohio, he graduated from West Point in 1852. After serving in Texas and California, Stanley was with the 1857 Sumner campaign against the Cheyennes in western Kansas. He was stationed at Fort Smith at the outbreak of the Civil War. Rejecting a high commission in the Confederate Army, he took part in Emory's retreat of Union forces from Indian Territory. He was prominent during the Missouri campaign, taking part in the battle of New Madrid and others. Later he was with Sherman's march through Georgia, being wounded at Jonesboro. He was wounded again at Franklin, Tennessee. This ended his battle service. In 1873 he led the expedition into Yellowstone and was active in settling Indian disputes in Texas. In 1884 he was made a brigadier general in the U.S. Army. He died in Washington, D.C., March 13, 1902.

John Mix Stanley

John M. Stanley, Indian artist who visited Oklahoma and painted scenes of Indian life, was born in New York State in 1814. Orphaned at age fourteen, he was apprenticed to a wagon maker in Detroit. He began drawing sketches of Indians at Fort Snelling. He accompanied Governor Pierce M. Butler to Tahlequah in 1843 to attend an Indian council. In 1846 he joined a Santa Fe–bound wagon train, and there was assigned to the scientific staff of Colonel Stephen Kearny's California expedition under the command of Captain William S. Emory. During the summer of 1847 Stanley was in Oregon, barely missing the massacre of Dr. Marcus Whitman and eleven others. In 1848 Stanley voyaged to Hawaii, where he painted the portraits of King Kamehameha III and his queen. In 1853 Stanley was appointed to a U.S. railroad surveying expedition that explored the Northwest. Stanley made many paintings of Indians and western subjects. He also produced some of the first daguerreotype images. He died in Detroit, April 10, 1872.

Enoch Steen

Enoch Steen, a dragoon officer and member of several ventures into the wild frontier of Indian Territory, was born in

Kentucky. He became a second lieutenant in the U.S. Rangers in July 1832. He made first lieutenant in March 1836, captain in December 1846, and major of the Second Dragoons in July 1852. Steen fought in the Mexican War and was commended for his gallantry and meritorious conduct at the Battle of Buena Vista. He died January 22, 1880.

Montford Stokes

Montford Stokes, U.S. commissioner at the Treaty of Camp Holmes in 1835, was born in Virginia on March 12, 1762. It is believed that he served in the Revolutionary War. Afterward he became a planter near Salisbury, North Carolina. He served as county clerk and clerk of the county court until 1804. Elected as a trustee of the University of North Carolina, he also served as a Democratic presidential elector. He became a major general of state militia during the War of 1812, thereafter serving as a U.S. senator from 1816 to 1823. He continued in politics and was elected governor of North Carolina in 1830. He resigned his office when he was appointed an Indian commissioner by Andrew Jackson. In 1836 Stokes became subagent for the Cherokees, Senecas, and Shawnees; later he became full agent for the Cherokees. Stokes remained in Indian Territory until his death on November 4, 1842, and is buried at Fort Gibson.

James Edwin Brown Stuart

J. E. B. Stuart, who kept a diary of a military excursion he led up Wolf Creek in 1859, was born in Virginia on February 6, 1833, and entered West Point in 1850. He saw action on the frontier with Colonel Edwin V. Sumner's campaign against the Cheyennes in 1857, receiving a minor wound. Stuart was sent to assist Colonel Robert E. Lee when John Brown attacked Harper's Ferry in 1859. When the Civil War began, Stuart resigned from the U.S. Army and became a colonel in the Confederate Army. He distinguished himself at the First Battle of Bull Run and was soon promoted to brigadier general in command of cavalry for the Army of Northern Virginia. Stuart won numerous victories and great laurels as a cavalryman until he was finally killed at Yellow Tavern on May 10, 1864.

Edwin Vose Sumner

Edwin V. Sumner, an officer member of the 1834 Leavenworth expedition, was born in Boston on January 30, 1797. After attending Milton Academy in Massachusetts, he became an officer in the Second Infantry in 1819. He served in the Black Hawk war, becoming a captain in the Second Dragoons in 1833. Following his service in Indian Territory, Sumner commanded a cavalry school in Pennsylvania. He served in the Mexican War, being wounded as he led the charge at Cerro Gordo. He was brevetted colonel, and after the war he commanded the military department of New Mexico in 1851–1853. He was sent to Europe on military business before being named colonel of the First Cavalry in 1855. He commanded Fort Leavenworth and led a campaign against the Cheyennes in July 1857. After commanding the Department of the West, he was put in charge of President Lincoln's escort from Springfield to Washington. During the Civil War Sumner commanded the left wing at Yorktown and was involved in many other battles, being wounded at Antietam. He was made a major general of volunteers in 1862. Asked to be relieved when another officer was appointed over him, Sumner was reassigned to the Department of Missouri. However, he died en route at Syracuse, New York, on March 21, 1863, at the age of sixty-six.

James Augustus Suydam

James A. Suydam was born in New York on March 27, 1818, of an old and well-known Dutch family. During his early studies as an artist, he traveled through Greece and Turkey. He was elected to the National Academy of Design and Art in 1858 and named an academician in 1861, an office he held to his death on November 15, 1865. He bequeathed the "Suydam Collection" to the academy in addition to a large sum of money. Suydam, a much-loved man of gentle nature, was especially known for his coastal landscapes.

William Henry Swift

William H. Swift, who accompanied Lieutenant Wilkinson down the Arkansas River in 1820, was born in Taunton, Massachusetts, November 6, 1800. He was an engineering cadet at West Point when he was ordered to join the Long expedition. After graduation he surveyed railroads and constructed a map of post offices and post roads. He had a long and highly successful career as an engineer with the Topographical Corps. He resigned from the army in 1849 and became president of several railroads. He resided in New York for many years and died there on April 7, 1879.

Zachary Taylor

Zachary Taylor, onetime commander of Indian Territory military forces, was born in Orange County, Virginia, November 24, 1784. His father, an officer in the American Revolution, moved the family to Kentucky, where Zachary received his little formal schooling from a tutor. After taking part in the Aaron Burr disturbance, he was appointed first lieutenant in the Seventh Infantry. Taylor served in the War of 1812, Black Hawk conflict, and Seminole War before being given command of the Western Division of the Army at Fort Smith as a brevet brigadier general. He was stationed on the Mexican border when that war broke out, and he quickly defeated the Mexicans at Palo Alto and Resaca de la Palma and later bested Antonio López de Santa Anna at Buena Vista. Taylor ran for president as a Whig candidate in 1848 and was elected as the twelfth U.S. chief executive. Taylor was in office only two years, dying from exposure and intestinal disorder on July 9, 1850.

Victor Tixier

Victor Tixier, who visited northern Oklahoma in 1840, was born in France on March 24, 1815. He studied medicine in Paris and passed his exams with high marks. But as he was beginning his internship, he suffered a small wound on his finger while dissecting. The wound would not heal, and continued fever interrupted his studies. On the suggestion of a friend, as a recuperating interlude he sailed for America in 1839. He remained in the United States for nearly a year, returning to take up a medical practice at Saint Point, France. In addition he wrote articles and books and was active in excavation of Gallo-Roman tombs in France. He died July 16, 1885.

Joseph Updegraff

Joseph Updegraff, an officer member of Marcy's 1849 survey of the Canadian River, was born in Virginia. He entered the army as a private and was quickly promoted to sergeant. He was commissioned as a brevet second lieutenant in the Fifth Infantry in June 1848. He was promoted to first lieutenant in 1854, to captain in 1861, and to major in 1863. He died June 19, 1866.

Earl Van Dorn

Earl Van Dorn, who led punitive military excursions across western Oklahoma, was born near Port Gibson, Mississippi, September 17, 1820. He graduated from West Point in 1842. As an officer in the Seventh Infantry, he took part in the military occupation of Texas during 1845–1846. During the Mexican War he was brevetted captain for his service at Cerro Gordo and as major for action at Contreras and Churubusco. He was wounded in the battle for Mexico City. Van Dorn also served in the Seminole War. After his Indian Territory service, he became a major in the Second Cavalry. At the outbreak of the Civil War, he resigned from the U.S. Army and became a colonel of cavalry in the Confederate Army. After seeing action in Texas, he was raised to the rank of brigadier general. As such, he was involved in Rebel defeats at Pea Ridge, Arkansas; Corinth, Mississippi; and Franklin, Tennessee. Van Dorn died May 8, 1863, when shot by a Dr. Peters because of a personal grudge.

Pierre Vial

Pierre Vial (or Pedro Vial), one of the earliest explorers of the country among St. Louis, San Antonio, and Santa Fe, was a native of France who became a Spanish subject. Just when he came to America is not clear, but he was active in America by 1786 as an explorer of the Southwest. Vial bravely traveled alone or with a single companion in his trail-breaking jaunts among Natchitoches, San Antonio, and St. Louis. Becoming ill on one occasion, he spent several weeks in the lodge of a Tawakoni chief, and he was known to visit at length among the Comanches. He traveled through Comanche country at least five times and did much to open the trade route between Missouri and New Mexico and develop relations with the Plains Indians. He died in Santa Fe in 1814 and is buried there.

Thompson B. Wheelock

Thompson B. Wheelock, an officer journalist for the Leavenworth expedition of 1834, was born in Massachusetts in July 1801. He graduated from West Point in 1822, tenth in his class. He served with the Third Field Artillery at various assignments, including a year as an instructor at West Point. In 1829 he resigned his commission and became a professor of mathematics at Woodward College in Cincinnati. He reentered the service in 1833 as a first lieutenant with the U.S. Dragoons. Following the Leavenworth-Dodge expedition, Wheelock fought with the dragoons against the Seminoles. He was killed in battle at Fort Micanopy, Florida, June 15, 1836.

Amiel Weeks Whipple

Amiel W. Whipple, a conductor of a railroad surveying expedition up the Canadian River in 1853, was born in Greenwich, Massachusetts, in 1817 and graduated from West Point in 1841. As an officer with the Topographical Engineers, he helped survey both the Canadian and Mexican boundaries of the United States. Whipple rose to the rank of brigadier general of volunteers during the Civil War. After commanding a brigade assigned to defend Washington, D.C., he was honored by having Fort Whipple carry his name. He was a divisional commander at the Battle of Fredericksburg. He was wounded at Chancellorsville, dying in Washington on May 7, 1863, two years before the war was over. His promotion to major general reached him a day before his death.

James Biddle Wilkinson

James B. Wilkinson, who led a detachment across northeastern Oklahoma in 1806, was the eldest son of General James Wilkinson. The younger Wilkinson was born in Maryland in 1784 and attended school in Philadelphia. He was commissioned as second lieutenant in the Fourth Infantry on February 16, 1801, and was promoted to first lieutenant on September 30, 1803. He was made captain in 1808, following the Pike expedition. He died September 7,

1813, two years before his father was dishonorably discharged as commander of the army and exiled to Mexico.

Israel C. Woodruff

Israel C. Woodruff, 1849 surveyor of the Creek boundary, was born at Trenton, New Jersey, in 1815. An 1836 graduate of West Point, he was appointed first lieutenant in the Topographical Engineers. In addition to his survey of the Creek boundary, he made reconnaissances of military roads to the South Pass of the Rocky Mountains and to New Mexico. For a time he was chief engineer and inspector of lighthouses on the Great Lakes. During the Civil War he was stationed at Washington, D.C., and took part in the defense of the U.S. Capitol against General Jubal Early's advance. Woodruff was brevetted for meritorious service and appointed to the rank of brigadier general. He died at Tompkinsville, New York, December 10, 1878.

Notes

Introduction

1. Bolton, *Coronado*, 305.
2. Lewis, "DuTisne's First Expedition," 319–323.
3. Lewis, "LaHarpe's First Expedition," 347.
4. Pike, *Sources of the Mississippi*, pt. 2, Map 3.
5. Weber, *Spanish Frontier*, 289–291.
6. Ibid., 294.
7. Flores, ed., *Jefferson*, 125.
8. Weber, *Spanish Frontier*, 299.
9. Rister, "Federal Experiment," 437–438; Gibson, *America's Exiles*, 4.
10. *American State Papers, Indian Affairs*, vol. 2, 14th Cong., 2d sess., 125.
11. Ammon, *James Monroe*, 538.
12. Ibid., 539–540.
13. Speech by Senator Sam Houston, *U.S. Congressional Globe*, Appendix, 33d Cong., 1st sess., February 14–15, 1854.
14. Gibson, *America's Exiles*, 9–10.
15. Meserve, "Indian Removal Message," 65.
16. *U.S. Register of Debates*, 20th–21st Cong., HofR, May 19, 1830, 1072–1074.

17. *U.S. Register of Debates*, HofR, May 19, 1830, 1061; Meserve, "Indian Removal Message," 64.

18. Gibson, *America's Exiles*, 4–5.

19. *Report of Committee of Congress on Indian Affairs*, May 20, 1834, cited by Murray, *Encyclopedia of Geography*, 3:585.

Chapter One

1. Bolton, *Coronado*, 288–289.

2. Weber, *Spanish Frontier*, 48–49.

3. Thomas, "Spanish Exploration," 190; Bolton, *Coronado*, 246; Bolton, *Athanase de Mézières*, 2:280.

4. Cutler, ed., *History of Kansas*, 48.

5. Winship, *Coronado Expedition*, 367.

6. Ibid., 380–381.

7. Bolton, *Coronado*, 280.

8. Ibid., 335–342.

9. Hammond and Rey, eds. and trans., *Coronado Expedition*, 1:416–419, 755, 838, 940.

10. Hammond and Rey, eds. and trans., *Don Juan de Oñate*, 1:417.

11. Wedel, *Kansas Archeology*, 21.

12. Hammond and Rey, eds. and trans., *Don Juan de Oñate*, 2:746.

13. See Oñate's map, which appears to support this line of reasoning.

14. Hammond and Rey, eds. and trans., *Don Juan de Oñate*, 2:752. Some scholars have suggested that these were Kaw Indians, but this seems unlikely in view of the tribe's known location well to the north of the Arkansas River, as indicated by the Joliet map of 1673–1674.

15. Ibid., 753, 856.

16. Ibid., 753–754, 843.

17. Weber, *Spanish Frontier*, 82.

18. Hammond and Rey, eds. and trans., *Don Juan de Oñate*, 2:753–754, 843.

19. Ibid., 758, 867.

20. Ibid., 758, 848.

21. Thomas, trans. and ed., *After Coronado*, 8.

22. Ibid., 195–196.

Chapter Two

1. Houck, *History of Missouri*, 1:255–258.
2. Thomas, "Spanish Exploration," 200–201.
3. Lewis, "LaHarpe's First Expedition," 331–349.
4. Schafer, "French Explorers," 397.
5. Lewis, "DuTisné's First Expedition," 319–323; Margry, *Découvertes*, 6:307–318; Wedel, *Deer Creek Site*, 25–32; Gregg, "Missouri Reader," 505.
6. Smith, trans. and annot., "Account of the Journey," 532–534.
7. Thoburn and Wright, *Oklahoma*, 1:42.
8. Cutler, *History of Kansas*, 48–49, containing translation of Le Page du Pratz's account of Bourgmond's journeys in Kansas.
9. Ibid., 47–48.
10. Schafer, "French Explorers," 400; Margry, *Découvertes*, 6:193–194; Nasatir, *Before Lewis and Clark*, 2:28. Pike's map indicates that it was the Red River that the Mallets descended by bark canoe in June 1740. It would have been extremely difficult for them to have made their way through the great raft of uprooted trees that clogged the Red River for miles above present-day Shreveport, Louisiana.
11. Schafer, "French Explorers," 397–401.
12. Bolton, "French Intrusions," 400–404.
13. Ibid., 396–398; Bolton, *Athanase de Méziéres*, 1:48.
14. Thoburn, "Collection of Relics," 353–356; Wright, "Pioneer Historical Archaeologist," 401–411.
15. Gibson, *Oklahoma*, 34–35; Westbrook, "The Chouteaus," 950.

Chapter Three

1. Bolton, *Athanase de Méziéres*, 1:270; 2:85.
2. Harper, "Taovayas," 287.
3. Allen, "Parrilla Expedition," 65–66.
4. Harper, "Taovayas," 282–283; Bolton, *Texas*, 90.
5. Harper, "Taovayas," 287.
6. Ibid., 272.
7. Bolton, *Athanase de Méziéres*, 2:188 n. 135.
8. Ibid., 207.
9. Ibid., 204.

10. Ibid., 201–203.

11. Ibid.

12. Ibid., 1:298.

13. Ibid., 2:174–182.

14. Ibid., 141–147.

15. John, ed., "Inside the Comanchería," 27–56.

16. Houck, *Spanish Regime*, 1:354–358.

17. Ibid., 357.

18. Barry, *Beginning of the West*, 37–38; Loomis and Nasatir, *Pedro Vial*, 393–405.

19. John, "Portrait," 412–433.

Chapter Four

1. Flores, *Jefferson*, 3–90.

2. Ibid., 100; *An Account of the Red River*, 1.

3. Ibid., 25.

4. Flores, *Jefferson*, 282.

5. Ibid., 125.

6. Jackson, ed., *Journals of Pike*, 2:277.

7. Pike, *Sources of the Mississippi*, pt. 3:14.

8. Ibid., pt. 2:18.

9. Ibid., 23–24.

10. Jackson, ed., *Journals of Pike*, 1:vii–ix, 285–287.

11. Pike, *Sources of the Mississippi*, Appendix to pt. 2:11–12.

12. Ibid., 22.

13. Ibid., 23.

14. "Extracts from the Diary," 205–206.

15. Ibid.

16. Ibid.

17. Ibid., 206.

18. Pike, *Sources of the Mississippi*, 150.

19. Hollon, *Lost Pathfinder*, 286–287; Blackburn, "Wilkinson," 6.

20. Jackson, ed., *Journals of Pike*, 2:161.

21. Pike, *Sources of the Mississippi*, Appendix to pt. 2:26.

22. Ibid., 29.

Chapter Five

1. *Message from the President*, 12.

2. Stoddard, *Sketches*, 401–403.

3. Ibid., 404.

4. "Extracts from the Diary," 196–218; see also Brooks, ed., "Sibley's Journal," 172–178.

5. Kappler, *Indian Treaties*, 95–99.

6. Ibid., 98–99; Gregg, "Fort Osage," 343.

7. "Extracts from the Diary," 196–218.

8. Isern, "George Sibley," 20–21.

9. "Extracts from the Diary," 210.

10. Ibid., 213–214.

11. Ibid., 217.

12. Thwaites, ed., *Bradbury's Travels*, 193.

13. Isern, "George Sibley," 27–28, citing Brooks, ed., "Sibley's Journal," 199–205. It is interesting to note that at the Cooper site only a few miles to the south on Beaver Creek, archaeologists have recently uncovered a buffalo (bison) kill site dating back 10,800 to 10,200 years earlier. These were giant buffalo, nearly half again as big as present-day buffalo.

14. Sibley to Rector, 1814, Ltrs. Recd., Sec. of War, Indian Affairs, M-271, National Archives.

15. Gregg, *Road to Santa Fe*, 93–94.

Chapter Six

1. Williams, "Louis Bringier," 112–113.

2. Bringier, "Notices of the Geology," 32–33. An ad ran in the February 19, 1820, issue of the *Arkansas Gazette* announcing a public sale at the Six Bulls salt works for all the personal property of the late Elijah Earheart.

3. Bringier, "Notices of the Geology," 27.

4. Bearss and Gibson, *Fort Smith*, 17.

5. *Imperial Magazine* (December 1825): 1133–1139.

6. Graustein, *Thomas Nuttall*, 59–77.

7. Ibid., 131.

8. Lottinville, ed., *Journal of Travels*, 136–137.

9. Ibid., 154.

10. Ibid., 167.

11. Ibid., 167–168.

12. Graustein, *Thomas Nuttall*, 144.

13. Lottinville, ed., *Journal of Travels*, 180–181.

14. Ibid., 188.

15. Thoburn and Wright, *Oklahoma*, 1:84–86.

16. Graustein, *Thomas Nuttall*, 145.

17. Lottinville, ed., *Journal of Travels*, 194.
18. Ibid., 228.
19. Ibid.
20. Ibid., 230
21. Ibid., 232.
22. Graustein, *Thomas Nuttall*, 148–152.
23. Williams, "1820 Letter," 351.
24. Ibid., 352. See also Miller letters, *Arkansas Gazette*, March 18, July 15, 1820.

Chapter Seven

1. Thwaites, ed., *James's Account*, pt. 3:114–115.
2. *American State Papers, Indian Affairs*, 2:595–609.
3. James, *Account of an Expedition*, 1:404–423.
4. Ibid., 425.
5. Ibid., 2:210.
6. Smallwood, "Major Long," 55.
7. Thwaites, ed., *James's Account*, pt. 3:110.
8. Ibid., 137.
9. Ibid., 141–142.
10. Ibid., 143.
11. Ibid., 150.
12. Ibid., 175.
13. Ibid., 181.
14. Berthrong, *Southern Cheyennes*, 20–21.
15. Thwaites, ed., *James's Account*, pt. 3:198.
16. Ibid., 217.
17. Ibid., 220.
18. Ibid., 233–236.
19. Wright, "Pioneer Historical Archeologist," 404–408; Wright, "Collection of Relics," 353–356.
20. James, *Account of an Expedition*, 2:230–231.
21. Bell, "Journal of Bell," 279–284.
22. James, *Account of an Expedition*, 2: 239–251.
23. *Niles' Weekly Register*, October 28, 1820.
24. Smallwood, "Major Long," 51, 59–60.

Chapter Eight

1. "Book Reviews," 100–102.
2. James, *Three Years*, 94–95.
3. Ibid., 102–103.

4. Three trading posts were in operation at Three Forks: one by Joseph Bougie; another by Glenn and two partners, Nathaniel Pryor and Samuel Richards; and one by Henry Barbour and George W. Brand. Gibson, *Oklahoma*, 35.

5. Thomas, "James, Glenn, and Fowler," 70 n. 30.

6. James, *Three Years*, 116–118.

7. Ibid., 118.

8. Ibid.

9. Ibid., 120.

10. Ibid., 123–124.

11. Ibid., 124.

12. Thomas, *Forgotten Frontiers*, 62–63.

13. James, *Three Years*, 125.

14. Ibid., 136–137.

15. Coues, ed., *Journal of Fowler*, 60–61.

16. Lottinville, ed., *Journal of Travels*, 2.

17. Coues, ed., *Journal of Fowler*, 2.

18. Ibid., 4–7.

Chapter Nine

1. James, *Three Years*, 190–192.

2. Ibid., 192.

3. Ibid., 195

4. Ibid. In 1839 Josiah Gregg called the site Spring Valley and made reference to a fort that "an unfortunate trader named McKnight" had erected in 1822. Gregg, *Commerce*, 235.

5. James, *Three Years*, 198.

6. Ibid. The Comanches possessed ample captives of Mexican descent who could communicate using the Spanish and Comanche tongues.

7. Ibid., 201.

8. Ibid., 202.

9. Ibid., 206.

10. Ibid., 215.

11. Ibid., 217.

12. Ibid., 227.

13. Ibid., 231.

14. *Arkansas Gazette*, July 22, 1823. This places the trading venture between February and July 1823.

15. Journal of Union Mission, November 22, 1823, entry.

Chapter Ten

1. Foreman, *Indians and Pioneers*, 169–170.

2. Morrison, "Fort Towson," 226–227.

3. Menard, whose wife was the sister of Jean Pierre Chouteau's wife, was one of the founding partners of the St. Louis Missouri Fur Company. It appears that Menard, a highly influential merchant, politician, and statesman in Missouri, was the namesake of Bayou Menard, a settlement site once located between Fort Gibson and Tahlequah.

4. Foreman, *Indians and Pioneers*, 154–155 n. 13.

5. *Arkansas Intelligencer*, May 19, 1849; Fort Gibson Post Returns for October 1826, Archives/Manuscripts, Oklahoma Historical Society.

6. "Remove Indians Westward," 11–48.

7. *Arkansas Gazette*, January 18, 1832.

8. Foreman, "Unpublished Report," 328–330.

9. Ibid., 329.

10. *Arkansas Gazette*, March 9, 16, 1831.

11. Gardner, "One Hundred Years," 779.

12. Irving, *Tour*, xvii.

13. Alderman, Kleinfield, and Banks, eds., *Complete Works*, 2:728.

14. Gregory and Strickland, *Sam Houston*, 135.

15. Day and Ullom, eds., *Autobiography of Houston*, 76–77, citing Journal of Washington Irving, Notebook no. 6, New York Public Library.

16. Irving, *Tour*, 21–22.

17. The settlement site of Beatte's Prairie once existed near Maysville. Foreman, *Advancing the Frontier*, 143 n. 4, states that Beatte's name was really Alexo and not Pierre as Irving gives it.

18. In addition to that of Irving, Ellsworth, Pourtalès, and Latrobe all penned accounts of the journey. See Ellsworth, *Washington Irving*; Pourtalès, *Western Tour*; and Latrobe, *Rambler*.

19. Irving, *Tour*, 44.

20. Ibid., 57 n. 5.

21. Ibid., 47–48.

22. Ibid., 48.

23. Alderman, Kleinfield, and Banks, eds., *Complete Works,* 729.

24. Ibid., 41–42.

25. Irving, *Tour,* 128.

26. Ibid., 100.

27. Latrobe, *Rambler,* 163.

28. Irving, *Tour,* 106. See also Chlouber, "Search for Fountain Camp," 137.

29. Ellsworth, *Washington Irving,* 62.

30. Chlouber, "Search for Fountain Camp," 139.

31. Latrobe, *Rambler,* 121–122.

32. Ibid., 125.

33. Ibid., 180–182.

34. Irving, *Tour,* 127–130.

35. Ibid., 138.

36. Ibid., 146–150.

37. Ibid., 184–192.

38. Ibid., 212.

39. Alderman, Kleinfield, and Banks, eds., *Complete Works,* 2:731.

40. Day and Ullum, eds., *Autobiography of Houston,* 77.

41. Pike's descriptive account of his journey and a previous one by Fort Towson resident Aaron B. Lewis appeared in the *Arkansas Advocate,* April 17, 24; May 1, 8, 15, 22, 29; June 5, 19, 1835. In September 1831 Lewis and two other men had escorted a young doctor and his wife, along with eleven Cherokee hunters, from Fort Towson to the Washita country. All turned back except Lewis and his two friends, who continued on to Santa Fe. Morrison, "Journey Across Oklahoma," 333–337.

42. *Arkansas Advocate,* April 17, 1835.

43. Foreman, "Nathan Boone," 328.

44. Foreman, *Pioneer Days,* 103–104.

45. Ibid., 117–119.

46. Mooney, *Calendar History,* 257.

47. Foreman, *Pioneer Days,* 104–105.

48. Young, "Ranger Battalion," 468–469.

49. Ibid.

50. Foreman, *Pioneer Days,* 116–119.

51. Gardner, "One Hundred Years," 766.

Chapter Eleven

1. Catlin, *Letters and Notes*, 50.

2. Hildreth, *Dragoon Campaigns*, 105.

3. Catlin, *Letters and Notes*, 51.

4. Perrine, ed., "Journal of Evans," 183.

5. Catlin, *North American Indians*, 2:37; *Daily National Intelligencer*, July 28, 1835.

6. Wheelock, "Dodge Report," 73–74; Catlin, *North American Indians*, 2:75.

7. Lottinville, ed., *Journal of Travels*, 194 n. 12.

8. Wheelock, "Dodge Report," 75.

9. Ibid., 76; Perrine, ed., "Journal of Evans," 183.

10. The force under Dodge consisted of six incomplete companies of First U.S. Dragoons totaling only around 250 men. This force was soon reduced 60 or 70 count by men falling ill on the trail. Field and staff officers were Major Richard B. Mason; First Lieutenant James W. Hamilton, adjutant; Surgeon Clement A. Finley (who would rise to brigadier general in 1865); and Lieutenant Thompson B. Wheelock, who was attached to Dodge's staff as journalist. First Company was commanded by Captain Edwin V. Sumner and Second Lieutenant John Henry K. Burgwin; Second Company, by Captain Matthew Duncan, First Lieutenant Stephen W. Moore, and Second Lieutenant Burdett Turrett; Third Company, by Captain David Hunter and Second Lieutenant Enoch Steen; Fourth Company, by Captain David Perkins and First Lieutenant Jefferson Davis; Fifth Company, by Captain Nathan Boone, First Lieutenant James F. Izard, and Second Lieutenant Lucius B. Northrop; and Sixth Company, by Captain Jesse B. Browne and Brevet Second Lieutenant Albert G. Edwards.

Remaining at Fort Washita in addition to Brigadier General Henry Leavenworth, who died July 22, 1834, were Lieutenant Colonel Stephen Watts Kearny, along with Captain Eustace Trenor; First Lieutenant Thomas Swords; Second Lieutenant John S. Vanderveer; Second Lieutenant Elbridge G. Eastman, Second Infantry; Second Lieutenant Asbury Ury; Brevet Second Lieutenant Gaines P. Kingsbury; Brevet Second Lieutenant James M. Bowman; Second Lieutenant James W. Schaumburgh; Brevet Second Lieutenant George W. McClure; Assistant Surgeon Samuel W. Hales;

and Lieutenant James West, Seventh Infantry. Many of them were ill but recovered. McClure died at Fort Washita on July 21; West, Leavenworth's aide–de–camp, expired on September 28, 1834; Lieutenant Eastman on October 6; and Hales on January 30, 1835. S. C. Stambaugh ltr., August 26, 1834, *Daily National Intelligencer,* September 30, 1834; Wheelock, "Dodge Report," 73–74; Heitman, *Historical Register.*

11. Catlin, *North American Indians,* 1:53.

12. Wheelock, "Dodge Report," 77; Perrine, ed., "Journal of Evans," 185.

13. Wheelock, "Dodge Report," 79; Catlin, *North American Indians,* 2:59–60.

14. The location of Camp Comanche is discussed by Griswold, "Camp Comanche," 322–337.

15. Catlin, *North American Indians,* 2:66.

16. Ibid.

17. Ibid., 60.

18. Ibid., 68.

19. Griswold, "Camp Comanche," 337, states that Catlin remained in the sick camp when the expedition continued on. Catlin's narratives and his sketch of the village clearly show that he did not visit the Wichita camp on the North Fork. Catlin, *North American Indians,* 2:70–75

20. Ibid., 71.

21. Ibid., 72.

22. *Arkansas Advocate,* October 31, 1834. This account was probably written by Captain Matthew Duncan, company commander, First Dragoons.

23. Catlin, *North American Indians,* 2:74.

24. Wheelock, "Dodge Report," 89.

25. Ibid., 84.

26. Catlin, *North American Indians,* 2:76.

27. Wheelock, "Dodge Report," 91.

28. Catlin, *North American Indians,* 2:80–81.

29. *Daily National Intelligencer,* October 23, 1834.

30. Catlin, *North American Indians,* 2:52. Because of so much sickness and death there, Gibson became known as the "Charnel House of the Army."

31. Ibid., 82–83.

Chapter Twelve

1. Jones, ed., "Diary of McPhail," 285.
2. Foreman, ed., "Journal of Proceedings," 394.
3. Ibid., 394–395.
4. Ibid., 396.
5. Ibid., 395.
6. Ibid., 402.
7. *Army and Navy Chronicle,* October 1, 1835.
8. Jones, ed., "Diary of McPhail," 283–284.
9. Ibid., 285.
10. Ibid.
11. *Army and Navy Chronicle,* October 22, 1835.
12. Jones, ed., "Diary of McPhail," 286.
13. Ibid., 288.
14. Ibid., 286.
15. Ibid., 285.
16. Ibid., 287. This could have been Red Hill in present-day Purcell.
17. Foreman, ed., "Journal of Proceedings," 396.
18. Jones, ed., "Diary of McPhail," 288.
19. Foreman, ed., "Journal of Proceedings," 396.
20. Ibid., 409; Kappler, ed., *Indian Treaties,* 435–439.
21. Foreman, ed., "Journal of Proceedings," 411.
22. Ibid., 413.
23. Ibid., 415.
24. Ibid.
25. Ibid., 416.
26. Foreman, *Pioneers Days,* 223–225.
27. Ibid., 225–226.
28. Ibid., 226.
29. Ibid., 227.
30. Kappler, ed., *Indian Treaties,* 489–490.
31. Ibid., 238.
32. *Daily National Intelligencer,* April 16, 1839.
33. Foreman, *Pioneer Days,* 238.

Chapter Thirteen

1. Gregg, *Commerce,* 225–229. See also Fulton, ed., *Diary of Gregg.*
2. Gregg, *Commerce,* 231.
3. Ibid., 232–234.

4. Ibid., 235.

5. Ibid., 239–241.

6. Ibid., 243–248.

7. Ibid., 249.

8. Ibid., 348.

9. Ibid., 238.

10. Horgan, *Josiah Gregg*, 11.

11. Foreman, *Marcy*, 4–5.

12. See McDermott, ed., *Tixier's Travels*.

13. Ibid., 224.

14. Ibid., 248.

15. See Foreman, ed., *Traveler*.

16. *Cherokee Advocate*, June 26, 1845. See also Hoig, *Sequoyah*.

17. Foreman, "Nathan Boone," 322–347.

18. "Captain Boone's Journal," 58–105; see also Pelzer, *Marches of the Dragoons*, 189–237.

19. Even though Boone refers to the record as "my journal" in his report, he is constantly referred to in the third person. Especially telling is the comment ("Captain Boone's Journal," 84) that "Capt. Boone showed us how to make one [a skin boat]." Furthermore, the journal reflects an advanced formal education that the frontier-experienced Boone did not possess. It is altogether logical that Boone would have assigned this task to one of his West Point–educated officers. Since the journal begins before Johnston, Anderson, or Simpson have joined the expedition, the evidence points to Buford as the one who wrote the report.

20. Ibid., 70.

21. Ibid., 90.

22. The Rock Salt region was visited again during the spring of 1844 by a party of Creek Indians under Rolly McIntosh. His account of the trip appears in the *Arkansas Intelligencer*, July 6, 1844.

23. Winfrey and Day, eds., *Indian Papers*, 1:251–275.

24. Clift, "Warren's Trading Post," 129–140.

25. Thoburn and Wright, *Oklahoma*, 2:787.

26. *Arkansas Intelligencer*, December 30, 1843.

27. *Arkansas Intelligencer*, January 6, 1844.

28. *Portraits by Stanley*, 53–55.

29. *Daily National Intelligencer*, March 3, 1852.

Chapter Fourteen

1. Galvin, ed., *Through the Country*, 5–7. See also "Journal of Abert."

2. See Montaignes, *The Plains*.

3. Galvin, ed., *Through the Country*, 5.

4. Ibid., 21.

5. Montaignes, *The Plains*, 104.

6. Galvin, ed., *Through the Country*, 40.

7. Ibid., 42.

8. Montaignes, *The Plains*, 113.

9. Galvin, ed., *Through the Country*, 47–48.

10. Ibid., 48–49.

11. Ibid., 50.

12. Montaignes, *The Plains*, 137–138.

13. Galvin, ed., *Through the Country*, 51.

14. Ibid., 57.

15. Montaignes, *The Plains*, 142.

16. Galvin, ed., *Through the Country*, 58.

17. Ibid., 61–62.

18. Ibid., 59; Montaignes, *The Plains*, 158–159.

19. Galvin, ed., *Through the Country*, 66–67.

20. Ibid., 74–75.

21. *Report of the Commissioner of Indian Affairs, 1848*, 136–140.

Chapter Fifteen

1. Marcy, *Prairie Traveler*, 194–195

2. Foreman, *Marcy*, 3–17; see also Marcy, "Account of Marcy's March."

3. *Niles' National Register*, October 25, 1848.

4. Foreman, *Marcy*, 21–22.

5. Ibid., 139.

6. Ibid., 152–155; Dott, "Simpson's California Road," 154–179; see also Simpson, "Route from Fort Smith."

7. Although Chouteau's was billed in Arkansas as the "Council Grove" of the Arkansas route, travelers discovered it now to be nothing but a few pieces of timber. *Arkansas Intelligencer*, April 7, September 1, 1849.

8. Foreman, *Marcy*, 195–205.

9. Marcy described the girl as a "belle of the prairie . . .

charming, vivacious, and possessing a fine education." Hollon, *Beyond the Cross Timbers*, 64–65.

10. Simpson, "Route from Fort Smith," 8.

11. Keim, *Sheridan's Troopers*, 300.

12. *Fort Smith Herald*, May 2, 1849.

13. Foreman, *Marcy*, 162–163 n. 12.

14. Ibid., 29.

15. Ibid., 238 n. III.

16. Ibid., 239 n. 12.

17. Ibid., 209–210 n. 15.

18. *Arkansas State Democrat*, September 7, 1849; *Washington Telegraph*, September, 12, 1849.

19. Foreman, *Marcy*, 90.

20. When Marcy's wife, Mary, learned of Harrison's death, she wrote grievingly to her daughter Mary Ellen, describing him as "one of the noblest young men I ever knew." Hollon, *Beyond the Cross Timbers*, 82–83.

21. Foreman, *Marcy*, 379.

22. "Reconnaissances of Routes," 30–39.

23. Ibid., 104 n. 27.

Chapter Sixteen

1. Foreman, ed. and annot., *Adventure*, 90–91.

2. Tomer and Broadhead, *Naturalist in Indian Territory*, 118.

3. Ibid., 30–31.

4. Rister and Lovelace, eds., "Diary Account," 268–301. See also Baker, "Northwest Boundary," 11–12.

5. Rister and Lovelace, eds., "Diary Account," 270.

6. A portion of Smith's diary is published in ibid.

7. Ibid., 288.

8. Ibid.

9. Foreman, ed. and annot., *Adventure*, vi–viii.

10. Ibid., v.

11. Glisan, *Journal*, 56.

12. Foreman, ed. and annot., *Adventure*, x.

13. Glisan, *Journal*, 81–82.

14. Ibid., 87.

15. Foreman, ed. and annot., *Adventure*, xii.

16. Marcy, "Exploration of Red River," 1.

17. This was likely New York artist James Augustus Suydam, then thirty–three, whose biography is included in the Appendix.

18. Foreman, ed. and annot., *Adventure*, 27 n. 8.

19. Marcy, "Exploration of Red River," 40–41.

20. Ibid., 25.

21. Ibid., 29.

22. Ibid., 36.

23. Ibid., 38–39. Marcy gave the latitude of the site as 35 degrees, 35 feet, and 3 inches and the longitude as 101 degrees and 55 feet. He described the bottle burial location: "We are near the junction of the last branch of any magnitude that enters the river from the north, and about three miles from the point where it debouches from the plains, in a grove of large cotton-wood trees upon the south bank of the river. Under the roots of one of the largest of these trees, which stand near the river and below all others in the grove, I have buried a bottle." Ibid.

24. Ibid., 55–56.

25. Ibid., 77.

26. Ibid., 78.

27. Glisan, *Journal*, 96; *Daily National Intelligencer*, July 28, 29, 1852.

28. See *Washington Telegraph*, July 28, 1952.

29. Foreman, ed. and annot., *Adventure*, 132–133 n. 9.

30. Glisan, *Journal*, 99.

Chapter Seventeen

1. *Report of the Commissioner of Indian Affairs, 1853*, 373.

2. Ibid., 359–371.

3. Kappler, *Indian Treaties*, 2:600–602.

4. Whipple, "Reports of Explorations," 19.

5. Wright and Shirk, eds., "Journal of Whipple," 248–249; Shawver, annot., "Stanley Explores," 260.

6. Whipple, "Reports of Explorations," 21.

7. Möllhausen, *Diary of a Journey*, 93.

8. Ibid., 261.

9. Ibid., 272.

10. Whipple, "Reports of Explorations," 22.

11. Ibid., 22–23.

12. Ibid., 24.

13. Ibid., 25. Two sketches resulted from the Whipple visit, one clearly an imitation of the other. The original was made by Möllhausen as the Whipple expedition passed by Rock Mary. It carries the notation "Natural Mounds near the Termination of the Cross Timbers." The second sketch, which was signed "Roberts SC," accompanied the expedition's official report. A committee from the Oklahoma Historical Society visited the site in 1960 and issued its "Rock Mary Report," 130–154.

14. Shawver, annot., "Stanley Explores," 267; Whipple, *Reports of Explorations*, 30.

15. Möllhausen, *Diary of a Journey*, 195.

16. Whipple, "Reports of Explorations," 31; Shawver, annot., "Stanley Explores," 268.

17. Whipple, "Reports of Explorations," 31.

18. Ibid., 33.

19. Ibid., 32.

20. Ibid. 33–34.

21. Ibid., 34–35.

22. Shawver, annot., "Stanley Explores," 269. See also "Diary of Stanley."

23. Ibid.

24. Foreman, *Pathfinder*, 90.

25. Ibid., 22–23.

Chapter Eighteen

1. Miller, ed., "Surveying the Southern Boundary," 104–139.

2. Thoburn, "Campaign," 30–38; Webb, *Texas Rangers*, 154–159.

3. Foreman, "Journal Kept by Cooper," 381–390.

4. Ibid., 387.

5. Foreman, ed., "Survey of a Wagon Road," 74–76; Beale, "Wagon Road," 25–26.

6. Foreman, ed., "Survey of a Wagon Road," 75–76.

7. Ibid., 89–90.

8. Ibid., 89.

9. Ibid., 92–93.

10. Beale, "Wagon Road," 24.

11. Ibid., 25–26.

12. Richardson, *Comanche Barrier*, 238–239.

13. Thoburn, "Battle with Comanches," 26.

14. Thoburn, "Indian Fight," 314–329.

15. Baker, "Northwest Boundary," 19–20.

16. Robinson, ed., "Kiowa and Comanche Campaign," 388.

17. Sedgwick's return route up the Beaver is not clear. Stuart notes that "Sedgwick had preceded us several days at Fort Larned and that the Expedtn. was broken up." Ibid., 398.

Chapter Nineteen

1. Beale, "Wagon Road," 10.

2. Richardson, *Frontier of Northwest Texas*, 197.

3. Ibid., 198.

4. Ibid., 199–200.

5. Ibid., 202.

6. Chapman, "Establishment of Wichita Reservation," 1048.

7. Thoburn and Wright, *Oklahoma*, 1:291.

8. Wright, "History of Fort Cobb," 55.

9. Emory to Townsend, May 19, 1861, *Compilation of Official Records*, I, 1: 648–649.

10. *Lawrence Republican*, June 13, 1861.

11. Ibid.

➤ _____

Bibliography

Government Documents

Abert, James W. "Notes of Lt. J. W. Abert." 30th Cong., 1st sess., 1847–1848. S. Exec. Doc. 7.

———. "Report of Expedition Led by Lieutenant J. W. Abert, on Upper Arkansas, and Through Country of Comanche Indians, in 1845." 29th Cong., 1st sess., 1845–1846. S. Doc. 438.

An Account of the Red River in Louisiana Drawn up from the Returns of Messrs. Freeman and Custis to the War Office of the United States Who Explored the Same in the Year 1806. Washington, D.C.: GPO, 1806.

American State Papers, Congressional Series, Class II: Indian Affairs. 38 vols. Washington, D.C.: Gales and Seaton, 1832–1861. Microfilm. Ann Arbor, Mich.: University Microfilms.

Beale, Edward F. "Wagon Road from Fort Smith to Colorado River." 36th Cong., 1st sess., 1859–1860. H. Exec. Doc. 42.

Carter, Clarence Edwin, ed. *The Territorial Papers of the United States.* 28 vols. Washington, D.C.: GPO, 1934–1948.

Compilation of the Official Records of the War of the Union and Confederate Armies, War of the Rebellion (1880–1891).

Fort Gibson Post Returns. National Archives.

Hodge, Frederick Webb. *Handbook of American Indians.* Bureau of American Ethnology. Smithsonian Bulletin 30. 2 vols. Washington, D.C.: 1910.

"Map of the United States and Texas Boundary and Adjacent Territory." *Bulletin of the United States Geological Society* 194 (1902).

Marcy, Randolph B. "Account of R. B. Marcy's March from Camp Scott to New Mexico and Return." Report of Secretary of War. 35th Cong., 2d sess., 1858–1859. S. Exec. Doc. 1.

———. "Exploration of the Red River of Louisiana in the Year 1852." 32d Cong., 2d sess., 1852–1853. S. Exec. Doc. 54.

Message from the President of the United States Communicating Discoveries Made in Exploring the Missouri, Red River, and Washita by Captains Lewis and Clark, Doctor Sibley, and Mr. Dunbar, February 19, 1806. Washington, D.C.: A&G Printers, 1806.

New American State Papers, Indian Affairs, 1789–1860. 13 vols. Wilmington, Dela.: Scholarly Resources.

"Reconnaissances of Routes from San Antonio to El Paso." 31st Cong., 1st sess., 1849–1850. S. Exec. Doc. 64.

"Remove Indians Westward." 20th Cong., 2d sess., 1828–1829. H. Report 87.

Report of Committee of Congress on Indian Affairs, May 20, 1834.

Report of the Commissioner of Indian Affairs, 1845–1861.

———. "Report of Exploration for a Railway Route from the Mississippi River to the Pacific Ocean." 33d Cong., 1st sess., 1853–1854. H. Exec. Doc. 129.

Simpson, James H. "Route from Fort Smith to Santa Fe." 31st Cong., 1st sess., 1849–1850. H. Exec. Doc. 45.

Sitgreaves, Lorenzo, and Israel C. Woodruff. "Report of Survey of Creek Indian Boundary Line." 35th Cong., 1st sess., 1857–1858. H. Doc. 104.

U.S. Register of Debates in Congress.

Wedel, Waldo R. *An Introduction to Kansas Archeology.* Bureau of Ethnology. Smithsonian Bulletin 174. Washington, D.C,: GPO, 1959.

Wheelock, Thompson B. "Colonel Henry Dodge Report of Leavenworth Expedition." 23d Cong., 2d sess., 1834–1835. S. Doc. 1.

Whipple, Amiel W. "Reports of Explorations and Surveys to Ascertain the Most Practicable and Economical Route for a Railroad from the Mississippi River to the Pacific Ocean." 33d Cong., 2d sess., 1854–1855. S. Exec. Doc. 78.

Periodicals

Arkansas Advocate (Little Rock)
Arkansas Gazette (Little Rock)
Arkansas Intelligencer (Little Rock)
Arkansas State Democrat (Little Rock)
Army and Navy Chronicle
Cherokee Advocate (Tahlequah)
Daily National Intelligencer (Washington, D.C.)
Daily Oklahoman (Oklahoma City)
Fort Smith Herald
Imperial Magazine (London, England)
Lawrence Republican
Missouri Republican (St. Louis)
Niles' (Weekly and National) Register
St. Louis Daily Democrat
Washington (Arkansas) *Telegraph*

Books and Articles

Agnew, Brad. "Brigadier General Henry Leavenworth and Colonel Henry Dodge, 1834–1835." In *Frontier Adventures: American Exploration in Oklahoma*, ed. Joseph A. Stout Jr., 91–100. Oklahoma City: Oklahoma Historical Society, 1976.

Alderman, Ralph M., Herbert L. Kleinfield, and Jenifer S. Banks, eds. *The Complete Works of Washington Irving, Letters, 1823–1838*. Vol. 2 of 3. Boston: Twayne, 1979.

Allen, Henry Easton. "The Parrilla Expedition to the Red River in 1759." *Southwestern Historical Quarterly* 43 (July 1939): 65–71.

Ammon, Harry. *James Monroe, the Quest for National Identity*. New York: McGraw–Hill, 1971.

Bailey, Minnie Thomas. *Reconstruction in the Indian Territory*. New York: Kennikat Press, 1972.

Baker, Marcus. "The Northwest Boundary of Texas." *Bulletin of the U.S. Geological Survey* (1902): 11–21.

Barry, Louise. *The Beginning of the West: Annals of the Kansas Gateway to the American West, 1540–1854*. Topeka: Kansas State Historical Society, 1972.

Bearss, Edwin C., and Arrell M. Gibson. *Fort Smith, Little Gibraltar on the Arkansas*. Norman: University of Oklahoma Press, 1969.

Beers, Henry Putney. *The Western Military Frontier, 1815–1846*. Philadelphia: Porcupine Press, 1975.

Bell, John R. "The Journal of John R. Bell, 1820." Far West and Rockies Series 6: 279–284.

Bell, Robert E. *Oklahoma Archaeology: An Annotated Bibliography*. Norman: University of Oklahoma Press, 1969.

Berthrong, Donald, J. *The Southern Cheyennes*. Norman: University of Oklahoma Press, 1963.

Blackburn, Bob L. "First Lieutenant James B. Wilkinson, 1806–1807." In *Frontier Adventures: American Exploration in Oklahoma*, ed. Joseph A. Stout Jr., 6–18. Oklahoma City: Oklahoma Historical Society, 1976.

Bolton, Herbert E. *Athanase de Mézières and the Louisiana-Texas Frontier, 1768–1780*. 2 vols. Cleveland: Arthur H. Clark, 1914.

———. *Coronado, Knight of Pueblos and Plains*. Albuquerque: University of New Mexico Press, 1949.

———. "French Intrusions into New Mexico, 1749–1752." In *The Pacific Ocean in History*, ed. Henry Morse Stephens and Herbert E. Bolton. New York: Macmillan, 1917.

———. *Spanish Exploration in the Southwest, 1542–1706*. New York: Scribner's, 1925.

———. *Texas in the Middle Eighteenth Century*. New York: Russell and Russell, 1962.

Bolton, Herbert E., and Thomas Maitland Marshall. *The Colonization of North America, 1491–1783*. New York: Hafner, 1971.

"Book Reviews." *Chronicles of Oklahoma* 1 (January 1921): 100–102.

Brackenridge, Henry Marie. *Views of Louisiana Together with a Journal of a Voyage up the Missouri River in 1811*. Pittsburgh: Craner, Spear, and Eichbaum, 1814.

Bringier, Louis. "Notices of the Geology, Mineralogy, Topography, Productions, and Aboriginal Inhabitants of the

Region Around the Mississippi and Its Confluent Waters." *American Journal of Science and Arts* 3 (1821): 15–46.

Brooks, George R., ed. "George C. Sibley's Journal of a Trip to the Salines in 1811." *Bulletin of the Missouri Historical Society* 59 (April 1965): 172–178.

"Captain Nathan Boone's Journal." *Chronicles of Oklahoma* 7 (March 1929): 58–105.

Catlin, George. *Letters and Notes on the Manners, Customs, and Conditions of the North American Indians.* 2 vols. Reprint, New York: Dover, 1973.

———. *North American Indians.* 2 vols. Edinburgh: John Grant, 1926.

Chapman, Berlin B. "Establishment of the Wichita Reservation." *Chronicles of Oklahoma* 11 (December 1933): 1044–1055.

Chlouber, Carla. "The Search for Fountain Camp: Locating Irving's October 20, 1832, Encampment in Oklahoma." *Chronicles of Oklahoma* 74 (Summer 1996): 130–145.

Clift, W. H. "Warren's Trading Post." *Chronicles of Oklahoma* 2 (June 1924): 128–140.

Coues, Elliott, ed. *The Journal of Jacob Fowler, Narrating an Adventure Through the Indian Territory, Oklahoma, Kansas, Colorado, and New Mexico to the Sources of the Rio Grande del Norte, 1821–22.* Minneapolis: Ross and Haines, 1965.

Cutler, William G., ed. *History of the State of Kansas.* Chicago: Andreas, 1883.

Day, Donald, and Harry Herbert Ullom, eds. *The Autobiography of Sam Houston.* Norman: University of Oklahoma Press, 1954.

Dott, Robert H. "Lieutenant Simpson's California Road Through Oklahoma." *Chronicles of Oklahoma* 38 (Summer 1960): 154–179.

Ellsworth, Henry. *Washington Irving on the Prairie.* Ed. Stanley T. Williams and Barbara D. Simison. New York: American Book, 1937.

"Extracts from the Diary of Major Sibley." *Chronicles of Oklahoma* 5 (June 1927): 196–218.

Flores, Dan. *Jefferson and Southwestern Exploration: The Freeman-Custis Accounts of the Red River Expedition of 1806.* Norman: University of Oklahoma Press, 1974.

Foreman, Carolyn. "Colonel James B. Many, Commandant at Fort Gibson, Fort Towson, and Fort Smith." *Chronicles of Oklahoma* 19 (June 1941): 119–128.

———. "General Richard Barnes Mason." *Chronicles of Oklahoma* 19 (March 1941): 14–36.

———. "Journal of a Tour in the Indian Territory, 1844." *Chronicles of Oklahoma* 10 (June 1932): 219–256.

———. "Nathan Boone, Trapper, Manufacturer, Surveyor, Militiaman, Legislator, Ranger, and Dragoon." *Chronicles of Oklahoma* 19 (December 1941): 322–347.

———. "North Fork Town." *Chronicles of Oklahoma* 29 (Spring 1951): 79–111.

———. "Pierce Mason Butler." *Chronicles of Oklahoma* 30 (Spring 1952): 6–28.

Foreman, Grant. *Advancing the Frontier.* Norman: University of Oklahoma Press, 1933.

———. "Early Trails Through Oklahoma." *Chronicles of Oklahoma* 3 (June 1925): 79–119.

———. *Indians and Pioneers: The Story of the American Southwest Before 1830.* New Haven: Yale University Press, 1930.

———. "A Journal Kept by Douglas Cooper of an Expedition by a Company of Chickasaws in Quest of Comanche Indians." *Chronicles of Oklahoma* 5 (December 1927): 381–390.

———. *Marcy and the Gold Seekers.* Norman: University of Oklahoma Press, 1939.

———. "One Hundred Years Ago—Our First Treaty with Wild Indians." *Daily Oklahoman*, August 25, 1935.

———. *A Pathfinder in the Southwest.* Norman: University of Oklahoma Press, 1941.

———. *Pioneer Days in the Early Southwest.* Cleveland: Arthur H. Clark, 1926.

———, ed. and annot. *Adventure on the Red River.* Norman: University of Oklahoma Press, 1941.

———, ed. "Journal of Proceedings at Our First Treaty with the Wild Indians." *Chronicles of Oklahoma* 14 (December 1936): 393–418.

———, ed. "Survey of a Wagon Road from Fort Smith to the Colorado River." *Chronicles of Oklahoma* 12 (March 1935): 74–96.

———, ed. *A Traveler in Indian Territory: The Journal of Ethan Allen Hitchcock*. Cedar Rapids, Iowa: Torch Press, 1930.

———, ed. "An Unpublished Report by Captain Bonneville with Introduction and Footnotes." *Chronicles of Oklahoma* 10 (September 1932): 327–330.

"A Fragment of History." *Chronicles of Oklahoma* 13 (December 1935): 481–484.

Fulton, Maurice Garland, ed. *Diary and Letters of Josiah Gregg*. Norman: University of Oklahoma Press, 1954.

Galvin, John, ed. *Through the Country of the Comanche Indians in the Fall of the Year, 1845: The Journal of a U.S. Army Expedition Led by Lieutenant J. W. Abert*. San Francisco: John Howell Books, 1970.

Gardner, James H. "The Lost Captain: J. L. Dawson of Old Fort Gibson." *Chronicles of Oklahoma* 21 (September 1943): 217–249.

———. "One Hundred Years Ago in the Region of Tulsa." *Chronicles of Oklahoma* 11 (June 1933): 765–785.

Gibson, Arrell Morgan. *The American Indian, Prehistory to the Present*. Lexington, Mass.: Heath, 1980.

———. *America's Exiles*. Oklahoma City: Oklahoma Historical Society, 1976.

———. *Oklahoma, a History of Five Centuries*. Norman, Okla.: Harlow, 1965.

———. "Prehistory in Oklahoma." *Chronicles of Oklahoma* 43 (Spring 1965): 1–8.

Glisan, Rodney. *Journal of Army Life*. San Francisco: Bancroft, 1874.

Gragert, Steven. "Thomas Nuttall, 1819." In *Frontier Adventures: American Exploration in Oklahoma*, ed. Joseph A. Stout Jr., 38–50. Oklahoma City: Oklahoma Historical Society, 1976.

———. "Washington Irving, Henry Ellsworth, Albert–Alexandre de Pourtalès, and Charles Latrobe, 1832." In *Frontier Adventures: American Exploration in Oklahoma*, ed. Joseph A. Stout Jr., 80–90. Oklahoma City: Oklahoma Historical Society, 1976.

Graustein, Jeannette E. *Thomas Nuttall, Naturalist: Explorations in America, 1808–1841*. Cambridge, Mass.: Harvard University Press, 1967.

Gregg, Josiah. *Commerce of the Prairies.* Ed. Max L. Moorhead. Norman: University of Oklahoma Press, 1954.

Gregg, Kate L. "History of Fort Osage." *Missouri Historical Review* 34 (July 1940): 439–488.

———, ed. "The Missouri Reader—Explorers in the Valley." *Missouri Historical Review* 39 (July 1945): 505–543.

———, ed. *The Road to Santa Fe: The Journal and Diaries of George Champlin Sibley.* Albuquerque: University of New Mexico Press, 1968.

Gregory, Jack, and Rennard S. Strickland. *Sam Houston with the Cherokees, 1829–1833.* Austin: University of Texas Press, 1967.

Griswold, Gillette. "The Site of Camp Comanche." *Chronicles of Oklahoma* 72 (Fall 1995): 322–337.

Hammond, George P., and Agapito Rey, eds. and trans. *Don Juan de Oñate, Colonizer of New Mexico, 1595–1628.* 2 vols. Albuquerque: University of New Mexico Press, 1953.

———. *Narratives of the Coronado Expedition, 1540–1542.* Coronado Historical Series. 2 vols. Albuquerque: University of New Mexico Press, 1940.

Harper, Elizabeth Ann. "The Taovayas in Frontier Trade and Diplomacy, 1719–1768." *Chronicles of Oklahoma* 31 (Autumn 1953): 268–289.

Heitman, Francis B. *Historical Register and Dictionary of the United States Army.* 2 vols. Washington, D.C.: GPO, 1903.

Hildreth, James. *Dragoon Campaigns to the Rocky Mountains.* New York: Wiley and Long, 1936.

Hoig, Stan. *Sequoyah, the Cherokee Genius.* Oklahoma City: Oklahoma Historical Society, 1995.

Hollon, William Eugene. *Beyond the Cross Timbers: The Travels of Randolph B. Marcy.* Norman: University of Oklahoma Press, 1955.

———. *The Lost Pathfinder, Zebulon Montgomery Pike.* Norman: University of Oklahoma Press, 1949.

Horgan, Paul. *Josiah Gregg and His Vision of the Early West.* New York: Farrar Straus Giroux, 1941.

Houck, Louis. *A History of Missouri.* 2 vols. Chicago: Donnelley, 1908.

———. *The Spanish Regime in Missouri.* 2 vols. Chicago: Donnelley, 1909.

Irving, Pierre M. *The Life and Letters of Washington Irving.* New York: Putnam, 1864.

Irving, Washington. *A Tour of the Prairies.* Ed. John Francis McDermott. Norman: University of Oklahoma Press, 1956.

Isern, Thomas. "George Champlin Sibley, 1811 and 1825–1826." In *Frontier Adventures: American Exploration in Oklahoma,* ed. Joseph A. Stout Jr., 19–37. Oklahoma City: Oklahoma Historical Society, 1976.

Jackson, Donald, ed. and annot. *The Journals of Zebulon Montgomery Pike, with Letters and Related Documents.* 2 vols. Norman: University of Oklahoma Press, 1966.

James, Edwin. *An Account of an Expedition from Pittsburgh to the Rocky Mountains.* 2 vols. Ann Arbor, Mich.: University Microfilms, 1966.

James, Thomas. *Three Years Among the Mexicans and the Indians.* Chicago: Rio Grande Press, 1962.

John, Elizabeth A. H. "Portrait of a Wichita Village, 1808." *Chronicles of Oklahoma* 50 (Winter 1982–1983): 412–437.

———. *Storms Brewed in Other Men's Worlds.* College Station: Texas A&M University Press, 1975.

———, ed. "Inside the Comanchería, 1785: The Diary of Pedro Vial and Francisco Xavier Chaves." *Southwestern Historical Quarterly* 98: 27–56.

Jones, Harold W., ed. "The Diary of Assistant Surgeon Leonard McPhail on His Journey to the Southwest in 1835." *Chronicles of Oklahoma* 18 (September 1940): 281–292.

"The Journal of Elijah Hicks." *Chronicles of Oklahoma* 13 (March 1935): 68–99.

Kappler, Charles J., ed. *Indian Treaties.* New York: Interland, 1972.

Keim, DeB. Randolph. *Sheridan's Troopers on the Border: A Winter Campaign on the Plains.* Philadelphia: David McKay, 1885.

Latrobe, Charles. *The Rambler in North America.* 2 vols. London: Seeley and Burnside, 1836.

Lewis, Anna. "DuTisne's First Expedition into Oklahoma, 1719." *Chronicles of Oklahoma* 3 (December 1925): 319–323.

———. "French Interests and Activities in Oklahoma." *Chronicles of Oklahoma* 2 (September 1924): 253–268.

———. "LaHarpe's First Expedition into Oklahoma, 1718–19." *Chronicles of Oklahoma* 2 (December 1924): 331–349.

Loomis, Noel M., and Abraham P. Nasatir. *Pedro Vial and the Roads to Santa Fe.* Norman: University of Oklahoma Press, 1967.

Lottinville, Savoie, ed. *A Journal of Travels into the Arkansas Territory During the Year 1819.* Norman: University of Oklahoma Press, 1980.

Marcy, Randolph B. *The Prairie Traveler.* New York: Harper, 1859.

Margry, Pierre, ed. *Découvertes et éstablissements des Français dans l'ouest et dans le sud de l'Amérique Septentrionale.* 6 vols. Paris: D. Jouaust, 1879–1888.

McDermott, John Francis, ed. *Tixier's Travels on the Osage Prairie.* Norman: University of Oklahoma Press, 1940.

Meserve, John Bartlett. "The Indian Removal Message of President Jackson." *Chronicles of Oklahoma* 13 (March 1935): 65.

Miller, Nyle H., ed. "Surveying the Southern Boundary Line of Kansas." *Kansas Historical Quarterly* 1 (February 1932): 104–139

Möllhausen, Balduin. *Diary of a Journey from the Mississippi to the Coasts of the Pacific with a United States Government Expedition.* London: Longman, Brown, Green, Longman, and Roberts, 1858.

Montaignes, François Des. *The Plains, Being No Less Than a Collection of Veracious Memoranda Taken During the Expedition of Exploration in the Year 1845.* Ed. and intro. Nancy Apert Mower and Don Russell. Norman: University of Oklahoma Press, 1972.

Mooney, James. *Calendar History of the Kiowas.* Washington, D.C.: Smithsonian Institution Press, 1979.

Morris, John W., ed. *Boundaries of Oklahoma.* Oklahoma City: Oklahoma Historical Society, 1980.

Morrison, James D. "A Journey Across Oklahoma Ninety Years Ago." *Chronicles of Oklahoma* 4 (September 1927): 333–337.

———. "Travis G. Wright and the Leavenworth Expedition in Oklahoma." *Chronicles of Oklahoma* 4 (September 1927): 7–14.

Morrison, W. B. "Fort Towson." *Chronicles of Oklahoma* 8 (June 1930): 226–322.

Murray, Hugh. *Encyclopedia of Geography.* 3 vols. Philadelphia: Lea and Blanchard, 1839.

Nasatir, A. P. *Before Lewis and Clark.* 2 vols. St. Louis: St. Louis Historical Documents Foundation, 1980.

Neihardt, John S. *The Splendid Wayfaring.* New York: Macmillan, 1927.

Newcomb, W. W. Jr., and T. N. Campbell. "Southern Plains Ethnohistory: A Re–examination of the Escanjaques, Ahijados, and Cuitoas." *Oklahoma Anthropological Society, Memoir 3* (1943).

Pelzer, Louis. *Marches of the Dragoons in the Mississippi Valley Between the Years 1833 and 1850.* Iowa City: State Historical Society of Iowa, 1917.

Perrine, Fred S., ed. "The Journal of Hugh Evans, Covering the First and Second Campaigns of the United States Regiments in 1834 and 1835." Notes by Grant Foreman. *Chronicles of Oklahoma* 3 (September 1925): 174–215.

Pike, Zebulon Montgomery. *An Account of Expeditions to the Sources of the Mississippi.* Philadelphia: Conrad, 1810.

Portraits of North American Indians with Sketches of Scenery, etc., Painted by J. M. Stanley, Deposited with the Smithsonian Institution. Washington, D.C.: Smithsonian Institution, 1852.

Pourtalès, Albert–Alexandre de. *On the Western Tour with Washington Irving.* Norman: University of Oklahoma Press, 1968.

Richardson, Rupert Norval. *The Comanche Barrier to South Plains Settlement.* Glendale, Calif.: Arthur H. Clark, 1933.

———. *The Frontier of Northwest Texas, 1846 to 1876: Advance and Defense by the Pioneer Settlers of the Cross Timbers Prairies.* Glendale, Calif.: Arthur H. Clark, 1963.

Rister, Carl Coke. "A Federal Experiment in Southern Plains Indian Relations, 1835–1845," *Chronicles of Oklahoma* 14 (December 1936): 434–439.

Rister, Carl Coke, and Bryan W. Lovelace. "A Diary Account of a Creek Boundary Survey, 1850." *Chronicles of Oklahoma* 22 (Autumn 1944): 268–301.

Robinson, W. Stitt, ed. "The Kiowa and Comanche Campaign of 1860 as Recorded in the Personal Diary of Lt. J. E. B.

Stuart." *Kansas Historical Quarterly* 23 (Winter 1959): 382–400.

"Rock Mary Report." *Chronicles of Oklahoma* 38 (Summer 1960): 130–154.

Schafer, Delbert. "French Explorers in Oklahoma." *Chronicles of Oklahoma* 55 (Winter 1977–1978), 392–402.

Shawver, Lona, annot. "Stanley Explores Oklahoma." *Chronicles of Oklahoma* 22 (Autumn 1944): 259–270.

Shirk, George H. "Peace on the Plains." *Chronicles of Oklahoma* 28 (Spring 1950): 2–41.

Smallwood, James. "Major Stephen Harriman Long, 1820." In *Frontier Adventures: American Exploration in Oklahoma*, ed. Joseph A. Stout Jr., 51–60. Oklahoma City: Oklahoma Historical Society, 1976.

Smith, Alson J. *Man Against the Mountains*. New York: John Day, 1965.

Smith, Ralph A., trans. and annot. "Account of the Journey of Rénard de La Harpe: Discovery Made by Him of Several Nations Situated in the West." *Southwestern Historical Quarterly* 62 (July 1958): 75–86; (October 1958): 246–259; (January 1959): 371–385; (April 1959): 525–541.

Stoddard, Amos. *Sketches, Historical and Descriptive of Louisiana*. Philadelphia: Mathew Carey, 1812.

Stoddard, Francis R. "Amiel Weeks Whipple." *Chronicles of Oklahoma* 28 (Autumn 1950): 226–234.

Stout, Joseph A., Jr., ed. *Frontier Adventures: American Exploration in Oklahoma*. Oklahoma City: Oklahoma Historical Society, 1976.

Thoburn, Joseph G. "Battle with the Comanches." *Sturm's Oklahoma Magazine* (August 1910): 22–28.

————. "A Campaign of the Texas Rangers Against the Comanches." *Sturm's Oklahoma Magazine* (July 1910): 30–38.

————. "The Collection of Relics and Artifacts from Ferdinandina, Oklahoma's First White Settlement." *Chronicles of Oklahoma* 34 (Autumn 1956): 353–356.

————. "DuTisne's Expedition into Oklahoma, 1719." *Chronicles of Oklahoma* 3 (December 1925): 319–323.

————. "Indian Fight in Ford County." *Kansas State Historical Collections* 12 (1912): 313–329.

————. "The Prehistoric Cultures of Oklahoma." *Chronicles of Oklahoma* 7 (September 1929): 211–241.

———. *A Standard History of Oklahoma*. Chicago: American Historical Society, 1916.

Thoburn, Joseph G., and Muriel Wright. *Oklahoma, a History of the State and Its People*. 4 vols. New York: Lewis, 1929.

Thomas, Alfred B. *Forgotten Frontiers: A Study of the Spanish Indian Policy of Don Juan Bautista, Governor of New Mexico, 1777–1787*. Norman: University of Oklahoma Press, 1932.

———. "Spanish Exploration of Oklahoma, 1599–1792." *Chronicles of Oklahoma* 6 (June 1928): 187–213.

———, trans. and ed. *After Coronado: Spanish Exploration Northeast of New Mexico, 1696–1727*. Norman: University of Oklahoma Press, 1935.

Thomas, Phillip Drennon. "Thomas James, Hugh Glenn, and Jacob Fowler, 1821–1823." In *Frontier Adventures: American Exploration in Oklahoma*, ed. Joseph A. Stout Jr., 61–79. Oklahoma City: Oklahoma Historical Society, 1976.

Thwaites, Reuben Gold, ed. *Bradbury's Travels in the Interior of America, 1809–1811, Early Western Travels*. Cleveland: Arthur H. Clark, 1904.

———, ed. *James's Account of the S. H. Long Expedition, 1819–20, Early Western Travels, 1748–1846*. Vol. 16. Cleveland: Arthur H. Clark, 1905.

Tomer, John S., and Michael J. Broadhead. *A Naturalist in Indian Territory: The Journals of S. W. Woodhouse, 1849–50*. Norman: University of Oklahoma Press, 1992.

"The Tribes of the 35th Parallel." *Harper's New Monthly Magazine* 17 (September 1858): 448–453.

Tyson, Carl. "Captain Randolph Barnes Marcy, 1849–1852." In *Frontier Adventures: American Exploration in Oklahoma*, ed. Joseph A. Stout Jr., 138–150. Oklahoma City: Oklahoma Historical Society, 1976.

Unrau, William E. *The Kansas Indians: A History of the Wind People, 1673–1873*. Norman: University of Oklahoma Press, 1971.

Van Zandt, Howard F. "The History of Camp Holmes and Chouteau's Trading Post." *Chronicles of Oklahoma* 13 (September 1935): 316–340.

Wallace, Ernest, and E. Adamson Hoebel. *The Comanches, Lords of the South Plains*. Norman: University of Oklahoma Press, 1952.

Ware, James. "First Lieutenant Amiel Weeks Whipple, 1853." In *Frontier Adventures: American Exploration in Oklahoma*, ed. Joseph A. Stout Jr., 138–149. Oklahoma City: Oklahoma Historical Society, 1976.

Webb, Walter Prescott. *The Texas Rangers: A Century of Frontier Defense*. Austin: University of Texas Press, 1982.

Weber, David J. *The Spanish Frontier in North America*. New Haven: Yale University Press, 1992.

Wedel, Mildred. *The Deer Creek Site, Oklahoma: A Wichita Village Sometimes Called Ferdinandina—an Ethnohistorian's View*. Series in Anthropology no. 5. Oklahoma City: Oklahoma Historical Society, 1981.

Wedel, Waldo. *Prehistoric Man on the Great Plains*. Norman: University of Oklahoma Press, 1961.

West, C. W. "Dub." *Fort Gibson, Gateway to the West*. Muskogee, Okla.: Muskogee, 1974.

West, James. "Josiah Gregg, 1839–1840." In *Frontier Adventures: American Exploration in Oklahoma*, ed. Joseph A. Stout Jr., 101–123. Oklahoma City: Oklahoma Historical Society, 1976.

Westbrook, Harriette Johnson. "The Chouteaus." *Chronicles of Oklahoma* 11 (June–September 1933): 786–797, 942–966.

Williams, Stanley T., and Barbara D. Simison, eds. "Notes and Documents—a Journey Through Oklahoma in 1832: A Letter from Henry Ellsworth to Professor Benjamin Silliman." *Mississippi Valley Historical Review* 29 (December 1942): 387–393.

Williams, W. D. "1820 Letter from Governor Miller Describing Arkansas Territory." *Arkansas Historical Quarterly* 42 (Winter 1983), 349–354.

———. "Louis Bringier and His Description of Arkansas in 1812." *Arkansas Historical Quarterly* 48 (Summer 1987): 108–136.

Winfrey, Dorman H., and James M. Day, eds. *The Indian Papers of Texas and the Southwest, 1825–1916*. 4 vols. Austin, Tex.: Pemberton Press, 1966.

Winship, George Parker. *The Coronado Expedition, 1540–1542*. Chicago: Rio Grande Press, 1964.

Wright, Muriel H. "A History of Fort Cobb." *Chronicles of Oklahoma* 28 (Autumn 1950): 53–63.

———. "Pioneer Historical Archaeologist of the State of Oklahoma." *Chronicles of Oklahoma* 24 (Winter 1946–1947): 404–408.

Wright, Muriel H., and George Shirk. "The Journal of Lieutenant Whipple." *Chronicles of Oklahoma* 28 (Autumn 1950): 235–285.

Wyckoff, Don G., and Robert Brooks. *Oklahoma Archeology.* Norman: University of Oklahoma Press, 1983.

Young, Otis E. "The United States Mounted Ranger Battalion, 1832–33." *Mississippi Valley Historical Review* 41 (December 1954): 453–470.

Manuscripts

"Diary of D. S. Stanley, U.S. 2d Dragoons." Typewritten manuscript. Archives and Manuscripts, Oklahoma Historical Society, Oklahoma City, Oklahoma.

Journal of Union Mission. Archives and Manuscripts, Oklahoma Historical Society, Oklahoma City, Oklahoma.

Whipple Collection. Journals and Diaries. Archives and Manuscripts, Oklahoma Historical Society, Oklahoma City, Oklahoma.

Index

References to illustrations are in boldface type.

Index

Marshall, Okla., 241
Martin, Judge Gabriel N., 158
Martin, Matthew Wright, 158;
 rescue of, 172
Mary's Rock, 142
Mason, Maj. Richard B., 165, 177,
 179–82, 184, 336n.10; biography, 311
McAlester, Okla., 35
McClellan, Capt. George B., 246,
 248; river named for, 249; survey
 error of, 274
McCoy, Rev. Isaac, 139, 143, 268;
 biography, 312
McCoy, John, 206, 268
McIntosh, Rolly (Creek chief), 185,
 339n.22
McIntosh County, Okla., 43
McKnight, John, 117–18, 123, 126–30
McKnight, Robert, 117, 123, 126–27,
 130, 135, 137
McNees Creek, 270
McPhail, Asst. Surg. Leonard, 180,
 181–84; biography, 313
Medford, Okla., 104
Medicine Bluff Creek, 286
Menard, Pierre, 138, 334n.3
Mexico, 5, 7, 23, 55, 61, 64, 75, 81,
 117, 123, 144, 179, 185, 187–88,
 192–93, 195–96, 203, 215, 218, 228,
 232, 262; church of, 263;
 independence of, 123; Indians of,
 23; mountains of, 75; trade of,
 59, 195–96, 206, 209
Meyhew, William C., 238, 240
Mézières, Gov. Athanase de, 51–53,
 55; biography, 313; death of, 56;
 names village, 54
Michler, Lt. Nathaniel: biography,
 313; exploration by, 234–35
Miller, Gov. James, 102
Miller, William, 84
Minco, Okla., 207, 290
Mississippi River, 6–7, 9–10, 12–13,
 42, 51, 59, 71, 93, 95, 117, 137, 140,
 256; explored by La Salle, 33
Missouri, 6–7, 10, 15, 38–40, 45–46,
 52, 56, 58, 71, 79, 82–84, 112, 139,
 155, 157–58, 192, 197, 202, 206, 223,
 270; rangers of, 155
Missouri Indians, 40
Missouri River, 40, 56, 63–64, 68,
 77, 83–84, 103–104, 108, 116, 215;
 tribes of, 40
Möllhausen, Heinrich B., 257, 259,
 261, 266, 343n.13; biography, 314

Monroe, James: addresses
 Cherokees, 11; Indian removal
 plan of, 10
Moore, Okla., 220
Mushalatubee (Mankiller)
 (Choctaw chief), 186
Muskogee, Okla., 39
Mustang Creek, 243

Natchez, Miss., 64
Natchitoches, La., 34, 52, 56, 58–59,
 62, 65, 122, 126
Neighbors, Robert, 234, 285;
 removes Texas Indians, 287
Neosho River, 82, 139. *See also*
 Grand River
New Mexico (New Spain), 5–7, 9,
 18, 20, 23–25, 27, 31, 33–34, 40,
 43, 49, 56, 58, 63, 67–68, 76, 90,
 106, 118, 123–25, 192, 196, 215,
 232–33, 235, 243–44, 255, 262, 265,
 268, 270, 275, 278; armies of sent
 to intercept Americans, 9;
 Comanche trade with, 120;
 military of, 122; mountains of,
 266; pueblos of, 29; Spanish
 claim to, 9; traders of, 205, 270
Nidiver, George, 138
Nix, General, 145
Norman, Okla., 152, 220
Norteños, 49, 52
North Canadian River (North Fork
 of the Canadian), 4, 110–11, 119,
 129, 132, 134, 139–40, 142, 151–52,
 193–94, 207, 221, 227, 229, 242,
 245, 275
Norrh Fork Town, 229, 276
Northrop, Lt. Lucius B., 189,
 336n.10; biography, 314
Nuttall, Thomas, 15, 39, 93, **94,**
 95–101, 149; biography, 314

Oilton, Okla., 149
Okeene, Okla., 242
Oklahoma, 3, 6, 18, 23–25, 28, 30–32,
 34–35, 37–40, 43, 46–48, 51–53,
 56, 58–59, 63, 67, 69, 76, 79–81,
 84, 86–87, 89–90, 96, 100, 102–103,
 108, 112, 115, 118, 124, 139–40, 145,
 153, 156, 158, 163, 181, 191, 203, 207,
 212–14, 223, 230, 234–37, 247,
 269–70, 281, 288, 290; claimed by
 U. S., 9; native life of, 211
Oklahoma City, Okla., 128, 152, 220,
 227